Jean Baudrillard is a pivotal figure in contemporary cultural theory and the whole field of the social sciences. Without doubt one of the foremost European thinkers of the last fifty years, his work has provoked debate and controversy across a number of disciplines, yet his significance has so far been largely ignored by feminist theorists. *Baudrillard's Challenge* is an attempt to redress this balance, presenting the first systematic feminist reading of Baudrillard's work.

Victoria Grace argues that Baudrillard's critique of signification, the economy, and the construction of identity offers a vital point of departure for any serious analysis of the problematic of patriarchy in contemporary western societies. Drawing on the full range of Baudrillard's writings the author engages in a debate with:

- the work of Luce Irigaray, Judith Butler, and Rosi Braidotti on identity, power, and desire
- the feminist concern with 'difference' as an emancipatory construct
- writings on transgenderism and the performance of gender
- feminist concerns about the objectification of women

Through this critical engagement Grace reveals a number of the limitations of some contemporary feminist theorising around gender and identity, patriarchy and power, and in so doing offers a way forward for contemporary feminist thought.

Baudrillard's Challenge will be essential reading for students of feminist theory, sociology, and cultural theory.

Victoria Grace is Senior Lecturer in Feminist Studies and currently serving a term as Dean of Arts at the University of Canterbury at Christchurch.

Baudrillard's Challenge
A feminist reading

Victoria Grace

London and New York

First published 2000 by Routledge
11 New Fetter Lane, London EC4P 4EE

Simultaneously published in the USA and Canada
by Routledge
29 West 35th Street, New York, NY 10001

Routledge is an imprint of the Taylor & Francis Group

© 2000 Victoria Grace

Typeset in Garamond by BC Typesetting, Bristol
Printed and bound in Great Britain by
Biddles Ltd, Guildford and Kings Lynn

British Library Cataloguing in Publication Data
A catalogue record for this book is available from the British Library

Library of Congress Cataloging in Publication Data
Grace, Victoria.
    Baudrillard's challenge: a feminist reading/Victoria Grace.
        p.   cm.
    Includes bibliographical references and index.
    1. Baudrillard, Jean.   2. Feminist theory.   I. Title.
    HQ1190.G67 2000
    305.42'01–dc21   99-059084

ISBN 0–415–18075–9 (hbk)✔
ISBN 0–415–18076–7 (pbk)

Contents

Acknowledgements

In the acknowledgements to their book, *The World of the Gift* (1992), Jacques Godbout and Alain Caillé note how it is customary, particularly in works within the social sciences and humanities, to name the many individuals to whom one is indebted for 'an idea, a criticism, a comment, some information or material, or emotional support'. They draw out the connection between gift-giving and gratitude. In the case of this book, it has been a very different experience from that implied by the custom to which Godbout and Caillé refer.

I was first introduced to the ideas and work of Jean Baudrillard by my partner, Louis Arnoux, when we first met in 1987. Louis is French, spent the first twenty-five years of his life in France, and was educated in Marseilles and Paris. I have lived in New Zealand for the most part. Louis has studied Baudrillard's work systematically, and read his books in French when first published. When Louis and I met, I was working on my doctorate in sociology, and found our discussions and engagement with Baudrillard's work of central importance to my thesis research. Since that time my understanding of Baudrillard's work has been inextricably linked with my conversations with Louis. I joined the Department of Feminist Studies at the University of Canterbury in 1993, and by 1995 a project was starting to form in my mind; to write a book on the work of Baudrillard from the perspective of feminist concerns. My gratitude and indebtedness lie wholly with Louis, from whom (and with whom) I have learnt more than I could have imagined. Louis has contributed immeasurably to my ideas on Baudrillard, and especially to the importance of a critique of the 'economic', which in my own work I have come to see has profound importance for feminism. Louis has also contributed suggestions for French references that I would not have otherwise stumbled across.

I have a research interest in feminist critiques of medicalisation, psychosomatic medicine, and theories of embodiment, and a specific research background in women's experiences of, and medical discourses on, chronic pelvic pain. I could list numerous individuals who have contributed to my work in this area; I feel surrounded by a truly rich and dynamic intellectual world of ideas and challenges in this connection, and have the privilege of working with postgraduate students whose work is inspirational. But in connection with this work on Baudrillard, I have not had these conversations with colleagues. Probably the most exhilarating moment was receiving the comments from Routledge reviewers who had read the proposal and the first chapter. This was the first contact (apart from Louis) with peers who were knowledgeable about Baudrillard's work, and as such was one of the most encouraging points in this journey. I am very grateful for their generosity of engagement and enthusiasm. My sincere gratitude also goes to Jean Baudrillard for writing a paragraph in strong support of the book proposal, which accompanied my submission to the publisher.

The one other person I want to acknowledge is my friend and colleague Chris Prentice (Department of English, University of Otago). Although Chris and I had not discussed the work of Baudrillard prior to her reading a complete draft of this book, her reaction to the manuscript made us both realise the extent to which our conversations about our work over the years have played an important role in the way our ideas have evolved. I realise how much Chris's support has encouraged me to continue with this critical stance, especially in the face of feminist discouragement regarding the value of Baudrillard's work. I am hugely grateful to Chris for the insightfulness of her comments on the draft, and for reflecting back a reading of the book that appears to see what I am seeing.

I am also grateful to two other colleagues, Patricia Elliot (Wilfrid Laurier University, Ontario) and Renée Heberle (University of Toledo, Ohio), for reading a draft of the manuscript and providing comment and engagement with the work. I am clear that this will not be a book that feminist colleagues will necessarily think sits easily within a feminist theory frame (although I think it should!), and therefore I particularly appreciate the opportunity to learn how this book will 'trouble' many feminist readers. It has been useful to reflect on this in the light of comments received.

The book was written over the summers of 1996 and 1997, then during a sabbatical leave from September 1998 till mid-1999. I am very grateful to the University of Canterbury for this study leave period.

Finally I would like to express my sincere appreciation to members of the Routledge publishing team who have provided useful assistance and excellent communication throughout the publishing process. My thanks go particularly to Senior Editor, Mari Shullaw, who was also the Commissioning Editor for this volume. Her encouragement and advice have been most welcome and important.

Abbreviations

Abbreviations of works by Baudrillard (full references are found in the bibliography):

AM   *America* (1986)

CM   *Cool Memories 1980–85* (1987)

CS   *The Consumer Society. Myths and Structures* (1970)

EC   *The Ecstasy of Communication* (1987)

EOP   The end of production (1990)

FF   *Forget Foucault* (1977)

FS   *Fatal Strategies* (1983)

IE   *The Illusion of the End* (1992)

MOP   *The Mirror of Production* (1973)

PC   *The Perfect Crime* (1995)

PES   *For a Critique of the Political Economy of the Sign* (1972)

SE&D   *Symbolic Exchange and Death* (1976)

SEDN   *Seduction* (1979)

SIM   *Simulations* (1981)

SO   *The System of Objects* (1968)

SSM   *In the Shadow of the Silent Majorities, or the End of the Social* (1978)

SV   *Suite Venitienne* (Sophie Calle) and *Please Follow Me* (Baudrillard) (1983)

TE   *The Transparency of Evil. Essays on Extreme Phenomena* (1990)

Introduction

The purpose of this book is to develop a critical reading of the work of Jean Baudrillard, and to argue that the epistemological approach he takes, the method of critique he pursues, the substantive problematics he identifies, are important to feminist scholarship and theory. I read Baudrillard 'in his own terms', as argued recently by Rex Butler (1999) to be the only way to read Baudrillard. I am in agreement with Butler on this point. Reading Baudrillard 'in his own terms' means, for me, that one attempts a reading that continually modifies and refines one's understanding of his concepts and use of language and rhetorics in the light of their repeated appearance throughout his own work. It means starting from an assumption that his works are theoretically and epistemologically consistent. I then interrogate that assumption through a reading that both seeks to refine concepts through assuming this consistency, and at the same time seeks to find inconsistencies when such a reading is not possible. Using this method of analysis and engagement, I have to say that I have not found inconsistencies in his work. Baudrillard goes rock bottom, and keeps going. He unravels, sometimes quite brutally and uncompromisingly, every illusory ontological notion, every moralistic premise, including the sacred lexicon of rights and liberation on which the discourses of the 'left' have tended to rest their case.

Baudrillard is critical on and on. He does not rest his case. His 'critique of critique' reveals the problem whereby a critique of the status quo ideology that purports to define a new truth is not only epistemologically flawed, but in political terms is historical. An assumption of the transformative role of critique and social revolution or change (and hence the role of an intelligentsia) no longer animates the landscape that has been called 'political'. This argument is developed in Chapter 3.

Some critics appear to be disturbed by the question of truth or fiction in relation to Baudrillard's work. To ask if Baudrillard is really saying something about what is going on in the world is to understand the process of critique differently from the way intended here. Critique precisely reveals how the 'what's going on' is constructed and the problematics of the attendant assumptions; this certainly tells us something about 'what's going on' and indeed opens up a space for action and engagement that has no need of a positive 'theory' about any social reality conceptualised in static, ontic terms.

Another method of analysis I have used is to create a 'conversation' between Baudrillard (or my reading of his work) and his critics. I use the texts of those who are critical of Baudrillard's work to see how well their arguments stand up when confronted with a 'reading of Baudrillard in his own terms'. Quite simply, they do not stand up at all well, but the process is a useful one in that it furthers the aim of progressing a reading of Baudrillard that strengthens, through interrogation, an understanding of what, at heart, is at stake in his work.

Baudrillard's writing, his 'theorising' has to be understood as an active challenge to the real (examined further in Chapter 1). To date, no one has understood this better than (apart from?) Rex Butler (his book is called *Jean Baudrillard. The Defence of the Real*):

> Baudrillard's writing, that is, like the terrorism it speaks of, attempts to form a relationship with that with which it cannot form a relationship, attempts to describe something that at once is excluded to allow it to be represented and only exists after the attempt to do so. In a sense, therefore, it must seek to represent *nothing*. But the risk and the strategy of writing – as of terrorism itself – is that it is only by daring to represent nothing, to offer nothing in exchange for the appearances of the world, that the world necessarily recognises itself in it, that we catch the world up, bring about an exchange with it.[1]
>
> (Butler 1999: 96)

I think it is a profound uneasiness with this feature of Baudrillard's work that leads many writers to be dismissive of his work on the grounds of 'nihilism'. The criticism of nihilism is frequently posed on what are argued to be substantive grounds in relation to what Baudrillard actually has to say. But in my assessment, in relation to Baudrillard's work this is never a very convincing position to adopt. I wonder, rather, if it isn't easier to criticise Baudrillard for 'nihilism' than it is to attend to the epistemological issues arising when Baudrillard on the one hand seems to be saying a lot about 'what is going on in the world', but on the other hand offers nothing by way of 'theory'.

Baudrillard has this to say on the matter:

> What I do is more of a thought experiment which tries to explore an unknown field by other rules. This doesn't mean it's nihilistic in the sense in which nihilism means there are no longer any values, no longer any reality, but only signs: the accusation of nihilism and imposture always relates to that point. But if you take nihilism in the strong sense, the sense of a nothing-based thinking, a thinking which might start out from the axiom 'why is there nothing rather than something?' –

overturning the fundamental philosophical question, the question of being: 'why is there something rather than nothing?' – then I don't mind being called a nihilist.

(Baudrillard in Petit 1997: 34)

This is not a book *about* Baudrillard; it is an engagement with his work. For this reason I neither spend time 'introducing' Baudrillard (something Rex Butler deems impossible anyway, although the 'introduction' to his book is well worth reading), nor situate his work relative to other authors or trends in intellectual writing, schools of thought. For readers who are interested, Gary Genosko (1999) discusses Baudrillard's work in relation to that of Marshall McLuhan; Mark Poster (1994) discusses it in relation to that of Habermas on critical theory and technoculture; Charles Levin (1996) introduces his book with some contextual analysis for his examination of Baudrillard's work as 'a study in cultural metaphysics'; Douglas Kellner (1994) provides an overview of the historical development of Baudrillard's work, as does Rex Butler (1999); Sadie Plant's exceptional book (1992) on *The Situationist International in a Postmodern Age* examines at least one aspect of the intellectual milieu surrounding the emergence of Baudrillard's work; and the work of Guy Debord (1967, trans. 1994, and 1988, trans. 1990) on the *Society of the Spectacle* also needs to be mentioned in this context.

Baudrillard's works are all, of course, written in French, and I have read his work in English translation. My partner, who knows Baudrillard's work through and through, has French as a first language, and is fluent in English. He and I have, over the years of reading Baudrillard's work (he in French and English and I only in English), discussed differences he has identified in English translations where they differ from his own interpretation. This has led to the curious phenomenon whereby I have a strong sense of what I would call a 'good' translation of Baudrillard compared to a 'poor' one, without apparently having any basis for this judgement, and possibly unsurprisingly my partner systematically agrees with my judgement on this. But for all that, I am clear on the important fact that my reading is of Baudrillard's work as it has been translated in English. It is the English-language texts that this work engages. Does that mean I cannot refer to 'Baudrillard'? I'm not sure, ultimately, that this question can be answered adequately. I will refer to 'him' as such, and possibly only he can protest.

Rey Chow (1995) writes on 'translation and the problem of origins', referring to the etymology of 'translation' as it pertains to the notion of 'traitor', 'betrayal', 'infidelity'. She critiques what she calls the common assumption that translation is a 'rendering of one language into another language' (p. 183), and refuses the notion of one-way relationship between the language of 'origin' and the language into which it is translated. This 'traffic', she argues, is in fact two-way; she is critical of the notion that the translation is 'derivative', or in some sense 'unoriginal'. Translation, she claims, 'is an activity that immediately problematizes the ontological hierarchy of languages'

(p. 184). Chow cites Walter Benjamin to elucidate further the process of reciprocity between the 'original' and the 'translation', to suggest that both the 'original' and the 'translation' become, through their interaction, 'recognizable as fragments of a greater language' (p. 188). The current reading, resulting as it does from a critical interaction with Baudrillard's texts in English translation, and with other readers who have read Baudrillard both in French and in English, has to be read more on its own merits, and less as a vehicle for the 'original' text of Baudrillard.

As a feminist reading, this book asks what and how Baudrillard's work contributes to feminist critique. In particular, I explore Baudrillard's refusal of the fetishisation of 'women', and analyse selected feminist writing from this critical point of departure. My own history has been one of immersion in the intensely critical impulse of feminism, but also one of caution and distancing when some new orthodoxy has emerged and when dogmatic 'positions' have been taken and defended. Kristeva (1998) calls this phenomenon of a foreclosure of questioning the 'suspension of thought', and refers to Hannah Arendt's analysis of this same concern. Kristeva is thus critical of this rejection of the old that is followed by a cult of the new (and which thus 'suspends thought' and ceases a process of questioning).

The feminist texts I have chosen to discuss and examine through the lens of my reading of Baudrillard have been selected partly because they are frequently cited, thus playing a key role in framing directions for feminist theory, and partly because they engage the issues that are pursued in the chapters of the book. Chapter 1 sets the scene, establishing the groundwork for any serious consideration of Baudrillard's ideas, by examining his early work. To understand Baudrillard's work, I argue, it is vital to confront the historically and culturally specific interweaving of the logics of economic value, linguistic representation, and constructions of the subject and the object. In Chapter 2 I engage the work of Luce Irigaray, Rosi Braidotti, and Judith Butler to consider the implications of Baudrillard's critique of contemporary discourses on identity, subjectivity, power, and desire. The concern of numerous feminist authors with the problem of 'difference' is critically examined in Chapter 3 through Baudrillard's claim that the more 'difference' circulates in our contemporary hyperreal world as an emancipatory construct, the more we see the inevitability that it will be rendered more of the same, recaptured by a process of simulation. The simulation of gender is the focus of Chapter 4, where I debate the salience of the assumptions transgenderists claim they bring to feminist politics and critique. Judith Butler's arguments for gender as 'performative' are critically examined in relation to Baudrillard's overarching critique of the performative as archetypal icon of the productivist logic of contemporary systems of economic value and signification.

Against the backdrop of discussion in Chapters 2, 3, and 4, Chapter 5 presents Baudrillard's concept of 'seduction' and develops an argument for its importance for feminism; this, in turn, in critical engagement with feminist concerns about woman as object, women as objects of exchange by men, women as objects of sacrifice. Chapter 6 pursues this emphasis further; I try to bring the full force of Baudrillard's critique of the 'political economy of the sign', underpinned by the importance of symbolic exchange and seduction, into view in terms of its implications for feminist thinking. If feminist critique claims an intellectual and political agenda to go to the core of the problematic of patriarchy, then it cannot ignore Baudrillard's work.

If I have not written this book from the ostensible standpoint of engaging those feminist authors whose work is 'close to' that of Baudrillard, it is because I have not found them; certainly not among the feminist theoretical texts cited and cross-referenced within what might broadly be called 'feminist theory'. I read Baudrillard's work indeed as a challenge to feminist theorising and critique, and wish to argue that it is a challenge that should be picked up. To try and find the points of 'similarity' could, even though they are so tenuous, potentially serve to obscure the points of departure, and those are what I have chosen to emphasise. There is no place to seek refuge when reading Baudrillard, and I have deliberately constructed this text in a way that minimises the allure of that prospect. I point instead to where, for example, Irigaray 'comes close' but stress how she backtracks and retraces those steps over and over to erase them effectively. Then again, the work of an author like Marilyn Strathern (1988), possibly not well known outside feminist anthropology, arguably develops insights into gender and the gift that could well be developed further in the light of Baudrillard's work in the sense that there are productive consistencies between them; but that is the work of another time, place, and possibly author. My inclination was to write this kind of book first.

1 Ideologies of Meaning and Value

To claim, to argue, that Baudrillard's work is of central importance to feminist theory, it is necessary to begin with his theoretical analysis of the relationship between the coded structure of value in political economy and the parallel structure of the linguistic sign. In recent years many feminist theorists have created a distinct and powerful trend within feminist thought by avidly appropriating concepts of 'post'-Saussurian linguistics, advocating 'post'structuralist approaches to theorising and critique. Feminists have claimed that the poststructuralist critique of language not as a medium that reflects or represents reality, but as an active discourse that constructs social realities and subjectivities, has empowering possibilities for women, for those cast as 'other' in a phallocentric, humanist semiology. Such a critique, it is argued, has the potential to demystify meta-narratives of objectivity and truth, to open the field of discourse to a plurality of competing meanings, and to make explicit the politics of knowledge. Challenges to oppressive discursive practices can reconfigure the meanings that characterise and give shape to events, to processes of gendering, to what gets done and why.

In this chapter I argue that consideration of Baudrillard's critique of the 'political economy of the sign' reveals serious problems with feminist endorsement and appropriation of these poststructuralist assumptions, problems which become evident in the work of important contemporary feminist theorists as different as Luce Irigaray and Judith Butler. Baudrillard's critique of the 'political economy of the sign' does not, of course, incite a defence of modernist or structuralist political and epistemological assumptions in the face of a 'post'structuralist challenge. Rather, it questions assumptions about the nature of meaning which are common to both structuralist and poststructuralist theories. It is these assumptions that Baudrillard analyses and deconstructs. I will argue that, in doing so, he reveals a gendered politics of meaning-making.

In this first chapter I establish an understanding of the key concepts and theoretical arguments in Baudrillard's early work, concepts and theoretical insights which provide the grounds for his later work. I begin the process of drawing out the implications of this critical work for feminist theory, a process that is subsequently developed throughout the book from a variety of angles. At least since Simone de Beauvoir wrote *The Second Sex* (1949), feminist theorists have been concerned to critique the object status of women, of the feminine, within a binary of subject/object where subjecthood is masculine. To explore this concern and progress this critique, there has been a primary focus on the way subjectivity is constructed within language, examining how a grammar of gendered positioning is integral to the structure of language. This has led to theoretical considerations of how subjects are created within discourse through the articulation of subject positions as politically invested significations. Feminists ask how the politics of this process that positions 'women' as invariably 'other', not men, as objects rather than subjects, can be subverted. How can women create a wholly different logic that is not subsumed within a phallocentric order? How is the binary of subject/object constituted and reproduced? What are the structural pre-conditions of the existence of this binary?

Baudrillard presents a case that the structure of economic value, as this has been constructed (and has changed) over the last few hundred years in the west, parallels, and is related to, the structure of signification. In other words, axiology and semiology have to be understood in terms of how they share a logic, a strategy, and a politics. Further, the very possibility of the construct of *subjects* and *objects*, and the relationship between them, has to be understood through an analysis of the social process of instituting economic value in conjunction with the structure of systems of signification. How these are interrelated and why the notion of a linguistic subject and an economic object is so problematic will be the focus of this chapter.

The Constitution of the Economic Object and the Linguistic Subject

Where does the *value* of an object come from? The so-called 'science' of economics and the mythology of economic exchange that constructs our knowledge of objects and their worth would have us believe that an 'economy' exists as a natural given in much the same way as societies, tool-making, history, or biological organisms for that matter. Objects with value to human beings are assumed to precede our human, social process of exchange of these objects. The exchange of these objects is called an 'economic exchange' and the structure of this exchange is assumed to vary across history and across culture. What is assumed to transcend history and culture, however, is the existence of objects and their exchange between human actors as a calculus of value based, ultimately, on the utility of those objects.

Baudrillard turns this edifice on its head and argues that it represents a pervasive ideological construct that has precisely sustained the progressively hegemonic and totalising economic structure of capitalism. He critiques Marx for making the same fatal assumptions and therefore perpetuating the ideology of a productivist logic of accumulation and growth to infinity (and certain end!). Rather than assuming objects exist and have value prior to the social institution of mechanisms of economic exchange, Baudrillard argues that objects are constituted *as objects* by virtue of the construct of value that precedes them. This critique is at the heart of his work, and given the significance to feminism of the concern regarding women's situatedness within a problematic subject/object dichotomy, it is important to examine the basis of this claim and to consider its implications.

The object as an object of economic exchange has an ontological status that is assumed to exist prior to, and in ontological terms independent of, systems of economic exchange. As such, the object has a singular and unchanging phenomenal being. If it changes, it is transformed from one object to another (a pile of ash is no longer a wooden chair). What Baudrillard points to is the way the construction of this status of the object cannot be understood independently from the representational system that establishes the meaning of objects. The mode of signification is inseparable from this process of constructing the status of objects. The key insight Baudrillard proposes is that both the signifying practice that institutes a linguistic subject and the ontological assumption that constructs objects as objects of economic exchange are structured according to a coded form; a code or logic that is the structural imperative constituting objects in the world and subjects who enter into (economic) exchanges of objects.

The coded form constructing the object of economic exchange assumes that exchange value is predicated on a prior use value. In other words, the question of where the value comes from in economic exchange (when money changes hands) is resolved through recourse to the assumption of a natural and given use value: the utility of the object to the 'individual' (for the logic of utility to work there has to be an *individual* whose psychology accords with the logic of interest to maximise his or her 'utility': 'use' of objects; an individual *subject* of economic exchange). Use value and the logic of utility are predicated in turn on the assumed inalienable status of human 'needs'. A loaf of bread, considered as basic staple food, is assumed to have 'use value' for someone who is hungry and thus deemed to 'need' it, and prepared to buy it at a given price corresponding to its 'exchange value'. (I elaborate on the significance of this assumption of 'needs', and Baudrillard's critique, below.)

So what exactly is the code? The code instantiates this process whereby, relying on the dichotomous separation of exchange value from use value, a logic of equivalence structures the scale of value which is then necessary to establish the relationship between exchange value and use value. For example, it is necessary to establish the relative 'exchange value' of a loaf of packaged bread and a jar of instant coffee, by recourse to a scale where three of this can be said to be worth one of that. Economics mythically postulates that this relationship is derived from the use value, or utility, consumers place on these goods. Baudrillard argues that this structure is paralleled by the positing of a subject as dichotomously separate from an object, which implies one then has to institute the concept of 'need' to establish the subject/object relation. Economics, of course, assumes that 'need' comes prior, and this assumption serves to postulate the natural status of the subject/object relation. The code, therefore, is the structural, dichotomous split, the bar that simultaneously separates and constitutes its terms as present/absent, identity/difference, 1/0.[1]

Poststructuralist linguistic theories, as these have been appropriated by feminists, critique the notion of the fixity of meaning, and rather assume that meaning is fluid, plural, and multiple (see Weedon 1987). This leads to the question of how this apparent plurality and multiplicity could be conceptualised by Baudrillard as coded. Saussure's structuralist theory of linguistics, for all its confusions and contradictions, has been interpreted as claiming, in simple terms, that meaning does not inhere in the object world, but is created within language. Vicki Kirby (1997) is an example of an author who, from a feminist perspective, engages Saussure's writings with careful scrutiny to reveal the problematics of such a rigid distinction of language and object world, claiming that Saussure's work is actually traversed by the tensions produced by such a rigid formulation. Generally, however, it is understood that the central thesis of Saussure's theory of linguistics is that language is made up of signs which form a system of meaning by virtue of a dichotomous structure of identity/difference (or same as, different from) distinguishing signs from each other and simultaneously establishing their 'identity'. Accordingly, a sign as a unit of meaning comprises a signifier (an acoustic sound or visual mark completely devoid of meaning) and a signified (a concept or meaning associated with that signifier). The signifier (Sr) and the signified (Sd) are a dichotomous binary, but according to Saussure, they are like two sides of a sheet of paper whereby the Sr conjures the Sd in an inevitable fashion, although their relationship is deemed to be arbitrary. This structure parallels that described above with respect to the dichotomous separating of exchange value and use value, and then the establishing of their relationship through a logic of equivalence. Similarly here, the dichotomous separation of the Sr and the Sd (Sr/Sd) presents the problem of their relationship, which is then resolved by establishing their equivalence.

This observation has to be followed quickly by the concern that the poststructuralist critique of the fixed nature of the relationship between Saussure's Sr and Sd renders this notion of a relationship of equivalence simply wrong; according to the poststructuralist critique the meaning (Sd) associated with any signifier is continually deferred, and is never fixed. Further, there is a multiplicity of possible Sds that might be 'read' from a Sr, and it is precisely this plurality of possible meanings of signs that makes the active use of language so political, as meanings are continually contested. Baudrillard argues, however, that this critique simply shifts the code from one of equivalence to one of polyvalence and leaves the fundamental structure intact. The fundamental structure is the dichotomous separation of the Sr and the Sd, and the codified nature of the construction of meaning according to a *polyvalent* logic of identity/difference (identities/differences). The structural assumptions about the construction of the meaning of 'objects' remain the same whether our meaning is assumed to be the same as, or different from, that of 'others'; assumed to be fixed or floating and fluid. Equivalent or polyvalent, meaning is still 'valent', that is, has the propensity to register a positive identity on a single scale of value; whether this is a single point or multiple points is irrelevant. It remains within a binary construct of identity/difference, Sr/Sd.[2]

Baudrillard argues that Saussurian linguistics created a semiology with an ideological force of the same magnitude as that of political economy.[3] It could perhaps be said, following Baudrillard's argument, that the 'post'structuralist critique of Saussure is of the order of Marx's critique of political economy. As Marx's critique leaves the assumptions of use value and the ideology of needs intact (and in fact more firmly reconstitutes them), similarly the post-structuralist critique leaves the assumption of the dichotomy of Sr/Sd intact, which reinscribes the codified logic of meaning.

From this brief introduction it is possible to see how Baudrillard focuses on the structural interweaving of political economy and signification. He insists that the critique of the system of political economy has also to be a critique of the political economy of the sign.[4] Before considering his analysis and critique of this system, it is probably useful to give some consideration to what exactly is problematic about the code by introducing the concept of 'symbolic exchange', which Baudrillard counterpoints to economic exchange.

The *Shorter Oxford English Dictionary* definition of 'code' is wonderfully ambiguous and ironic when considered in the light of the current discussion: 'set of rules *on any subject*' (my emphasis); a set of rules, a code that pre-determines the form of the subject (here linguistic subject as well as 'topic'). The very possibility of economic exchange, Baudrillard argues, is predicated on the existence of such a code: a rule that structures the relationship between objects and the relationship of objects to subjects on a scale creating differential positions that *identify* the object. The object must exist as an autonomous entity that can be so positioned; simultaneously, the subject must exist as an autonomous agent whose need or desire constitutes the benchmark for the utility of the object, providing the basis for its value.

This dichotomous structure of subject/object is a precondition for the existence of economic exchange, in other words for a form of exchange that functions through the codification of value according to a scale that can position objects in terms of their equivalence and difference. This parallels the structure of identity/difference in linguistic terms, whereby identity constitutes the positive or marked term and difference is the negative or unmarked term: a binary structure that designates *the same* or *not the same*.[5] This structure is assumed and naturalised within political economy and within Saussurian linguistics. It is not possible to critique such a structure from 'nowhere'; the critic must take a stance that provides a view on that structure, and

Baudrillard's critique is from the viewpoint of, or by way of contrast to, what he calls 'symbolic exchange'.

Symbolic exchange is the radical 'other' of economic exchange in all respects. The 'symbolic' character of the exchange means there is no autonomous object, no autonomous subject, no code, no possibility of economic value. The object takes on its meaning in the relationship of exchange. This meaning is always and only ambivalent – it is neither this nor that; the object has no 'identity' in a positive (+) sense. Symbolic exchange is a process of non-essentialist, dynamic challenge and seduction; a social process whereby objects seduce, meanings are continually exchanged, the meanings and status of subjects are always ambivalent. Power is squandered and laid to waste.

I am very aware that numerous questions are raised by this characterisation of symbolic exchange, questions that will be addressed throughout this book. What is meant by 'symbolic'? What is meant by 'power'? What is 'seduction'? What is the significance of 'ambivalence' in this context? How, in what way, are these conceptualisations important to feminist inquiry? Precisely how symbolic exchange differs from economic exchange is discussed in this chapter in more detail below, to provide a background for the exploration of these questions.

The Ideology of Needs

> Metaphysics itself has never done anything else in western thought but posit the subject and tautologically resolve its relation to the world.
>
> (PES: 71)

The entire logic of economic exchange value is predicated on the inalienable assumption of use value. In other words, to be able to assign an economic value to a commodity (a structural precondition of the commodity form), it has to be placed on a scale of value (more than this, less than that, equivalent to itself and others that are the same – have the same identity); so the question then becomes 'Where does the value on this scale actually come from?' In the discourse of classical and neo-classical economics, in the critique of Marx, in the assumptions of western metaphysics, it comes from the usefulness of the commodity to the individual. The individual is assumed to have 'needs' and these needs (and desires) are, *a priori*, the natural basis of the logic of economic value, a logic of utility, or use value (I am thirsty; I need a drink; a glass of water is useful to quench my thirst). As Baudrillard writes, the postulate that humans are 'endowed with needs and a natural inclination to satisfy them' is never questioned (PES: 73).

Crucial to an understanding of Baudrillard's critique (of economic *and* Marxist ideology) is his argument that the presumption that human beings have needs is simply that; a presumption, an ideology. Rather than accept this axiomatic origin, Baudrillard constructs an extraordinary and compelling argument of immense import, that the notion of humans as subjects with needs that are satisfied by objects in the world is an ideology. Baudrillard was not the first to identify the importance of such a critique but developed his argument building on the observations of Bataille (1967, trans. 1988). Baudrillard argues that, rather than preceding economic exchange value as the point of origin from which all economic systems and modes of production derive their meaning and *raison d'être*, the notion of needs, the notion of use value, *follows* the ideological construction of exchange value. Use value acts as an 'alibi' for exchange value, providing a naturalised rationale for its existence, in much the same way, I would add, as feminists have argued that (biological) 'sex' has provided a naturalised alibi for 'gender'.

Following on from his earliest work on objects and social dynamics of consumption (SO and CS), Baudrillard develops this critique of the ideology of needs in his book *For a Critique of the Political Economy of the Sign*. He claims that to '[speak] in terms of need is magical thinking' (PES: 70) pre- cisely because of its status as a kind of origin myth. Here he argues that the positing of subject and object as autonomous and separate entities creates the necessity to devise a myth to establish their relation. This, he says, is accomplished in the concept of need and its allied concepts of mana, instinct, motivation, choice, preference, utility. The syntax of *subject needs object* is a tautological means of resolving the relationship between the subject and the object, whereby the one is defined in terms of the other: 'positing the autonomy of the subject and its specular reflection in the autonomy of the object' (PES: 71).

The logic of equivalence (axiomatic to economics) is an abstraction, a code, a rule. For objects to be abstractly and generally exchangeable, they must be thought and rationalised in terms of utility (PES: 131). The code equates the object to its useful end; its function becomes its ontological finality. According to Baudrillard's analysis, this is where the economic is born (PES: 132). In the same movement, the social relation of use value requires the existence of the abstract *individual* who becomes not only the person with needs, but also the one with desires, with motivations, with a 'self' (and an unconscious) in the privacy of 'his' or 'her' psychological finitude.[6] I have placed the gendered pronoun in inverted commas here to signal what, I want to argue, is the provisional nature of the gendering of this individual. In the same way as the 'subject' is an abstraction necessitated by this dichotomous splitting of 'subject' and 'object', the notion that gender constitutes an *identity* of the *individual* is equally an abstraction. The abstract (gendered) individual with a 'self' has to have a relation to 'him' or 'her' self, a relation which Baudrillard argues is itself structured by the utilitarian imperative:

> In the process of satisfaction, he [*sic*] valorises and makes fruitful his own potentialities for pleasure; he 'realises' and manages, to the best of his ability, his own 'faculty' of pleasure, treated literally like a productive

force. Isn't this what all of humanist ethics is based on – the 'proper use' of oneself?

(PES: 136)

In his critique of the naturalised assumption of utility and human needs, and its role in providing an anchoring point for the system of economic exchange value, Baudrillard also analyses the relationship between the two forms of value as two terms of a binary opposition. He points out, as many have before and since, that the structural logic of binary oppositions always privileges one term, which becomes the dominant term. In this context, the logic of equivalence, articulated within a dichotomous structure of 'same as' or 'different from', is necessary for the construction of 'identity': identity *is* the dominant term ('same as'). Here we see the powerful significance of the parallel structure of identity/difference; same as/different from; equivalent to/not equivalent to; positive/negative; present not present. This rationalisation which permits the identity of objects to be rendered in their functionality also permits the object to enter the field of political economy as a positive (+) value (PES: 134).

Baudrillard characterises the parallel structural form of economic value and signification in the terms of two equivalent dichotomies: EV/UV = Sr/Sd. The ideological form of economic exchange value (EV) is to assume that EV obtains its value from use value (UV), whereas in fact, Baudrillard has argued, UV is an artefact of the social institution of a codified system of EV.[7] In the same way, rather than assuming that the meaning of the Sr obtains in the Sd, Baudrillard argues that the Sd is an artefact of the social institution of a codified system of representation. UV and Sds are only *effects* of EV and Sr respectively, and neither UV nor the Sd is an autonomous reality that either EV or the Sr 'would express or translate in their code' (PES: 137). Here Baudrillard argues that UV and the Sd are only simulation models, produced by the play of EV and Srs, providing the latter with the 'guarantee of the real, the lived, the concrete' (PES: 137). As political economy needed UV to institute the order of EV (in the same movement establishing equivalence as an abstract equation of all values), so the Sd was needed to institute an order of meanings making possible the naturalisation of the relationship Sr–Sd. This naturalisation could then produce the appearance that concepts (Sds) exist and precede the Srs that name them.[8] In Baudrillard's words:

The system of use value involves the resorption without trace of the entire ideological and historical labour process that leads the subject in the first place to think of himself [*sic*] as an individual, defined by his needs and satisfaction, and thus ideally to integrate himself into the structure of the commodity.

(PES: 138)

The inalienable point of origin instantiated by the myth of utility is not only parallel to, but inextricably coexistent with, the assumption of the unsurpassable 'nature' of meaning. As I mentioned above, whether the Sd conjured by a Sr is assumed to be fixed in Saussure's terms, in the semantic conventions of a particular language, or whether the Sd is conceptualised as plural in its possibilities, inevitably deferred in poststructuralist, Derridian terms, the dichotomous structure of Sr/Sd remains, the bar that separates them is re-marked, and the assumption of a codified system of meaning continues to underwrite the mode of representation. I hope that the significance of this critique becomes clearer as we consider Baudrillard's notion of symbolic exchange and seduction.

Before moving on to look at Baudrillard's articulation of specific logics of value and signification, it is useful here to signal how the argument presented so far points to the importance of developing a critique of the political economy of the sign as much as a critique of the political economy of value, labour, production. In this connection, his comment on the 'magical thinking of ideology' is pertinent. He proposes that the concept of ideology needs to be theorised radically differently from a Marxist formulation of infra–superstructural relations. Baudrillard understands this relation to be precisely structured in accordance with the very form and logic that, in his argument, need to be critiqued. Rather, he construes ideology as that form traversing *both* the production of signs and material production (in other words both the super- and infrastructural realms in Marxist terminology): specifically, the bifurcation into two terms as EV, Sr, on the one hand and UV, Sd, on the other. The ideological form is that bar that simultaneously splits EV/UV and Sr/Sd to place EV and Sr on one side of the dichotomy and UV and Sd on the other.

> Ideology lies already whole in the relation of EV to UV, that is, in the logic of the commodity, as is so in the relation of the Sr to the Sd, that is, in the internal logic of the sign.
>
> (PES: 144)

And, in what in my view is the key statement here, Baudrillard writes: 'ideology is the process of reducing and abstracting symbolic material into a form' (PES: 144). Both the abstraction of value instantiated through the economic exchange of supposedly autonomous objects by supposedly autonomous (needing and desiring) subjects, *and* the abstraction of meaning instantiated through the circulation of signs as a mode of representation, rest on the ideological separation of EV from UV and the Sr from the Sd. These two dichotomies form one structure, an ideological structure that stands in radical opposition to the symbolic (the system's ultimate exclusion).

The Logics of Value and Signification

Baudrillard distinguishes three logics of value and signification which can be contrasted to that of the symbolic, or symbolic exchange. First is use value, which accords to a logic of utility or practical operations, and whereby the object is an instrument to an end, the satisfaction of a (naturalised) need. Second is economic exchange value, with its logic of the market and of equivalence, where the object is a commodity. Third is sign value, which accords to a logic of status and of difference, where the object is a sign.

UV	[utility]	practical operations	(*instrument*)
EV	[market]	equivalence	(*commodity*)
SV	[status]	difference	(*sign*)

In each of these three orders of value, the object takes on its value/meaning according to its location within a codified system, and according to a specific, structured logic: the *instrument* within a field of practical operations according to a logic of utility; the *commodity* within the field of the market according to a logic of equivalence; and the *sign* within a hierarchical field of status according to a logic of difference. Baudrillard points out that each configuration of value 'is seized by the next in a higher order of simulacra' (SE&D: 2), thus the hegemony of each 'phase' of value is supported by the logics of the prior phase appearing as a phantom reference. Baudrillard analyses this as an ideological process whereby each previous phase serves as an alibi to justify and mask the contemporary operation of the law of value. A mythical UV is brought to bear to justify EV, and EV is promoted to institute the 'law of the market' when prevalent social dynamics are actually best understood in terms of sign value (SV).

Within a logic of symbolic exchange, by contrast, the object does not take on a value or a meaning from an *a priori*, codified, abstracted field. The 'object' does not circulate within an economic field which inaugurates subjects and objects; it cannot have an economic value; its meaning is both established and abolished in the relationship of exchange. The logic of ambivalence and the field of symbolic exchange creates the 'object' and the 'subject' as neither this, nor that; it abolishes the positivity of identity and the accompanying cumulative investment in the individual self. The symbolic nature of the object cannot be 'known' (discursively) and cannot be represented.

Central to Baudrillard's entire theorisation of the contemporary political economy of the sign is the ascendancy of sign value in this era of the explosion of consumption. The previous dominance of an economic logic of equivalence in the era of early capitalism has been subordinated to a logic of difference: the logic of the sign, where the meaning of the sign is achieved through its differential status within a chain of signifiers. The object as an item of consumption is no longer a commodity with its originary, anchoring reference in utility, it is rather a sign; 'liberated' from any reference point, it floats and accumulates in a relentless positivity. If the object enters the field of political economy as a commodity with positive (+) value because of its rationalisation as use value under the sign of its functionality, it still has a relation of 'reference'; it still obtains its positive value, its identity, by virtue of a logic of reference. But the object as sign is sublimely released from any such referent to exist as pure positivity. The sign's positivity is irreducible, obtaining its equivalence to itself through its difference to other signs. This concept of the positivity of the sign is a crucial one, but before considering Baudrillard's critique (or movement towards a critique) of the political economy of the sign, it is important to say something about 'production'.

The Production of Production

Baudrillard argues that use value is an 'alibi', or naturalised rationale, for the construction and reproduction of economic exchange value. If use value – the idea that objects have value to humans because of their irreducible utility – is the anchoring point for economic exchange value, the notion of a 'subject', who makes objects that have use value and which can be exchanged, follows. 'Production' is axiomatic and instantiates the inevitability of utility, and neither production nor utility was really critiqued by Marx; obviously he critiqued the relations of production, but not, as Baudrillard points out, the form of production, not the possibility and politics of its very construction. Production is assumed to be as irreducible as utility. In *The Mirror of Production* Baudrillard examines the interdependent construction of the autonomous individual as an economic agent and as labour power, the object of economic exchange as discrete, having utility, and able to be represented in terms of its 'identity' (equivalence to itself), and the ideology of production. An understanding of how these constructs are linked and inter-dependent, and an appreciation of the significance of this cultural formation, are, I want to argue, vital to our understanding of the politics of the 'production' of gendered subjects in the contemporary world.

'Production' enables objects to be rendered visible in their positive (+) identity (as 'this' and not 'that'), and to be released into the domain of economic exchange. For example, fresh, pasteurised (thus safe) skim milk in an easy-to-use/dispose-of/or-recycle container, defines at once a production process, a product, and a set of social relationships determining the value at which this product can be traded at a given point in time and a given place. However, in the exchange as ideologically defined, both production processes and social relationships are occulted, and the product is produced as on a stage, positively appearing as object of desire and use. Production also enables the construction of the individual as 'labour power', as producer. The principle of 'production' is one of indefinite accumulation; value is only meaningful as 'more', positive, additional. Within this logic, the production of items for consumption and use can only be understood as neutral, obvious, natural, transhistorical, and transcultural; as an irreducibly 'good thing'. The social processes associated with the 'mode of production' have been the subject of Marxist-inspired critique and political activism for decades, but the notion of production, the assumption of its natural and inevitable status, had, until Baudrillard's critique, not been the focus of systematic critical scholarly inquiry. What is of particular interest here is to tease out the implications of the way the object is constructed within western capitalist 'political economy'. The object-that-is-'produced' is the object-to-be-consumed, is the object that has an 'identity'. To have an identity means it *is* something (albeit deferring any absolute meaning): its ontology is fixed within a semiology structured in accordance with the dichotomy of identity/difference, in other words, it cannot be both this and not this at the same time. The construction of objects (and subjects) as identifiable within this semiological structure creates the possibility of 'production'.

A substantial part of Baudrillard's early work involved characterising and theorising the shifts and changes since the eighteenth century that have transformed the structure of capitalism, the construction of economic value, and the mode of representation. Baudrillard's critical standpoint and concern have focused on the ideological processes, remembering that, in Baudrillard's terms, in talking about ideology we are talking about the semiological reduction of the symbolic: reducing that which cannot be contained and represented within a dichotomous +/− structure of identity/difference to a codified form, and specifically how this ideology simultaneously structures a mythological economic object and linguistic subject. This 'history' provides a basis for constructing an understanding of the contemporary configuration of signification, subjectivity, and economic value.

To predicate a theory of the object on the existence of human needs and their satisfaction implicates another dichotomy; one that was vital to the flourishing of a discursive practice of production in the eighteenth and nineteenth centuries: culture and nature. 'Nature' became the great, primary referent, the great signified (MOP: 54). 'Nature' was cast as the *reality* from which utility was extracted, from whence value obtained its ultimate reference, and which science was destined to know. Indeed, beyond and common to each of these, 'nature' provided the reference point as object against which 'man' could register as subject.[9] The contradictions inherent in the status of 'man' as both subject of (the conditions of) knowledge and the object of knowledge (anatomy) as theorised by Foucault (1966, trans. 1970), are more complex and politically potent for 'woman', who is positioned in a more ambiguous position within the culture/nature (human/not human) dichotomy. This split of 'man' and 'nature', a split that objectifies 'nature' and inaugurates the subject, is predicated on, and in turn institutes, a relation of necessity and an economic 'law' of scarcity. In *The Mirror of Production*, Baudrillard refers to Weber, who locates historically this rupture that makes the 'rational calculus of production' possible, in Christian times (MOP: 65). Baudrillard's point is that 'political economy' could be characterised as a kind of actualisation of this break.

Baudrillard constantly returns to a comparison with what he calls 'symbolic exchange'. I am firmly of the view that it is unhelpful, inaccurate, and misleading to interpret his point of comparison as a kind of romanticism for a previous 'golden age'. Baudrillard uses a notion of the symbolic, engaging to some extent with the works of Mauss (1966), Sahlins (1974), and Bataille (1967, trans. 1988), as a point of departure for the purpose of critique of the contemporary world he inhabits and the ideological processes that mark it; a point of departure chosen precisely because of its ability to throw into relief the interrelated nature of the institution of the economic object and the construction of the linguistic subject. He uses the notion as a device to present a theorised, critical interpretation of the problem at the heart of our postmodern age: the codified, ideological underpinnings of economic value and the mode of signification, and how this codification institutes and makes possible relations of power.[10]

It is a position or standpoint that precisely disallows and deconstructs the romanticisation of 'liberation', 'freedom', 'the market', 'democracy' – the signifiers of the (or one) history of the 'west'. It allows a critical stance from which to view our contemporary social order. To turn it around and suggest that Baudrillard is wanting to return to the horrors of the social relations of 'obligation and reciprocity' of feudal Europe, the torturing, ritualistic bodily mutilations associated with many tribal practices, or the 'symbolic exchange' of 'women', is to have grasped the wrong end of the telescope, and, I might add, in a way that prevents (avoids?) engagement with the issues at stake. It is also a flaw of logic; to take a critical stance with respect to an object of inquiry does not mean one endorses its 'other'. To critique exploitation by contrast to domination does not mean one advocates the latter. My reading of Baudrillard prompts me to ask if there is something about the concept of the symbolic as he articulates it which has potential for exploring gendered power relations and the problematics of gender identity.

Symbolic exchange is the radical other from the economic. According to Baudrillard, the economic, in its classical and neo-classical form,[11] is born when what the object 'is' is assumed to reside within it, it has an essence; when the object attains its value in accordance with an abstract code that enables its relation to other objects to be ascertained through a logic of equivalence which in turn obtains its rationale from the ideology of utility and use value; and when the individual emerges as a 'subject' whose relation to the world of objects is articulated primarily through the ideology of need (and, with psychoanalysis, desire). From this critical viewpoint, the notion of the 'individual' as it emerged from the Enlightenment period with needs, 'liberated' from the ties and constraints of a previous era, is an abstraction. And the discourse of liberation can be understood as a process of interiorising subjectivity resulting from the dichotomous separation of subject and object. This 'subject' of industrialising modernity has an essence, 'an abstract essence over which the identity of the subject comes to fix itself' (MOP: 95).

By contrast, symbolic exchange is a form of exchange, a form of construction of objects and their meaning, that is antithetical to the economic. The poles of the exchange are not automatised; there is neither essence nor absolute separation of subject from object. Both are continually transformed through the exchange. There is no identity.[12] The ontology of objects is inexorably ambivalent. Goods are not produced, nor do they exist as commodities or products. Most importantly, goods are destined to circulate in a social process of exchange that augments the social in terms of the creation and destruction, the giving and returning or passing on, of the 'gift'. This process negates the possibility of power through accumulation. The individual is not an 'individual' with an interior psychology, a subjectivity, an identity, with needs and desires. Within this construct of the symbolic exchange, language is symbolic, similarly ambivalent, and must be exchanged. Words evoke, point, seduce, act rather than connote and denote. And they circulate. Stockpiles of words that do not circulate and are not exchanged are, as Baudrillard writes, more deadly than the accumulation of waste from industrialisation (SE&D: 203). The logic of the symbolic and symbolic exchange is one of ambivalence and transformation through circulation; the positive and the negative, presence and absence (if one can talk in these terms), are always activated.

I have taken time to elaborate a little more on symbolic exchange, not to invoke another era or culture (I will discuss this construct of 'otherness' in relation to culture and 'difference' in Chapter 3), but to provide some characterisation of what I believe to be central to Baudrillard's evocation of the 'symbolic' for the purposes of my own argumentation. I think there is something here that is profoundly important to feminism, especially at this time, and I will gradually build a case for this claim as I proceed.

Returning more specifically to the theme of production, during the first century of the transition to capitalism, as the utilitarian ethos and productivist machinery were gathering momentum, the mode of representation (Sr/Sd) and the ontological presumptions of its grammar, as well as the code of economic value, were solidly formulated according to a logic of representation and reference. The Sr and EV were both conceptualised as representational formulae that referred to something else, and that something else was 'reality'. The Sr represented the Sd – the concept, or the sign (Sr/Sd) represented the real thing, the referent (in the form of 'nature'); EV was a proxy that relied on UV as its referent, again a thoroughly naturalised construct; the Sd of production was the subject who laboured. This period was marked by the object-as-commodity, whereby the materiality of the commodity was obtained through this structural formulation of EV/UV; language referred to things where reality (Sd or referent) preceded its representation. Indeed, the representation of an object could be questioned and altered by reference to that-which-was-represented: the map had to fit the territory and could be altered to achieve a more accurate representation. Similarly, reference to the function of UV (which of course would only work if 'individuals' experienced themselves as 'subjects' with 'needs') was the ultimate benchmark.

From the Natural Real to the Hyperreal

From a critical standpoint that does not assume the natural status of utility, production, objects as commodities, subjects as labour power, and so on, modernity takes on an even greater weight of ideological manipulation than Marx theorised. Beyond the exploitative relations of capitalist and neo-classical economics, modernity constructed a social relation of economic exchange, of 'political economy' with all its permutations, that instituted a logic of accumulation and power at its core.[13] By the early decades of the twentieth century, it was evident that the imperatives of a logic of production would collapse without an escalation of consumption. And as Baudrillard writes, '[s]omething in the capitalist sphere has changed radically, something Marxist analysis can no longer respond to' (MOP: 118). The explosion of consumption over the course of the twentieth century has been accompanied by a severance of the sign from the referent, the Sr from reference to the Sd, and in practice while not in ideological form, UV, 'utility', has been abandoned to create an economic structure of exchange where values float free from their anchoring point, are no longer tied down by a fixed logic of equivalence relative to a fixed referent of value, but can find their level in a sea of differences. It is a kind of throwing overboard of heavy and superfluous items to stop the ship from sinking – we don't even need the referent, we don't need the gold exchange standard, in fact without them the logic of consumption can expand unimpeded.

The proposition of such a transformation and its implications requires careful discussion. First, I think it useful to say something about why I believe the analysis Baudrillard develops is so important. My own introduction to Baudrillard's work was in the late 1980s or so, when I was grappling with a question that became the basis for my doctoral research. I was perplexed and bewildered by what I observed to be the failure of a politics of opposition, where those of us involved in the women's health and community health movements in New Zealand and around the world were attempting to challenge and overwhelm the vested interests of the medical establishment in relation to a number of demands. We assumed these demands were related to our oppressed and minority status, and we wanted to apply pressure to the systemic dominance of medical authority to insist on our own status as subjects of our own bodies. My experience and observations over a period of a few years in the late 1970s and early 1980s led me to question why it was that our attempts were not exactly met with opposition, there was not even really a sense of a battle to be won; rather, the urgency and determination with which we articulated our concerns were met with a kind of unidentifiable neutralising force. It was very hard to say whether we had made any progress when the boundaries between 'us' and 'them' became progressively more blurred, and 'they' started to use 'our' discourse and try and tell us that our concerns were really their concerns too. We could all work together under the formulation of a new relationship of providers and consumers which, it seemed, would give us all we 'wanted'. Beyond a simple yet inadequate explanation in terms of co-option, this process represented a massive implosion of the polarisation of power, and had the uncanny capacity to absorb and recapture any form of opposition. My sense was that this process was similar to many other so-called 'political' antagonisms I observed around me; it created the feeling of a *pretence* of political challenge: it *looked* like a political challenge, we went through the motions, but at root the systemic processes seemed to be regulated by something quite 'other'. The stakes had changed and could disappear and reappear in another guise with a different name. The structural logic of the very terms of power seemed to have changed, or at least to be very different from those underpinning the discourses of liberation, emancipation, and empowerment articulated in the 1960s. Reading Baudrillard's work, I came to develop a theoretical understanding that helped make sense of all of this in sociological and political terms.[14]

Baudrillard confronts and engages with what he presents as tendencies or trends produced by major transformations in the structural logic of capital, economic value, signification, and the construction of subjects and objects. If this analysis has some potential to produce insights into some of the most dramatic and compelling contradictions of our era, then surely it's worth pursuing. Later in this chapter I will address the important epistemological question of how we know whether he has a point or not. In leading to this question I want to outline briefly another problematic that might speak to some readers. If production is still firmly grounded in labour, if we work because the products of our labour are needed (desired) by people, and if the extraction of surplus value is still *the* mechanism of capitalist exploitation, then how come it appears that 'work', its availability and practice, is not in fact regulated by this ideology, or should I say, how come it *appears* that this explanatory framework itself constitutes only an appearance? As Baudrillard writes in 'The end of production' (the first part of *Symbolic Exchange and Death*), 'labour power is no longer brutally bought and sold: it is "designed", "marketed" and "merchandised", linking production with the consumerist system of signs' (EOP: 105)[15]. In this chapter he foregrounds the shift whereby 'labour' seems to function more to 'locate individuals in a social nexus where nothing ever converges, except perhaps in the immanence of this functional matrix' (EOP: 104) than to provide the means by which products are manufactured to fulfil needs, or as a labour exploited by the capitalist who owns the means of production and ruthlessly extracts profits. Baudrillard considers the possibility that knowledge, skills, and aptitudes, along with sexuality, the body, and imagination, are not so much mobilised for production but 'rather indexed, assigned and summoned to function as operational variables. They have become not so much productive forces, but chess pieces of the code, and checked by the same rules of the game' (EOP: 105).[16] The concerns I raised above in the first example regarding the apparent implosion of 'power relations' find their echo in the dislocation of labour from its role as the great signified of production.

> Whereas the axiom of production tends to reduce everything to factors, the axiom of the code reduces everything to variables. And whereas the former leads to equations and a balance sheet of forces, the latter leads to fluctuating and random combinations that neutralise by connection, not by annexation, whatever resists or escapes them.
>
> (EOP: 105)

The shift in the discourse of economic value from exchange value to sign value represents, in Baudrillard's view, a social transformation of virtually unparalleled magnitude. He uses the universalist assumptions of Saussure's theory of linguistics to locate Saussure's theory precisely in its historical context. In other words, what is accomplished by this appropriation is the demonstration that Saussure's theory of the linguistic sign can be understood to reflect the conditions in which it was formulated. The theory of the structural bar that splits the Sr and the Sd, but which in turn begs the question of how these terms are related (equi-/polyvalence), prefigures the possibility of the increasing autonomy of the Sr. The Sr takes its meaning less from the anchor point of the Sd (the sign from the referent), and more from its (fluid and hence plural) location within a chain of signifiers. Rather than with reference to a Sd, difference from other Srs locates the meaning of the Sr; a meaning that is fleeting, secured only in the moment of its invocation. The play of Srs, of positive values, constructs meaning; another way of looking at it is that the Sr precedes the Sd, rendering the Sd meaningless as the referent of the Sr. The *sign* is the word Baudrillard uses to evoke that entity, that construct which exists in its pure positivity, as 'identity' with no 'other', no 'difference', no reference point that limits the freedom of meaning and value. It is, of course, a myth. This mythical character, however, does not seem to circumscribe or defuse the potency of this structural code to underwrite economic value, and in the same movement to volatilise social contradictions and have them reappear in simulated form. Before discussing the important phenomenon of simulation, I want to continue this depiction of the sign and sign value until the interconnected political, ontological, and epistemological facets are clarified.

The structure of the sign, in Baudrillard's terms, is the same code as that which excludes reference to utility from the calculus of economic exchange, leaving EV as the form parallel to the signifier. Economic value obtains through a logic of difference; like the meaning of the signifier, value floats in a randomised set of possibilities, taking a particular 'position' only ephemerally, forever plural and contestable, with no specific reference to UV, to the relativity of needs, of desires, but only by its position within a field of differences. How, then, could I state an apparent contradiction above, that the sign form (and here the commodity form) exists as pure identity with no 'difference'? It is crucial to point out here that these 'differences', which, in Saussurian terms, create the possibility of 'identity', are conceptualised by Baudrillard as *parallel positivities* (my term); they are not differences that have a negative valence relative to a positive, but rather they represent an infinity of positive values that never converge, never engage, that can never transform an 'other' or be transformed, but rather jostle around in an endless, shifting, arbitrary hierarchy. Baudrillard calls this a logic of difference, as did Saussure in his theory of signification, but this is a difference that separates and distinguishes positive identities and not a difference that constitutes otherness.

Ontology: what we assume to be real, the nature of reality, the discussion of, and definition of, what 'is'. Clearly this concept is problematised in Baudrillard's theorisation. To analyse ontological assumptions, we have to engage critically with the form and structure of language, which, as we have seen, Baudrillard argues is inextricably related to the structure of value and processes of exchange. Sign value, a mode of representation whereby positive values, positive signifiers, circulate and designate difference, issues an ontology which is both essentialist and at the same time fluid, plural, multiple. The word 'is' simultaneously constructs a sign that is pure identity (a dollar is a dollar is a dollar), and opens the possibility of its rejection or its multiple interpretation (or value). But what is radically excluded from this grammar of the sign by virtue of the structural logic of difference is its transformation through encountering an 'other'.[17] This identity which can only be displaced and replaced but not subverted, transformed, seduced, is, I want to argue, a phallic identity (an argument I will develop in Chapter 2).

The abstract code that regulates sign value in the contemporary political economy of the west, a code that creates the systemic programme for infinite consumption and proliferation of identities, is a form of social control that Baudrillard describes and writes about as absolute. Absolute in the totalitarian sense, but not by virtue of a form of domination that can always, at the limit, be reversed; rather, totalitarian in its exclusion of the possibility of reversion. Reversion has been written out, deleted, eradicated from the system; at least this is the myth that sustains its rule, and while this myth structures the construction of economic value and economic agents, the only possibility of challenge is at the level of the logic of the system itself. Any other mode of transgression will be recaptured by the system and reproduced as another market niche, another identity, another lifestyle. It is this 'absolute' character of a social order structured in accordance with sign value that Baudrillard remarks on so vehemently as one which is hegemonic in the extreme; to a point that makes earlier capitalist exploitation (and historical materialism) positively benign. There is no dialectic here, but rather an endless proliferation of different identities and constantly shifting value. 'Things' come and go, but equally there is a market (and a place and time) for frozen identities. 'I am who I am' unproblematically coexists with 'I can be anything I want'. Sign logic operates by internal differentiation *and* by general homogenisation (PES: 101). It is this homogenisation that, in the guise of a proliferation of simulated differences, creates an abstract totalisation that, Baudrillard argues, permits the functioning of signs to 'establish and perpetuate real discriminations and the order of power' (PES: 101).

This brings us to the question of politics and an understanding of power. I will discuss Baudrillard's conceptualisation of power in more depth in Chapter 2. Here I will just note Baudrillard's observation that power, as it is manifested in the contemporary social order (as distinct from the symbolic realm), is that which cannot be reversed. For example, an ontological or epistemological assertion (this *is*; I *know*) that is *produced* and prohibits or refuses any possibility of its transformation, its challenge or seduction,[18] is of the order of power. A physical constraint or violation that is rendered absolute, as irreversible, or equally protestations of 'love', might instantiate power and construct the 'other' as 'subjected' to the authority of that power. If reversion negates power, then a social order that structurally eliminates the possibility of reversion at the very core of its logic turns 'politics' into bland simulation that reverses nothing, but serves to perpetuate continually the power of the system, partially through its pretence that something 'political' is in fact going on.

In the final chapter of *For a Critique of the Political Economy of the Sign*, Baudrillard brings together the strands of his argument to reassert that the logic of political economy is at the very heart of the sign, and that the structure of the sign is at the very heart of the commodity form. The interpenetration of value and signification simultaneously makes it possible for signs to function as exchange value (sign value) and for the commodity to function as sign. The subsuming of value within codified systems of signification centres on the functionality and operational character of contemporary life. In the same way as sign digits in electronic circuitry enable a computer to function mindlessly by carrying out series of operations on digits (1/0), the meaningless circulation of sign values enables, indeed intimates, signifies to, producers and consumers to function mindlessly according to the hegemonic code of value. The sign is not as a 'message' that conveys something in a relation of representation, but, as Baudrillard writes, 'because its form establishes it as a total *medium*, as a *system of communication* administering all social exchange' (PES: 146). With the implosion of a relation of reference, the object, or commodity, *is* sign, and subjects structured as producers and consumers of signs are signified.[19] The interplay of signifiers and of exchange values is governed and structured by the same code, the same 'set of rules'.

Thus, Baudrillard is critical of Saussure's theory of the relationship between the Sr and the Sd, as idealist. The Sd/Referent is an effect of the ontological assumption of the representational code; a code that splits the Sr and Sd and in doing so effects a real that has a meaning that is pre-empted and controlled by the code. Far from being idealist himself, Baudrillard uses this critique to expose the reductionist nature of the semiological code and creates a space to wonder about the real. The idealism that instantiates the political economy of the sign is expanded by Baudrillard into his theory of the simulated nature of the real. While I will discuss his work, *Simulations*, more fully in Chapter 3, I will briefly relate this concept and its significance to the discussion thus far. The loss of the referent (or more accurately, the implosion of a relation of reference), the flotation of value and signification, the passing of a relation of reference to use value and to reality as an anchoring point for exchange value and signification as representational systems, has meant a displacement of the location of the real. The benchmark or reference point for reality has ceased to precede its representation; reality now is an effect of that representation. The play of signifiers, the play of sign values (signs that function as exchange values, and commodities that function as signs), is the location of the floating models that precede the real, so in a dramatic reversal, reality simulates its models. The (simulated) real is more real than (the old, natural, material) real. An example that provides a clear illustration is the synthesised emerald, which simulates a model of the perfect emerald; the structural perfection of the emerald does not precede its representation but rather the *most* real emerald is preceded by its own model. It is *hyper*real. 'The process of signification is, at bottom, nothing but a gigantic simulation model of meaning' (PES: 160). Meanings, signifieds, concepts, notions of reality structure reality in accordance with a code that semiologically reduces the symbolic; that eliminates ontological and epistemological ambivalence, and eradicates the possibility of reversion.

> Of what is outside the sign, other than the sign, we can say nothing, really, except that it is ambivalent, that is, it is impossible to distinguish respective separated terms and to positivise them as such.
>
> (PES: 161)

Hyperreality is the word Baudrillard uses to evoke the ontological principle structuring contemporary economic value and signification where reality is preceded by a model(s) of the real, and is an effect of the operationalisation of such models. It is a perfectly idealist logic. Baudrillard is, as I hope is clear, profoundly critical of the explosion of sign value that characterises hyperreality, viewing it as an ultimate form of social control whereby:

> the fundamental code of our societies, the code of political economy (both commodity form and sign form) does not operate through alienation of consciousness and contents. It rationalises and regulates exchange, makes things communicate, but only under the law of the code and through the control of meaning.
>
> (PES: 147)

The 'law of the code' structures the communication as an input/output, encoder/decoder system that transmits bits of positivised information; bits that accumulate and disseminate on and on. As I mentioned above, the sign is not just a 'semiological supplement' to the exchange value of commodities but, according to Baudrillard, 'it is an operational structure that lends itself to a structural manipulation compared with which the quantitative mystery of surplus value appears inoffensive' (MOP: 121–2). The illegibility of this ideological structure makes its manipulation more subtle and more total through its production of meaning and difference.

Symbolic Exchange

In *For a Critique of the Political Economy of the Sign* and *The Mirror of Production* Baudrillard has highlighted how what he has called symbolic exchange is incommensurate with any form of economic exchange. In *Symbolic Exchange and Death* he has stressed and analysed further this incommensurability by reference to the work of Freud, Mauss, and Saussure in their respective fields of psychoanalysis, sociology, and linguistics. He points out that '[e]verywhere, in every domain, a single form predominates: reversibility, cyclical reversal and annulment put an end to the linearity of time, language, economic exchange, accumulation and power . . . Neither mystical nor structural, the symbolic is inevitable' (SE&D: 2). In a footnote, Baudrillard further stresses that this reversibility is fatal to the contemporary economic order and related social processes: 'This is exactly what the term symbolic "exchange" means' (SE&D: 5, footnote 2).

From this critical stance of symbolic exchange, Baudrillard is not concerned to create a 'positive' knowledge of a pre-capitalist (feudal) or tribal exchange of 'objects' and then to valorise this social form. Rather, as I suggested earlier, to engage in a process of critique one has to stand somewhere, and it is possibly more helpful to conceptualise Baudrillard's 'symbolic' as the 'somewhere' that emerges as radically 'other' through critique of the naturalised constructs of utility, production, needs, desire, and the social relations of 'political economy' instituted by economic value and signification. Although Baudrillard does refer frequently in these early texts to 'primitive societies' structured around the 'symbolic exchange' of gifts, he does not pretend to develop a strictly 'historical' analysis of subsequent shifts and transformations, or an anthropological one of cultural meanings and social processes. He uses these references as a point of departure to evoke that which is excluded by the contemporary institution of the economic, of economic value. Whether such references succeed in this respect is an open question, but to argue that they don't, and to get bogged down in concerns about rather obvious problems with valorising 'primitive' societies as some kind of bizarre pataphysics[20] for postmodernity, is decidedly beside the point.[21] One of the main theoretical strands of the present project is to explore the potential of Baudrillard's notion of the 'symbolic' as a *critical* construct for feminist theory and politics, and this will be developed in the next chapter, and explored further in Chapter 5. Here I will begin this discussion by considering a few references to symbolic exchange and 'the symbolic' in *For a Critique of the Political Economy of the Sign* and *The Mirror of Production*, and reflecting on criticisms of this aspect of Baudrillard's work specifically.

To talk or write of the symbolic is an extremely problematic task. As Baudrillard himself writes: 'the symbolic, whose virtuality of meaning is so subversive of the sign, cannot, for this very reason, be named except by allusion, by infraction. For signification, which names everything in terms of itself, can only speak the language of values and of the positivity of the sign' (PES: 161). Clearly to treat the notion of the symbolic as a positive signifier is not only a doomed and contradictory project, but one which (although by appearances only) negates its subversive position. Thus, it is not a matter of 'definition' but rather of evoking through analogy, or through words that point to but do not actually 'identify'. This is at the heart of the process of critique.

The logic of signification represented in Saussurian and neo- or post-Saussurian linguistics, and the logic of economic exchange, according to Baudrillard, exclude, or bar, the symbolic. By instituting a bar that separates the Sr and Sd, the subject and the object, and then articulating their relationship in terms of equivalence, or in terms of need or desire, the symbolic is negated, is excluded. To put it another way, the possibility, for example, that meaning might be abolished in the process of exchange is negated; the possibility that the process of (inter)action simultaneously constructs and vaporises 'subjectivity' in a way that is only ambivalent and continually 'unknowable' is excluded.

Symbolic exchange in what Baudrillard refers to as 'primitive societies' involves the continual cycle of giving and receiving: that which is not exchanged '(taken and not returned, earned and not wasted, produced and not destroyed) risks breaking the reciprocity and begins to generate power' (MOP: 143). Baudrillard claims that this social process of reversion, although barred by 'political economy' (of value and signification), cannot be eradicated. The more the structural positivity of the sign is asserted, the more that which is negated will haunt and undermine a social order predicated on the assumption that it is not only possible but natural to strive for more, to accumulate, to have gain without loss, to produce without waste, to create without destruction, to invest in a truly positive, linear calculus. Societies based on symbolic exchange actively avoid the accumulation of any surplus and institute its destruction through, for example, ritual encounters.[22] In a social order where objects are not discrete items conceptualised as referents of a representational system, language cannot be understood as a 'means' of communication,[23] nor, Baudrillard argues, are individuals 'thinkable as separated terms outside the exchange of language' (MOP: 97). This is the context in which Baudrillard claims that language is a symbolic form and 'it is so not, as is generally thought, in its coded signification function, nor in its structural agency' (MOP: 97). The symbolic is relational, and as such, the terms of the relation cannot be autonomised. Similarly, the object has no meaning outside the terms of the exchange; it takes its meaning from the terms of the relationship and has no ontological finality. Communication, in this sense, is not of the order of meaning. Marilyn Strathern (1988) analyses ceremonial gift exchange in Melanesian culture, in which the 'benefits' must be reabsorbed by one or other partner in order to create the condition for new action. This is also the case for Melanesian knowledge, she suggests, where '[r]elationships have to be hidden within particular forms – minds, shells, persons, cult houses, gardens – in order to be drawn out of them' (p. 344). Here, she insists, 'information does not exist in itself'.

Baudrillard's use of symbolic exchange in so-called 'primitive societies' as a counterpoint to 'political economy' is fraught with dangers, as he acknowledges himself,[24] and indeed has been a focus of concern for a number of critics. Charles Levin, in his introduction to *For a Critique of the Political Economy of the Sign*, presents a sympathetic and detailed overview of the core arguments in the book, but he distances himself from Baudrillard's deployment of symbolic exchange and the significance of 'ambivalence' in this context. Levin writes: 'the principle of reciprocity which for Baudrillard ruptures and transgresses the axiological determination and abstract finality of social exchange confronts us at the outset as that signification process most popularly associated with the "exchange of women" in kinship structures' (PES: 25). This is probably the most immediate and striking concern from a feminist perspective: why is it 'women' who are exchanged? Why are 'women' positioned as 'objects' of exchange and thus obviously 'men' as the 'subjects' who activate the exchange? These are crucial questions, but in connection with the current discussion, I do not think it is useful to try to address them in anthropological (feminist, political) terms. The question of gender and the symbolic will be the focus of a number of discussions in this book, especially in Chapter 5, where I will return to this question of the symbolic exchange of 'women' and engage with the feminist work of Gayle Rubin. My concern here is rather to refocus on why it is that this criticism does not necessarily undermine the importance of symbolic exchange as a logic that negates power. If we accept, even provisionally, Baudrillard's concept of power as a logic of inventing the social that institutes dichotomous, essentialist categories, as a structural logic which denies or negates (or seeks to avoid and endlessly defer the inevitability of) reversion, then it becomes clear that it is contradictory and incoherent to apply, or in Baudrillard's terms 'project' (MOP: 96), this concept of power onto other forms of domination. In other words, a society of symbolic exchange is not devoid of social relations of hierarchy and domination, but Baudrillard argues that this has to be distinguished from a social order of 'power'. The significance of this distinction, and its implications for feminist theorising, will become clearer in Chapter 2 in the context of a consideration of Baudrillard's concept of power.

Mark Poster, in his introduction to *The Mirror of Production*, is, like Levin, concerned about Baudrillard's postulating symbolic exchange as a counter-point to the law of value, to axiology and semiology. Poster is critical of Baudrillard's critique of Marx in so far as Baudrillard posits the profound dif-ference between 'production' within a capitalist structure and that which is created, is exchanged, and circulates within the social order of symbolic exchange, a difference Baudrillard claims Marx ignored. Poster argues that Baudrillard can't have it all ways: if he wants to argue for the profound 'other-ness' of a social exchange that is not predicated on 'production' and to criticise those who see production everywhere because of their own assumptions and lack of critical distance, then he has also to present a method or epistemology for the process of making radical discontinuities intelligible (MOP: 14). In this context Poster raises the spectre of Baudrillard courting the danger of 'pure relativism'. This criticism connects with and extends the debate above: how can we 'know' about a form of domination that is not of the order of power, if it is so fundamentally discontinuous? Possibly Baudrillard would say we can't, but that this isn't the point. It is not a matter of knowing but a matter of critique. How can we employ and mobilise concepts to critique the ideological assumptions and orders of power within which we live? In my assessment, Baudrillard's work is not positioned within a binary of relativism and absolutism, but adopts critical epistemological postulates. Baudrillard's work must be seen in the context of a whole body of research and critical analyses of the epistemological underpinnings of con-temporary social processes, in particular, economics (see Fradin 1976, 1978; Caillé 1989; Latouche 1973, 1979, 1984, 1986, 1989, 1991; Godbout and Caillé 1992; and the work of M.A.U.S.S.).[25]

Not only Baudrillard but this broader body of work make it clear that 'economics' is a myth, and a deadly one at that. With pretensions to scientific methods and knowledge, economics presumes a domain of inquiry which is 'natural' existing prior to human social deliberations (itself a construct of the economic – nature as the ultimate referent), inaugurates the grandiose dis-course of human needs and utility, and constructs a linear scale of value which constructs the individual subject and the ontologically discrete and meaning-ful object in terms of identity/difference: the institutionalisation of the binary code of one bar zero (1/0). Further, this critique is possible through engaging a standpoint which is not of the order of the economic, which Baudrillard characterises as symbolic exchange. Thus the symbolic can heuristically, and for my purpose here, be understood as that which is 'other' to the code; as that which is not predicated on a dichotomous, binary logic. It is a point of departure for critique that exposes the imaginary of political economy, and the ideology of semiological reduction inherent in the internal structure of the sign: Sr/Sd.

Questions of Epistemology and Theory

I highlighted earlier the importance of addressing the epistemological questions raised by Baudrillard's 'theory' of sign value, the structural law of value and signification: how, on what grounds, do we assess his claims? A number of epistemological questions have been raised in critiques of Baudrillard's work. Objections to the characterisation of the hyperreal are a case in point; concerns have been raised such as 'This sounds so global, surely all communication doesn't happen like this' – but people certainly do assume a calculus of economic value that is consistent with the commodity and not with sign value. Baudrillard's work has to be understood and engaged at the level of a structural critique. He says this himself (MOP: 121) and so much is clear from the epistemological assumptions he makes. What appear empirically to be the most significant structural tendencies influencing the social order are not necessarily so. Baudrillard refers to the work of Marx to make this point in relation to his own work:

> The objection that our society is still largely dominated by the logic of commodities is irrelevant. When Marx set out to analyse capital, capitalist industrial production was still largely a minority phenomenon. When he designated political economy as the determining sphere, religion was still largely dominant. The theoretical decision is never made at the quantitative level, but at the level of a structural critique.
>
> (MOP: 121)

This epistemological position is consistent with a realist postulate: that is, to assume that an understanding of structural tendencies or social processes at play, influencing the empirical events and discourses that we observe and interpret, involves an analysis at the level of a structural critique. This critical approach to the theory of knowledge assumes that our intellectual endeavour is to critique those social processes and precisely not to assume that the creation of a positive knowledge of the social is possible or, for that matter, that the illusion of such knowledge is desirable. On the contrary, to assert what 'is', in any way other than in a critical sense, can only be ideological. Consistent with this critical epistemology, it is most helpful to approach Baudrillard's work not from the question of whether sign value does or does not exist as he says it does, but to ask: what problematics are revealed through this characterisation? Do these issues speak to political concerns of importance in any way? If so, why and from what standpoint, in relation to what political investments? This is not to say that the question of the validity of the existence of sign value in the way Baudrillard characterises it is not an important question, but it is to argue that the most helpful route by which to address this question is not to assume he is positing a positive knowledge. Baudrillard's critique of political economy, like Marx's, is precisely that, a critique; in dislodging and disrupting the cornerstones of our contemporary construction of economic value, of subjects, of objects, and of meaning, Baudrillard generates an argument about the social processes that construct those cornerstones, and what is problematic about these social processes. Thus a critical epistemology is neither absolute (objective, employing a discourse of truth) nor relativist (an obscure epistemological stance that retains a notion of truth but relates it to the conditions of its articulation, thus assuming to place its truth claims beyond critique). By taking an uncompromising critical stance, Baudrillard engages in a critique of the contemporary social order while simultaneously activating a critical reflexivity regarding the historical locatedness of his rhetorics: in other words he engages in a meta-reflection on the contemporary onto-epistemological conditions that shape, make possible, indeed compel, his own discourse.

A keyword in Baudrillard's text (and in my discussion of his work) is 'logic'. His tendency to write in what appear to be global, universal terms is perhaps best understood through reflecting on this notion of logic, and his attempts to evoke and 'speak of' a logic that is the 'object' of a structural critique. For example, a statement that 'language is not a means of communication' has to be read through layers of meanings. It is not an assertion that can be proved wrong by an empirical instance to the contrary. Neither does it assume that language is never a means of communication; indeed, Baudrillard argues that in the hyperreal construction of signification, language is precisely that. This statement activates a *challenge* to the notion that language is a means of communication, but it is not *only* a political challenge, which would reduce theory to rhetorics. Rather, it coheres with his discussion of language as symbolic, the exchange of words as a form of symbolic exchange; in other words, the statement as a challenge (from the critical standpoint of the symbolic) evokes a 'logic' of the codification of linguistic signs implicit in the concept of 'communication'. Its coherence is to be understood in terms of dialectical and not formal logic.[26]

Criticisms of Baudrillard frequently stem from mistaken assumptions about the epistemological approach informing his work. Chris Rojek and Bryan Turner, in their introduction to a recent edited collection of essays on Baudrillard (1993), use the term 'preaching' to describe a style of assertion they read in terms of accuracy. They say 'Baudrillard has been wrong' (p. xiv) and cite a number of what they consider to be illustrations, including 'his unsupported statement that the body has become a mere extension of network television'. Rojek and Turner are, it appears, looking for theoretical substantiation in terms of formal logic ('Baudrillard fails the validity test', p. xv).[27] Levin (1996) is similarly of the view that Baudrillard's claims regarding the implosion of the masses and the end of the social 'are empirically false' (p. 131). As I indicate above, such an epistemological assumption will mean that if one can find instances contrary to the assertion, then the statement is 'wrong'. This kind of reading effects a detour away from Baudrillard's arguments and makes his work easy fodder for this kind of 'criticism'. The most striking example of Baudrillard's being 'wrong' in Rojek and Turner's list is 'his prediction of the impossibility of the Gulf War'. Of course the Gulf War happened, but this doesn't make Baudrillard 'wrong'; to assume so is a failure of hermeneutic interpretation, or again, an attempt to read dialectical logic in terms of formal logic.[28] Without reading his text on the Gulf War, familiarity with Baudrillard's theoretical writings on the nature of hyper-reality and the simulation of the real provides ample 'evidence' for the coherence of this statement. On the basis of this reading I would assume that Baudrillard meant that the Gulf War happened in simulated form prior to the actual detonation of missiles. Because the totality of this prior modelling of the war anticipated and structured its outcome, whether or not the war 'happened' is actually irrelevant in terms of political outcome. In fact, because of this prior modelling, the 'war' (as an agonistic encounter whose outcome cannot be predicted but emerges precisely from the fight) couldn't happen – it was destined never to 'happen' in this sense. This analysis means that the fact the war is 'actually' played out, that bodies are burned, and communities and families destroyed is all the more horrendous: an epiphenomenon as the war could have been (in fact was) won/lost without it. A side comment: this observation was clearly apparent to a 5-year-old Iraqi boy living in New Zealand who, when interviewed with his family on the television news in response to the US and UK air strikes on Iraq on 17 December 1998, said 'it's just a game, just a computer game, and people and children who have nothing to do with it are dying'.

Roy Porter, in a chapter from the Rojek and Turner collection (1993), contends that because there are numerous ways that non-rationalised discourses traversed and constructed the social in the historical period in Britain and Europe that saw the emergence of capitalism, the market, the individual as producer and consumer, etc. (and he provides very vivid and entirely convincing examples), it is therefore impossible to analyse the rise of market economies in terms of the rationality of utilitarianism. This is another example of the same epistemological disjuncture; reading Baudrillard by disavowing a level of structural critique. It is not a matter of taking issue with Porter's examples, but Baudrillard has always said that the symbolic cannot be eradicated, and that the totalising logic of 'political economy' is illusory and ideological. What Porter describes historically is unsurprising and entirely to be expected, in terms of Baudrillard's own texts. Porter goes on to argue that Baudrillard's concern for the well-being of our social world in the era of the hyperreal is all rather 'déjà vu', as historians know that all this has happened at different times in the past. 'Mass society, mass communication, the sign-saturated world have all been a long time coming' (p. 16), writes Porter, provoking the question of his understanding of 'sign-saturated'. It should be clear from the discussion developed in this chapter that Baudrillard, in his depiction of the hyperreal, is not referring to a proliferation of 'signs' in terms of media, advertising, and so on as merely a bombardment of mediated images of a type that might have occurred in the past. He is talking about an era or mode of representation imploding and displacing the real from its location of reference, and representation as simulation *becoming* reality. I think we can say quite categorically that this has not happened before; Baudrillard argues that this shift in the order of power from the ownership of the means of production to the hegemony of the code is a revolution as important as the industrial revolution (MOP: 122). There are numerous examples of such criticisms of Baudrillard's work, particularly in the Anglo-American, and specifically sociological, literature.

Baudrillard makes no claims that the phenomena characterised through his structural critique will determine specific instances of social life: assuming that the social is contingent and never fully determined (an epistemological assumption that is neither determinist nor anti-determinist). Furthermore, Baudrillard's stance is consistent with a view of the social as never fixed, but rather dynamic and in constant flux. This assumption places epistemological questions in the realm of the political, and his own theoretical discourse as one which does not presume to present a commentary on what 'is' but rather an active praxis of engagement, interpretation, and dialogue. For example, I do not read Baudrillard's critical characterisation of the control of meaning through the coded logic of the sign form as a 'theory' whose validity rests on its 'fit' with the empirical world (indeed, if it did we'd all be pretty 'dead'!), but rather as a critique of social processes that function ideologically to create certain possibilities and tendencies, and to obscure and annihilate others.

> To speak, in sorcery, is never to inform . . . It seems impossible to inform the ethnographer, that is to say, someone who affirms that he/she will not put the information to use, but who only naively demands to know for the sake of knowing. For it is a speech (and only a speech) that will undo the spell, and whoever sets him/herself in a position to say it is formidable . . . It is as well to say that there is no neutrality of speech: in sorcery speech is war. Whoever speaks of it is a warrior, the ethnographer like everybody else. There is no room for a neutral observer.
>
> (Favret-Saada 1977: xii)

Kellner's (1989) characterisation of Baudrillard's 'beliefs' about theory again too easily slip into untenable and superficial readings. Kellner has Baudrillard 'believing' that 'theory itself is simulation, a projection of models of the real as the real' (p. 178), without specifying *what* 'theory' Baudrillard is referring to ('theory' that is grappling with how to speak the truth without assuming a truth because a discourse of truth no longer constructs and circulates knowledge?), without making it clear that Baudrillard is talking about 'theory' not in a vacuum but in a specific temporal and spatial (hyperreal) context, without providing the next line in the text of

Baudrillard's that he cites (which would make some of these points clear), i.e. 'theory pays dearly for this in a prophetic autodestruction' (EC: 98). Clearly here Baudrillard is not talking about how he conceptualises theory for himself. Kellner then, in the same movement, does refer to a passage where Baudrillard writes about this conceptualisation, but constructs Baudrillard's stance as idealist (an intent to make the world fit the theory),[29] which represents a refusal to engage with Baudrillard's critical and active, strategic notion of the relationship between theory and the real. Baudrillard's entire work critiques the structural usurpation of the meaning and ontology of the object; to criticise him for idealism (as many do) seems to be a case of chasing one's tail.

In a 1989 interview with Judith Williamson, Baudrillard responds to a question on the 'status' of his theories.[30] Williamson is concerned to ask 'what do they explain?' In this context of talking about what is ostensibly an onto-epistemological question, Baudrillard makes it clear that he views the practice of theorising as an encounter, an active engagement. His relationship to the object of inquiry is neither neutral nor reduced to the confines of the interpreting subject. He views theory as:

> not so much a kind of lineage of references, a continuity, but rather a confrontation, an antagonism, a kind of duel between the object and theory, between the real and theory. So it's no longer so much the real or reality as a reference, but rather the reference would be the confrontation itself, the antagonism between the object and the theory. I don't think that the purpose of theory is to reflect reality, nor do I think its reference should be the history of ideas. We need something more adventurous, more direct, more aggressive if you like.
>
> (Baudrillard in Williamson 1989: 16)

I think this characterisation of theory, or the practice of theorising, picks up a number of challenges that have emerged from feminist critiques of mainstream assumptions about the politics of knowledge. From a feminist perspective, and commensurate with these epistemological assumptions, we need to ask what Baudrillard's work tells us about the way power relations are gendered. What does it make available for scrutiny and consideration that might lead to transformative understandings of gender politics, the construction of gendered subjects, or the objectification of women? My concern in the chapters that follow is to address precisely these questions, concluding that Baudrillard's work has importance for feminist theory. Baudrillard is certainly no neutral observer, and our engagement with his work must take up the full challenge of his discourse. To reject his work on 'empirical' grounds is simply missing the point; to reject it on political grounds from a feminist perspective is, I wish to argue, a 'political' mistake.

Conclusion: Axiology, Semiology, and Feminism

A feminist poststructuralist critique typically focuses on the hegemonic structure of logocentrism, that is, the binary form that privileges the dominant term and subordinates that which is cast as 'other'. Baudrillard's work, however, highlights that it is not just the nature of the code, but the very fact of the codification which is important in structural terms. It is not just the dichotomous configuration of the relation between male and female, masculine and feminine, men and women, which is patriarchal, but the very axiological and semiological codification that prefigures the possibility of a hierarchical form of representation and social practice. This has important implications for feminist theory. From engaging with Baudrillard's early work, I would argue that the subversion of a political, social process that positions women as 'other' requires a critique of gender as a 'logic' that is implicated in the (pre)dominant, interrelated semiological and axiological form in an historically and culturally specific context.

What might we make of the logic(s) of gender in the hyperreal, postmodern context? This question will be explored from a number of angles throughout this book. In the following chapter I will address this question with particular reference to Baudrillard's *Symbolic Exchange and Death*, and to his critique of Foucault's theory, or characterisation, of power. I will do so in close conversation with selected, influential contemporary feminist theorists who appear to be asking similar questions, and who are concerned with an historically and culturally specific theory of gender. It will become apparent through the next three chapters that the analyses of feminist theorists as different as Irigaray, Braidotti, Butler, and Ebert either fail to address the questions of the social relations of gender in a way that confronts a critique of the object form as an axiological construct, or, for those who are more inclined to do so, tend to articulate their 'materialist' concerns within the phantasmatic preoccupations of a prior logic of value and economic order.

Fictions of Identity,
...r, and Desire

> How can 'we feminists' affirm the positivity of female subjectivity at
> a time in history and in the philosophy of the west where our acquired
> perceptions of the subject are being radically questioned?
>
> (Braidotti 1989: 91)

Rosi Braidotti is not the only feminist voice raising concerns that post-
modernist proclamations that the subject is 'dead' undercuts the feminist
achievement in the recent past of finding ways to articulate the 'positivity
of female subjectivity'. Whether feminist theorists and activists have focused
their attentions on the phallocentric linguistic structure that bars women
from the position of subject, or on creating social, economic, and legal conditions for women's rights and possibilities for self-determination, there is
a suspicion of contemporary critiques of the meaningfulness of 'subjecthood',
particularly when these critiques are authored by male, 'postmodern' writers.
Feminist engagements with the politics of the gendering of subjectivity will
be elaborated below by focusing on a few influential arguments. Before
reviewing these, however, and given that Baudrillard appears to be one
such 'male postmodern writer', I want first to frame this chapter by looking
briefly at Suzanne Moore's criticisms of his work. Those very few feminists
who have commented on his work have focused in the main on his 1979 publication, *Seduction*. I will discuss these critiques in Chapter 5. Baudrillard's
work ranges far beyond the scope of *Seduction*. It may thus be that the substance and tenor of Moore's criticisms are symptomatic of feminist responses
more broadly, which explains their silence as complete dismissal.

'Baudrillard is, to my knowledge, the male French theorist who most
explicitly and most frontally adopts an adversarial relation to feminism'
(Gallop 1987: 113). At face value, feminist anger at what is interpreted to
be an undisguised anti-feminist discourse is not surprising. However,
before we rush to condemn Baudrillard and analyse his position in terms of
his own fears of the (loss of the) feminine (see, for example, Plant 1993),
feminists need to consider what exactly Baudrillard is referring to in his
alleged aversion to feminism, and think again about how we might evaluate

the position he develops. At the heart of Baudrillard's concern, attack, dismissal (challenge? despair?), is a critique of the desire of feminists to instantiate female subjectivity, female 'identity'. Whichever way feminist discourse approaches the political question of the erasure of the feminine in its position as the other of the masculine (and it is approached in a multiplicity of intensely critical ways), the signs of that desire are palpable. Moore, in her concern that Baudrillard's association of the feminine with the 'superficial', the 'masquerade', the 'simulacra' might obliterate women altogether, asks: 'where is female identity? Where is female desire?' (Moore 1988: 181). She vehemently asserts that feminism, which refutes the claim that the feminine is only lack, 'says women have identities, women have desires' (p. 182), but that 'because he has no coherent theory of power relations, Baudrillard cannot conceive that this [feminine as lack and appearance] is far from the ideal position' (p. 182). It is not convincing simply to assert that Baudrillard has no coherent theory of power relations. He does theorise about power. A critique must analyse that theory and argue coherently and systematically about its shortcomings. Baudrillard's arguments regarding power and the feminine require far more careful analysis and consideration.

Baudrillard and the Mathematics of Sex

In Chapter 1 I argue that Baudrillard presents a challenge to the limits of theoretical explorations of questions of 'identity' and 'subjectivity' that do not ask how these constructs are related to the codification of economic value and the structure of the production and exchange of objects. To extend Baudrillard's analysis of economic value and structures of signification into a more detailed theoretical discussion of the construction of sexual difference and gender identity in the west, this chapter will develop Baudrillard's concept of the symbolic (specifically in *Symbolic Exchange and Death*) and his critique of Foucault's concept of power (*Forget Foucault*).

In *For a Critique of the Political Economy of the Sign*, Baudrillard proposes that the construction of male and female, masculine and feminine, as a dichotomous structure that marks and demarcates individuals is an example of the semiological reduction of the symbolic; in other words it is a form of ideology barring the possibility of symbolic exchange and instituting the order of identity. According to Baudrillard, 'no being is assigned by nature to a sex' (PES: 99), but rather the very ambivalence of what might be understood to be of the order of the 'sexual' (for example, activity and passivity) traverses every 'subject', as 'sexual differentiation is registered as a difference in the body of each subject and not as an absolute term linked to a particular sexual organ' (PES: 99). In brief, sexual ambivalence is reduced by a violent instantiation of the biological organs (presence/absence) as the codified reference for sexual identity. I assume that Baudrillard's views on this matter refer to the post-Enlightenment era. This 'difference', or 'opposition', he argues, serves a simplistic, though grandiose, cultural logic whereby the absolute privilege of one sex over the other can be sustained. With reference to Laqueur (1990), I would add that this is not to say that such a relation of hierarchy and privilege was 'new' at this time, but rather that it took a new form from the eighteenth century.[1]

At first glance it might appear that there is nothing new here. Freud said as much with his notion of the polymorphous, bisexual infant and the construction of gender identity through the recognition of a sexed body (having or not having a penis) and the repression of desire. But in fact Baudrillard develops an analysis which, when used to understand gender and sexual difference, is radically different from that of Freud. His analysis starts from a different place and leads in quite a different direction. Baudrillard is not referring to a concept of 'bisexuality'. To discover the significance of this we need to consider more closely Baudrillard's (usually brief) references to gender or sexual difference in his early works, and develop his critique(s) of psychoanalysis.

In *Symbolic Exchange and Death*, Baudrillard cites a brief dialogue from 'a modern novel' (not referenced) where one character says 'so ultimately, why are there two sexes?' And the second character replies, 'what are you complaining about? Do you want twelve of them or just one?' (SE&D: 118). He uses this dialogue to point to the absurdity of the concept of *numbers* of sexes. Whether we are referring to Laqueur's one-sex model or two-sex model, the question of difference is predicated on the assumption of the one, against which more like it can be added, or those not like it can be differentiated. To use Baudrillard's example, we can logically ask 'why not six fingers on each hand?' Such a question assumes a unit which can be multiplied; which can be added to hypothetically, *relying on a standard against which relations of equivalence can be ascertained.* Sex, he claims (understood radically), simply does not have a calculable status. The two sexes – again, understood radically – cannot be added together, nor can they become part of a series; nor again are they terms of a dualism. To articulate sexual difference in terms of 'numbers' (two sexes as versions of one sex; the one-sex model) *or* in terms of a binary opposition (two sexes as the one that is incommensurably different from the other; the two-sex model), either way the construct is reliant on a standard against which relations of equivalence and difference can be asserted in accordance with a binary logic. This, according to Baudrillard, is precisely how sexual difference is constructed within the modern western cultural tradition. Thus Baudrillard's concept of sexual ambivalence traversing every subject cannot be understood in terms of a 'bisexuality'; not in terms of a calculus of two in one.

Feminist theorists, particularly recently and in many different ways, have pointed to the problem of binary logic, of logocentrism (to use Derrida's term), or of phallocentrism implicit in a semiological structure that posits the dichotomous terms of the one and the different from (identity/ difference) as the male and the female; the masculine and the feminine. What Baudrillard's analysis forces us to consider is that this structure cannot be understood only in semiological and psychoanalytic terms, nor can it be confronted only in terms of deconstruction, reinventing language, and reconfiguring the unconscious, by whatever means. These latter strategies are blind to the role of the code, to the role of the economic structuration of that codification in sustaining and reproducing this binary logic. Baudrillard's argument leads us to problematise not only the format of the coding of language and value, but the role of the codification itself.

As discussed in Chapter 1, to establish the exchange value of an item in a market relation where the object of exchange is a commodity, the necessary relation of equivalence requires a standard, an *a priori* (phantasmatic) benchmark, for the articulation of value to become meaningful. Gender identity and sexuality in the modern era of the west are, in Baudrillard's analysis, predicated on the relentless instantiation of the mythic finality of a phallic exchange standard to accomplish the parallel task of establishing who or what is or is not the same as or different from . . . what? On one level the 'what' is scarcely relevant; on another level, its consequences are deadly. The structural logic of gender in this instance marks individuals in accordance with the presence or absence of biological organs which form a naturalised alibi for the institution of a massive cultural ideology: in Baudrillard's terms, the phallic exchange standard. In *Symbolic Exchange and Death*, Baudrillard explores how this biological anchoring – this notion that the finality of the biological genital organs creates the inalienable basis for the apparently ensuing structure – enables the *structure* (male/female) to become confused with the privilege granted to the genital *function* (reproductive or erotic) (SE&D: 116).[2] To privilege the genital in a male-dominated social order does not simply serve to mark and remark *the* site of difference, but rather it serves to establish a general equivalence, 'the Phallus becoming the absolute signifier around which all erogenous possibilities come to be measured, arranged, abstracted, and become equivalent' (SE&D: 116).

The inextricable linkages in Baudrillard's analysis between the structural form of political economy and that of signification are implicated in the construction of sexual difference and sexuality. We have seen how, since the Industrial Revolution, the production and exchange of commodities are argued by Baudrillard to be governed by the structural form of exchange value, predicated on the assumption of the prior existence of use value; simultaneously, language becomes a 'means of communication', arranged into the separate orders of signifiers and signifieds where the exchange of signifiers is governed by the structural form signified-referent. However, as we also saw in Chapter 1, the progressive ascendancy of the sign form, of sign value, in the contemporary era of the explosion of consumption has been accompanied by the gradual disappearance of the 'objective' reference of utility, of the signified-referent, until the ontological finality of 'the real' is no longer structurally so compelling. To use Baudrillard's words, '[i]n the "neo-capitalist" (techno- and semiocratic) framework, this form [political economy] is systematised at the expense of "objective" reference: signifieds and use-values progressively disappear to the great advantage of the operation of the code and exchange-value' (SE&D: 115). Extrapolating the increasing functionality of the code to the phallic exchange standard, this would suggest that the form of sexual difference would become less and less underwritten by the presence or absence of the phallic organ and more and more governed by the signs of difference as these are regulated by the functional operation of the code. Thus sexual difference is no longer (predominantly) structured and articulated in accordance with a logic of equivalence whereby that which is on the wrong side of the bar – the feminine – is barred from occupying the place of identity. Rather, the signs of sex are exchanged in a veritable promiscuity of positivity where nothing is lost, where all signs are phallic, where all signifiers can claim their identities (in all their differences); the bar does not bar the (sign) feminine, but bars the symbolic.

The radical exclusion of the symbolic is pivotal to the central discussion of this volume, and therefore requires more detailed consideration. This chapter will work towards setting the scene for an analysis of gender and sexual difference in the contemporary hyperreal world as a simulation model, and pointing to the limitations of the notion of gendered power relations, a notion which in some of its usages is, I will argue, an already redundant conceptualisation. To do this scene-setting, I need first to consider in greater depth what is at stake in taking the symbolic as a critical point of departure for an analysis of gender and its assumptions of 'identity' and the 'subject'. I will then run this discussion against the theoretical work in selected texts of Irigaray, Braidotti, and Butler. Secondly, but relatedly, I will discuss Baudrillard's critique of Foucault's concept of power, of Deleuze's concept of desire, and Baudrillard's critical eye on the contemporary assumptions of psychoanalytic discourse. This discussion will lead to an analysis of gender and sexual difference as simulation models. This analysis will be explored further in Chapters 3 and 4, along with other signs of 'difference' currently prominent in feminist theorising.

Symbolic Exchange and Death

> Identity is untenable: it is death since it fails to inscribe its own death.
>
> (SE&D: 4)

Suzanne Moore's (1988) insistence that the 'pimps of postmodernism' (Baudrillard, Lacan, Barthes, Lyotard) can't see that women have 'identities' and 'desires', and their refusal to see the obvious – that the notion of women's lacking the possibility of identity and desire is problematic to say the least – is a perfect entry point into a consideration of the limitations of feminist theory when it comes to analysis of the symbolic, in Baudrillard's terms. My argument is not that feminism is inherently limited in this regard, but that the theoretical standpoints adopted by many feminist theorists and commentators systematically sever the possibility of thinking through

Baudrillard's very particular contribution. To follow Moore's concern, she exposes and opposes the presumed motives of those (especially French and philosophical) blokes who seem to think there is something in the association of the feminine with the realm of appearance, of lack, absence, seduction, the masquerade (possibly even chaos and death), that is worth hanging on to. She calls them 'pimps' to point to an essentially exploitative relationship whereby their apparent valorisation of the feminine, of 'women', thinly conceals what is better understood to be a desire and resolve not only to ensure that the 'other' of the man, the masculine, stays firmly in its place (thus ensuring his continued existence), but also that 'he' can make his postmodern excursions into the world of the feminine, getting his 'bit of the Other'. To use Gallop's words in response to Baudrillard: 'a line if ever I heard one' (Gallop 1987: 114).

While I fully support the need to be cautious and discerning when it comes to gendered investments, in particular theoretical configurations, alternative 'explanations' need to be explored to avoid repeating exactly the same pattern. In the case of Baudrillard, his intent is fairly unambiguous: to engage the symbolic to critique the order of (a phallic) identity. Considering such a project, it quickly becomes evident that the contemplation of that which is barred from the realm of a codified identity – the symbolic – might potentially hold as much anxiety for women as for men.

In *Symbolic Exchange and Death*, Baudrillard writes of the symbolic as an act, a social relation:

> The symbolic is neither a concept, an agency, a category, nor a 'structure', but an act of exchange and *a social relation which puts an end to the real*, which resolves the real, and, at the same time, puts an end to the opposition between the real and the imaginary.
>
> (SE&D: 133)

This quotation contains some of the central elements of Baudrillard's critique of the order of identity; elements that I want to approach from a number of different angles through the course of this chapter, developing specifically a critique of modern and postmodern western configurations of gender and/ or sexual difference, in Baudrillard's terms.

'Identity' is a concept that is reliant on the instantiation of a series of dichotomous separations, whose relationships are then determined in the specific instance in accordance with a code that establishes the possibility of that relationship. The separations Baudrillard discusses in *Symbolic Exchange and Death* include self/other, self/body, male/female, subject/object, life/ death. Such separations, or dichotomous splits, effect an ontological structure that is premised on the illusory construction of an essence. The 'identity' of one term is only possible within a structure that severs the 'being' of that term from its representation (and the subsequent creation of a signifier/ signified relationship), and that, in the same movement, crystallises the 'being' of that term as identical to itself and different from everything else (including its own death, its not-self). Regarding human beings, the multiplicity of an individual's 'identities' presumes a codified structure upon which their 'gender identity', their 'cultural identity', and so on might be ascertained in a structure of identity/difference, same as/different from, by virtue of characteristics that enable such a demarcation. At the level of the fundamental structure, or model, of identity/difference, whether these identities are singular or plural, enduring or fleeting, is beside the point. The possibility of plural, changing identities renders the structure no less essentialist, even if these identities might appear contradictory. Identity is premised on the notion of essence; not because it is singular and unified, but because it only becomes meaningful in a logic of the real where ontological status is separated, in Baudrillard's view superstitiously, from its (linguistic) representation. We have seen the interdependence of this structure and the emergence of the 'economic' in Chapter 1.

It might be useful at this point, in order to consider the way Baudrillard engages with understandings of 'symbolic exchange', to throw the problematic of 'identity' (and the 'economic') into relief by contrasting it to a social form without the preconditions for 'identity'. His theorising on this matter is of profound importance for feminist theory, where, for those theorists pursuing a project of 'sexual difference', the question of how to reinvent the feminine subject precisely not within the phallogocentric, dichotomous structure of identity/difference is considered central.

In Chapter 1 I introduced symbolic exchange as a form of social relation whereby the exchange of objects is predicated on the notion of the circulation of the gift. This cyclical process of reciprocity runs contrary to a logic of accumulation of wealth and the extraction of a surplus. The ontological status of things and persons cannot be understood within a differential calculus of identity and difference, but rather they take on their meaning through the terms of the exchange, the social relation, and are hence always ambivalent. Meanings, in this sense, are not embedded in coded structures of representation, but are rather more of the order of challenges. 'Challenge' and 'seduction' are words frequently used by Baudrillard to evoke a social process whereby existence and non-existence are not ontological poles but are rather concurrent, always already present, always in a continuing cycle of encounter and transformation. The social traverses persons and things; persons and things seduce and challenge each other, encounters are open and not prefigured by codified structures of meanings. Thus Baudrillard makes use of this (very specific) anthropological (re)interpretation of the social process of symbolic exchange to show how the eradication of the symbolic might be understood precisely to obliterate 'reality' by inscribing it within a codified structure that precedes the encounter. Hence we can make sense of his statement that the symbolic puts an end to the real, where the real is that specified by the signified, and where the signified is in fact, as he argues, *preceded* by the signifier – a codified, constructed meaning.

In societies of symbolic exchange, meanings activate, seduce, and transform, often in highly ritualised fashion. It is a mistake to view them as representational. Signs, or meanings, in this sense, traverse and circulate over the
entirety of forms present in that social sphere. This circulation is an active
articulation of gestures: no signifieds have 'precipitated' from this circulation
of signs, meanings, or challenges, and therefore there is no truth of the sign,
no real to which it refers; or in Baudrillard's words, 'signs are exchanged without phantasms, with no hallucination of reality' (SE&D: 95).

Baudrillard characterises this cyclical process of presence negated by
absence, and thus always ambivalent, by the word *reversion*. Reversibility at
once marks ontology as a process, things as inherently ambivalent, and the
inseparability of what something is from what it is not. This is neither of
the order of identity (A/Not-A), nor of the order of a death drive, or immersion into a non-differentiated state as this is understood in the mainstream
Freudian interpretation. In Baudrillard's conceptualisation of the principle
of reversion, that which *is*, is a gesture;[3] it is symbolic in that it cannot be
represented in a finite set of words, it is ambivalent in that its meaning is
never singular and positive (+), rather that which *is* contains the possibility
of its seduction, its transformation, its death. In *Symbolic Exchange and
Death*, Baudrillard refers to three social forms which typify this process: the
gift (radicalised against Mauss's original interpretation), the death drive
(radicalised against Freud's original interpretation), and the anagram (against
Saussure's stance). In all three cases he critically singles out the figure of reversion. The gift is reversed in the counter-gift, life (individuation) in death, the
term and value of the *langue* in the anagram. The reversion annuls, by contrast
to the linearity of the cumulative logic of production, time, economic
exchange, and their corollary, power.

Baudrillard's consideration of the body, sexuality, and death makes this
somewhat more concrete. In the era of the economic and the semiological,
the signs of bodies are not exchanged symbolically; rather they mark, and
demarcate, they signify identifications by virtue of separations and representations. In a society of symbolic exchange, marking the body as a masking
practice gives effect to, or actualises, symbolic exchange. The bodily signs,
or in this sense symbols, are exchanged, either within the group or with
the gods.[4] Baudrillard describes this negotiation as precisely not a negotiation
of identity by the subject behind the mask, and neither is it a question of a
subject manipulating signs, but rather, the masking 'consumes the subject's
identity' (SE&D: 107), so the social form is one of a reversion of possession
and dispossession, with the entire body becoming material (for want of a
better word) of symbolic exchange.

[F]or the body as material of symbolic exchange . . . *there is no model*, no
code, no ideal type, no controlling phantasm, *since there could not be a system*
of the body as anti-object.

(SE&D: 114)

Baudrillard contrasts this to our contemporary world, where the body specifically as object 'is sealed in signs' (SE&D: 107): the signs of the body contribute to augmenting the subject through abstracted systems of reference, establishing his or her 'identity' calculated within a codified, albeit floating and labile, system of value (and in terms of sex, the phallic exchange standard). In Baudrillard's terms, rather than being eliminated through the exchange, the subject is re-marked, or fetishised by the law of value (SE&D: 107). The practice of masking becomes a question of signification that takes its effect from the alleged truth or otherwise of its relation to its reference. As the costume becomes dress, the body becomes nature. This last point is tremendously significant when we consider signs of sexual difference.

With the separation of the body as a natural reference, Baudrillard argues that sexuality becomes 'functionalised', and thus an 'element in the economy of the subject' (SE&D: 115). In other words, as the body becomes that which is signified, or represented, sexuality becomes individualised as a function of the subject: sexuality becomes a function of self-expression or the expression of subjectivity, it becomes a function of personal equilibrium, 'mental health', a function of unconscious emanations. A discourse of 'sexual needs' and 'sexual satisfaction' explicitly evokes an 'economy' of sex. Sexuality becomes a kind of individualised production. Baudrillard's main point here is that this productive functionality of sexuality 'crystallises around the exercise of a particular sexual model' (SE&D: 115): its prerequisite is the model of that 'great opposition' male/female, which takes the phallic organ as its reference point, 'closing the play of the body's signifiers' (SE&D: 115).

At this point I want to return to Baudrillard's fundamental argument regarding the construction of the real, the 'hallucination of reality' that he suggests obliterates reality, or the establishment of the real on the basis of a series of ruptures that, through their separations, allow for systems of representation. He goes on to postulate that the archetypal disjuncture is that between life and death. What makes this particular disjuncture 'archetypal' is the structure of its form: death, phantasised as irreversible, relentlessly haunts and threatens the 'other' term. In other words, each dichotomous separation of terms involves the assertion of one as real in its positive value, excluding the other, but this realness is contingent on the imaginary of the other term. Every term for which the other is its imaginary is haunted by the latter as its death – if the *other* is real, then *it* is not – precisely the contradiction instantiated by the dichotomy. The ramifications of this observation are clear in relation to the male/female dichotomy and the mythologies that situate the female on the side of the dark, seductive, destructive, chaotic. '[T]he price we pay for the "reality" of this life, to live it as a positive value, is the ever-present phantasm of death' (SE&D: 133). I understand Baudrillard here as saying that the construction of the real within a dichotomous logic of the positive from which the negative is barred has its cost: to have life separated from death, we create death as irreversible, as ever-threatening, as the void.[5] In developing this critique Baudrillard points out obliquely that there is nothing *a priori* natural, real, or pre-existing in this opposition of life and death. This construction of life and death is concurrent with the construction of the private individual with needs and desires, as it is only within the confines of the individual, conscious subject that the irreversibility of death takes its meaning. He goes so far as to say 'our whole culture is just one huge effort to dissociate life and death, to ward off the ambivalence of death in the interests of life as value' (SE&D: 147). I pursue this discussion in a later section of this chapter, where I elaborate more fully on Baudrillard's argument regarding desire and death, and his critique of psychoanalysis.

Before the implications of this discussion can be utilised for understanding gender and/or sexual difference, it is useful at this point to consider the work of selected feminist theorists. I have chosen to focus on Luce Irigaray's project on sexual difference, Rosi Braidotti's reading of the work of Gilles Deleuze for her concept of the nomadic subject, and Judith Butler's analysis of gender as performative. What follows is by no means an exhaustive analysis of the works of these theorists, but rather an engagement with the key strands of their respective argumentations as these appear to me from the vantage point of an analysis of the work of Baudrillard.

Irigaray and the Project of Sexual Difference

> The question being how to detach the other – woman – from the otherness of sameness.
>
> (Irigaray 1977, trans. 1985: 169)

In her discussion of Irigaray, Grosz (1989) makes it clear that her organising and structuring of Irigaray's ideas not only reduces the complexity of her arguments but also, of necessity, structures her fragmented textual strategies, and imposes an 'order' on her otherwise 'polyvocal' texts. Grosz justifies this organising and ordering by claiming that Irigaray's writing, her 'project', is 'exceptionally difficult to re-present convincingly' (Grosz 1989: 102). Although my aim is not to 're-present' Irigaray's work, I do wish to acknowledge similar reservations and qualifications in my much more restricted discussion of her ideas.

In her early work, *Speculum of the Other Woman*, Irigaray develops a critique of the positioning of woman, of the feminine, as the 'other' of man, of the masculine (1974, trans. 1985). According to Irigaray, within the structure of representation in the west since the early Greeks, the dominant term designating identity takes its (phallic) presence by virtue of its unacknowledged and denied debt to its (usually) oppositional 'other'.[6] Hence 'woman' is characterised only in so far as she is the 'negative' of man, in Irigaray's terms. In this structural location of 'otherness', woman provides a mirror to man, reflecting back to him his presence against her absence. Irigaray is concerned to present a critique of this 'otherness' which is only an 'otherness of sameness'. In other words, her critique centres on her concern that this 'otherness' is not an 'other' with its own special presence, its onto-logical being, but is solely a 'negative', an absence that serves to reflect the presence of identity. Hence the phallic status of identity where the masculine is the dominant term, and the phallocentric status of this representational logic of identity/difference which inevitably locates woman as 'other', not man.

Grosz (1989) comments that Irigaray 'uses' psychoanalysis without being committed to its fundamental presuppositions (p. 104). Irigaray begins *Speculum* with a critical engagement with Freud's discussion on the 'dark con-tinent' of femininity. Her ambivalence in relation to psychoanalysis is evident in the depth of her critique, against a clear intent to employ psychoanalytic concepts to understand the masculine investments in a phallic ontology. She simultaneously denounces a theoretical schema in which 'woman' *is* (not) by virtue of her lack, absence, castration, and at the same time uses this very construction to expose the phallocentric foundations of the social order. In her own words, '[o]bviously Freud is right insofar as he is describing the status quo. But his statements are not mere descriptions. They establish rules intended to be put into practice' (p. 123). For my purposes here, the key concerns that emerge through Irigaray's reading of Freud appear to be the absence of women's desire (except for desire for the penis resulting from her castrated state), woman's displacement from her own origin and the denial of the debt to the maternal, the structural impossibility of women's access to a 'signifying economy' that would enable the representation of her sexual reality, and the associated lack of the auto-erotic with its connection to the mother and to a 'homo-sexual economy'. These concerns are con-ceptualised as interrelated and are, together, symptomatic of the demarcation of woman as the 'other' of the self-same, man.

Irigaray analyses the derivation of 'sexual difference' from the 'problematics of sameness', within the Freudian discourse (p. 26). The universality of the masculine is assumed to be the starting point for all human lives; all the same until that which is not-masculine is differentiated through the recogni-tion of castration. Thus a 'normal woman' is '[a] man minus the possibility of (re)presenting oneself as a man' (p. 27). Irigaray questions Freud closely on his assumptions about 'penis envy' in a way which accomplishes both a challenge to the psychoanalytic interpretation and a critique of the reality of 'otherness' that is (re)inscribed by the rehearsal of such interpretations. The inevitability of the lack of women's desire (of the representation of women's desire within a phallocentric representational system) is both accepted and questioned in a way that acknowledges the 'status quo' but points unmistakably to the stake invested in maintaining it:

> If woman had desires other than 'penis-envy,' this would call into ques-
> tion the unity, the uniqueness, the simplicity of the mirror charged with

sending man's image back to him – albeit inverted.

(Irigaray 1974, trans. 1985: 51)

In conjunction with the negation of desire, Irigaray contends that the trope of castration also leaves woman without recourse to 'valid, valuable images of her sex/organs, her body' (p. 55). Her positioning as 'other', the symbolic imagery of woman functioning as 'hole', lack, absence, deficiency, 'inevitably affords woman too few figurations, images or representations by which to represent herself' (p. 71). She lacks access to a 'signifying economy'. Furthermore, and according to Irigaray's analysis this is crucial, the state of castration is a prohibition against establishing 'one's own economy of the desire for origin' (p. 83). If subjecthood is reliant, at least in part, on a 'desire for origin', the barring of woman from entering the status of subject of desire and of representation also severs her, or prohibits her, from her (desire for her) maternal origin. This is reflected in a prohibition or depreciation of a desire for the 'self-same', and a lack of an 'auto-erotic, homo-sexual economy' (p. 102). The reduction and caricaturing of this (women's) desire is pivotal in establishing the dominance of the Phallus: in Irigaray's terms, women's relationship with her origin, her original relationship with her mother and her sex, must be 'cancelled', 'made secondary', for the purpose of instituting the single (non-maternal) origin necessary for the mastery of the phallic order.

Irigaray tracks the myth of the single origin back to Plato's cave, in the last section of *Speculum*. Her reinterpretation of Plato's myth can itself be read as a search for an origin of sorts; the originating moment of the dislocation of the connection to the maternal origin in western discourses, in western history. Plato's myth of the cave depicts a metaphoric scene designed to convey the relation between the realm of the real, or the form, and the realm of empirical reality, of discrete objects discernible through the senses. In Plato's ontology the world of the senses is a shadowy mimicry in which the realness of objects is known only by reference to the 'real' world of forms. For example, circularity and squareness are forms, the idea of a form that precedes the specific instance. An object may be called a circle or a square only in so far as it resembles the form circularity, or squareness. This is, of course, an idealist ontology where reality is constituted by the ideas we form of the real. In Plato's cave, prisoners are chained in the depths of the cave and all they can see (and have ever seen) is the back wall of the cave reflecting the shadows of everything happening in the light at the cave's opening. Because they haven't seen anything else the prisoners mistakenly take the reflections for the reality, until they are led into the light and see the 'real world'. Plato's shadowy world of the reflections on the inside of the cave is intended to be analogous to the world of the senses, which we might believe to be reality but which only represents a copy or imitation of the real. The light of day is analogous to the world of ideas, of true forms, which is indeed the real in Plato's perspective.

Irigaray re-reads Plato's myth as a story that metaphorically embodies an initial articulation of the single, ideal origin that dissociates the masculine (or lived experience, subjectivity) from the maternal origin and instantiates a single reference of truth accessible only to those positioned as readers of such a truth within this representational system. The imagery of the cave is analogous to the womb. The real, or the truth of the real, is deemed to have its origins, or Being, elsewhere; the split between the interior and the exterior is irrevocable, annihilating the connecting corridor (vagina); men (paternal) produce the real, women (maternal) (re)produce copies, fakes, imitations of the real. The general, the universal, the form (the one, indivisible) is the good, the true, the light, the real, whereas the specific, matter, body (dark, multiple), is not of this order, but rather takes the place of reflecting appearances, like a screen. Irigaray emphasises the relation of conformity, resemblance, or equivalence by which the reflections, duplications, are measured as proportions of a more-or-less correct relation to the sameness (of the Idea) (p. 262).

> The feminine, the maternal are instantly frozen by the 'like,' the 'as if' of that masculine representation dominated by truth, light, resemblance, identity . . . The maternal, the feminine, serve (only) to keep up the reproduction-production of doubles, copies, fakes, while any hint of their material elements, of the womb, is turned into scenery to make the show more realistic. The *womb*, unformed, 'amorphous' origin of all morphology, is transmuted by/for analogy into a circus and a projection screen, a theater of/for fantasies.
>
> (Irigaray 1974, trans. 1985: 265)

Clearly, numerous transformations of European (western) metaphysics since Plato wrote his myth of the cave mean a literal reading of the significance of this historical reference will miss Irigaray's point. Indeed, Foucault's work (1966, trans. 1970) on the shifts in modes of representation (the relation between words and things) from the classical through the Renaissance and to the modern makes Plato's idealist ontology truly historical; Laqueur's specific analysis (1990) of the construction of sexual difference across the same time span is similarly incompatible with an attempt to find the roots of contemporary renditions of identity/difference solely in the classical period. Irigaray invokes a myth, so the question I am concerned to ask here is not so much one of the appropriateness of the use of this historical reference to understand the present, but rather of what she is valorising through this invocation. What concept of 'otherness' as alternative to the 'otherness of sameness' is presented, or inferred? The mimetic function of the cave is predicated on 'otherness' that is only other to the same, so does Irigaray point to the possibility of an alterity that is not caught up in this logic of the same, or of 'identity' which assumes its prior reference (or in Baudrillard's terms, a logic whereby the world is separated into subjects and objects, requiring the tautological resolution of their relationship)? My reading is that she only partially moves in this direction, and here we see a significant source of tension in her work. Irigaray's desire for such an alterity seems to be conflicted, and passionately so. She appears to be motivated by a strong wish for an alterity, an 'otherness', not predicated on this binary logic, but simultaneously her discourse again and again, sometimes indirectly and sometimes very explicitly, articulates her wish to engender the 'feminine', 'women', in a site of non-reversible ontological presence. My argument is that these points of tension are incompatible. *Speculum of the Other Woman* provides the critical foundation for Irigaray's future work, which Rosi Braidotti (1991) characterises as 'positive' and 'constructive' with respect to envisioning a feminine subjectivity different from that produced by the phallogocentric patriarchal order. Evidence of the tension I have referred to in Irigaray's work becomes clearer if we turn to some of her subsequent writings.

Irigaray's reference to an alterity that is of a wholly other order from that of the structure of identity/difference appears in many contexts, including loving between men and women, the metaphor of copulation as that which cannot be divided in half, the need for a female divine, for another language, another economy. She most convincingly evokes something of this alterity in those few references where a reversibility of terms is fully implicated in the text; for example:

> Since we give each other (our) all, with nothing held back, nothing hoarded, our exchanges are without terms, without end. How can I say it? The language we know is so limited.
>
> (Irigaray 1977, trans. 1985: 213–14)

> She herself enters into a ceaseless exchange of herself with the other without any possibility of identifying either.
>
> (Irigaray 1977, trans. 1985: 31)

These quotations have the appearance of a reversibility, an on-going reversion of presence and absence, an annulment of self in the other which nullifies the possibility of 'identity'. This appearance is, however, undercut by what immediately follows:

> This puts into question all prevailing economies: their calculations are irremediably stymied by woman's pleasure, as it increases indefinitely from its passage in and through the other.
>
> (Irigaray 1977, trans. 1985: 31)

Within the overall context of her drive to establish and secure an ontological 'other' feminine, I read Irigaray here as saying that, contrary to a (prevailing) economy of debit and credit, we see a pure positivity of infinite increase of a pleasure which is identifiably that of 'woman'. To introduce a comment here from my reading of Baudrillard, rather than countering the logic of prevailing economies, such an 'indefinite increase' is precisely in accordance with the logic of production and capitalist enterprise. As Marx himself wrote, 'accumulate, accumulate, it is the law and the prophets'. Implicitly, however, Irigaray's use of the word 'indefinitely' seems to betray a sense of the symbolic, which she seeks to avoid. The extreme 'increase' in sexual ecstasy leads to the infinite where it rejoins the zero: nothing accumulates and the alterity is fully reversed.

Irigaray writes on the ethics of sexual difference, referring to Descartes' first passion: *wonder*. She refers precisely to the surprise, astonishment, and wonder in the encounter with the unknown, indeed, the unknowable. She writes: '*Who or what the other is, I never know*' (1984, trans. 1993: 13). Turning to Baudrillard's analysis, in the absence of a codified system of meaning instantiated in the split between the signifier and signified, this experience of wonder constructs the encounter as one which is open to challenge and seduction. Irigaray goes on, however, to say:

> But the other who is forever unknowable is the one who differs from me sexually. This feeling of surprise, astonishment, and wonder in the face of the unknowable ought to be returned to its locus: that of sexual difference.
>
> (Irigaray 1984, trans. 1993: 13)

Here the openness of the encounter with the unknowable meets an abrupt turnaround. Why would the location of the 'forever unknowable' reside with the sexually different? The question of the erasure of 'otherness' within the logocentric, phallocentric representational system does not privilege any particular sites of 'otherness'. Furthermore, to assume an endeavour of 'returning' this 'feeling to its locus of sexual difference' is precisely its undoing, since the instantiation of an identity of man/woman, male/female, masculine/feminine, articulates the vector of that which is known. Irigaray's association of the passion of wonder with the autonomy of the terms of sexual difference is undoubtedly problematic.

Another example of Irigaray taking a resolutely critical stance is a quotation frequently cited by Grosz in her discussion of Irigaray's work (1989):

> In other words, the issue is not one of elaborating a new theory of which women would be the *subject* or the *object*, but of jamming the theoretical machinery itself, of suspending its pretension to the production of a truth and of a meaning that are excessively univocal.
>
> (Irigaray 1977, trans. 1985: 78)

When this critical observation is placed alongside another statement by Grosz – that Irigaray's aim (amongst others) is 'the recategorisation of women and femininity so that they are now capable of being autonomously defined according to women's and not men's interests' (Grosz 1989: 105) – we have to question how the *autonomous* definition of *women* with their clearly defined *interests* is compatible with a theory in which women would be neither the subject nor the object. Grosz cannot be criticised for misrepresenting and distorting Irigaray through the use of her own terminology. Irigaray herself refers repeatedly to the need for women's 'autonomy', in contradistinction to valorising her ('woman') being 'neither one nor two', and 'resisting adequate definition' (1977, trans. 1985: 26). In *Speculum*, the notion of 'interests' appears to underpin her critique: 'We will continue to waver indecisively before this dilemma unless we interpret the interest, and the interests, involved here. Who or what profits by the credits invested in the effectiveness of such a system of metaphor . . . ?' (1974, trans. 1985: 270).

To assert the importance of the ontological specificity of 'woman', of 'women's sexuality', as Irigaray frequently does, must be to assume an essence. Concerns about essentialism in relation to Irigaray's work have typically focused on her morphological allusions; concerns about biological essentialism which have been countered by the claim that she is utilising these allusions metaphorically and hence strategically, or that she is writing in accordance with a particular, French form of rhetoric (Spivak 1989). More fundamentally, some critics have raised concerns about the inevitable essentialism implicit in the recourse to 'woman' or the 'feminine' in Irigaray's work (for example, Moi 1985). I want to raise a similar concern: to assert the ontological necessity of a positive presence, albeit in the context of a critique of the 'otherness of sameness', albeit plural instead of singular, apparently changing instead of fixed, involves the assumption of an essence. An essentialist ontology posits a 'core' that persists, where Being has a thingness quality to it, and has recourse to a unique origin, and a myth of its end. *It* prevails. 'Woman's sexuality', 'woman's desire', has a truth and an origin:

> one would have to dig down very deep indeed to discover beneath the traces of this civilisation, of this history, the vestiges of a more archaic civilisation that might give some clue to woman's sexuality. That extremely ancient civilisation would undoubtedly have a different alphabet, a different language . . . Woman's desire would not be expected to speak the same language as man's; woman's desire has doubtless been submerged by the logic that has dominated the West since the time of the Greeks.
>
> (Irigaray 1977, trans. 1985: 25)

It is buried, but its truth persists; an intact core that cannot be eradicated but can be overlaid, submerged. In *This Sex Which is Not One*, Irigaray suggests, with ironic understatement, that Freud, in his descriptions of feminine sexuality, 'overlook[s] the fact that the female sex might possibly have its own "specificity"' (p. 69). The notion of 'specificity' is used repeatedly in relation to female sex, women, the feminine, in Irigaray's work and conveys a sense of that which can be defined in its own right, on its own terms, without reference to anything else; defined autonomously. Such specifically identifiable 'things' require an origin, which is consistent with Irigaray's concern with the importance of the maternal origin, and indeed the denial of the debt to the maternal origin.

Irigaray is explicit in her wish: she 'want[s] to secure a place for the feminine within sexual difference' (1977, trans. 1985: 159). A place. Her writing is replete with references to 'woman's desire', 'woman's path', 'woman's pleasure', 'woman's body'. Irigaray states that the feminine has never been defined except as the inverse of the masculine, and that it is not a matter of woman 'installing herself within this lack' (p. 159) and certainly not of 'reversing the economy of sameness by turning the feminine into *the standard for "sexual difference"'*, but rather it is 'a matter of trying to practice [*sic*] that difference' (p. 159). The notion of 'practice' here gives a sense of process, action, a plea for that which is conceptualised as gestural rather than ontologically installed within a binary logic. Within Irigaray's discourse, however, we repeatedly come back to the female 'subject' which, no matter how much she tries to distance this new subject from the subject/object, identity/difference dichotomy, still rests on its essentialist premise with its essentialist origin while it continues to be articulated as a non-reversible positivity. This recourse to the notion of 'identity' becomes increasingly evident in her later writings. For example, in *Sexes and Genealogies* (1987, trans. 1993), Irigaray has numerous references to women's 'sexual identity'. In 'Body against body: in relation to the mother' from that volume, statements like the following appear: 'hold on to our identity' (p. 19); 'to discover our identity' (p. 19); 'to do so is to sever women from the roots of their identity and their subjectivity' (p. 20); 'much more in harmony with what women are, with their sexual identity' (p. 20); 'and be hallowed in her identity as a woman' (p. 21).[7]

Grosz's representation of Irigaray's work certainly reflects this trend. According to Grosz (1989) Irigaray's project is 'both to undo the phallocentric constriction of women as men's others and to create a means by which women's specificity may figure in discourse in autonomous terms' (Grosz 1989: 109). Grosz does not comment on what I am arguing is an implicit tension in the aims expressed here. Women are the others of men, at least in part, because of the specificity and autonomy granted the signifier 'man'; quite simply, if women have this too (which is precisely what I want to go on to argue is happening in the contemporary hyperreal context), there is no 'undoing' of the phallocentric construction. This tension remains unresolved and, as we have seen, is increasingly articulated in terms of the importance of women's positivity. For example, Grosz refers to Irigaray's project of 'reconceiving the female body as a positivity rather than a lack' (Grosz 1989: 110). Braidotti (1991) firmly embraces Irigaray's work in such terms.

Baudrillard is clear in his support for feminism when feminist critique and activism are aimed at the code, at the fundamental problem of the dichotomous logic that creates the split of male/female and makes the female the unmarked term (see MOP: 134–5). In the opening to this chapter I indicated that Baudrillard's objection to feminism stems from his critique of a movement of those on the 'other' side of the bar who articulate their desire to instantiate a subjectivity, a positive identity. Such a desire fails to oppose the binary logic instituting an essentialist and phallocentric ontology. In Irigaray's work we have seen an ambiguity with respect to this desire, but certainly the desire is articulated: a desire for women's subjecthood, and relatedly, a desire for the representation of women's desire. This is particularly evident in her insistence to carve out a positive (+) space for women, for the feminine, in the face of Lacan's assertion that 'woman does not exist' and that she, 'woman', cannot know or speak of her desire (see Irigaray 1977, trans. 1985: 86–105). This seems to arouse a degree of *ressentiment*; a form of indignation that compels opposition. However, to reiterate, the attempt to demand a subjecthood, to insist on a subjectivity as presence, fully positivised without a concept of reversion, will only succeed in reasserting an essentialist premise, in semiologically reducing the symbolic, and Lacan would probably still only see himself reflected back in the mirror.

The limitation of Irigaray's engagement with the concept of reversion, or reversibility, is possibly evident in her discussion of the work of Merleau-Ponty (1984, trans. 1993). Merleau-Ponty's use of the concept of reversibility is developed differently from that of Baudrillard, but aspects of Irigaray's commentary reveal a predisposition to this concept. Her comment on Merleau-Ponty's reversibility of the seer and the seen seems to indicate a two-field vision on her part, with individuation into the logos of subjecthood on the one hand, and the death drive, or immersion in a non-differentiated state, on the other. She writes:

> This reversibility of the *world* and the *I* (which Merleau-Ponty refuses to dissociate, to separate into two) suggests some repetition of a prenatal sojourn where the universe and I form a closed economy, which is partly reversible (but only in the opposite direction, if reversibility can have meaning: the in utero *providing* it, the *hypokeimenon*, is more on the side of the maternal-feminine, the future 'subject' or seer on the side of the world or of things), or some anticipation of a heavenly sojourn, unless it is a love pact between the world and things. [And later] I might say that Merleau-Ponty's seer remains in an incestuous prenatal situation with the whole.
>
> (Irigaray 1984, trans. 1993: 173)

The point about reversibility in Baudrillard's formulation is that both of these alternatives are inevitably linked, and both result from a non-reversible, essentialist ontology. Reversibility of the seer and that which is seen cannot be mapped on to a 'reversibility' conceptualised in terms of the incest or death drive without missing the point.[8] In conclusion to her discussion, Irigaray states that 'it is impossible to have relations of reversibility without remainder' (1984, trans. 1993: 184). Irigaray's concept of 'remainder' refers to the symbolic excess that cannot be confined within the phallogocentric system of representation; that which is unsayable in a logic of identity/difference. In Baudrillard's terms, and at least to some extent in Merleau-Ponty's, relations of reversibility are precisely those which symbolically exchange all terms so there is no 'remainder'; in this sense, relations of reversibility are indeed possible, but certainly unthinkable from an essentialist frame.

Braidotti: Deleuze and Desire

> Following Beauvoir, and at the same time displacing her problematic, feminists have posed the question close to my heart; given the fact that woman is the other, defined as being exterior, excluded from, the recognised circle of human experience, how can she come into a subjectivity of her own?
>
> (Braidotti 1991: 166)

Braidotti quotes Alice Jardine asking a similar question:

> Is there a way to think outside the patriarchally determined Same/Other, Subject/Object dichotomies diagnosed as the fact of culture by Simone de Beauvoir thirty years ago, and, in the process, still include women as a presence?
>
> (Jardine cited in Braidotti 1991: 214)

Like Irigaray, Braidotti is concerned about sexual difference and develops an analysis of the ways women in philosophy have grappled with the question of how to detach women from the 'otherness of sameness'. Where Irigaray is ambiguous in her critique, Braidotti is less compromising in embracing a discourse of positivity and in advocating a specificity of the 'embodied female subject'. For Braidotti, there is no question of a tension or contradiction inherent in a project that aims to articulate an embodied female subject in critical resistance to the 'otherness of sameness'. Braidotti describes Irigaray's project as that 'of expressing the positivity of sexual difference' (1991: 248), within 'another symbolic system, based on female, feminine specificity' (p. 252). The tensions surrounding the possibility of delineating the contours of such a system in Irigaray's work appear to be somewhat glossed over in Braidotti's interpretation.

To engage with Braidotti's discussion on the project of sexual difference would be to repeat a number of arguments already introduced through the discussion of Irigaray's work. What I do want to elaborate here is the way Braidotti engages with the work of Gilles Deleuze to develop her concept of nomadism; the 'interconnected nomad' being the new feminist, female-specific, subject. In doing so, I am commenting on Braidotti's interpretation and not on the work of Deleuze himself. The main concern raised with respect to Irigaray's work was her insistence on the positivity of the subject, a feminine-specific, desiring subject. Baudrillard's criticism of feminism as a social movement in a specific historical and cultural milieu, instantiating such a desire for subjectivity, is best understood in the context of his critique of the axiological and semiological structuring of such a subject position. In the light of symbolic exchange as his critical point of departure, we can see how Irigaray's concern to develop an 'other' form of alterity from that constrained with a reference point of sameness is not plausible without reconceptualising the relation between presence and absence, subject and object, positive and negative; a reconceptualisation that does not have the incestuous death impulse as its other pole. These same concerns remain in consideration of Braidotti's arguments for the importance of 'sexual difference' and 'female specificity', but her engagement with Deleuze and his theorisation of 'desire' adds another dimension of concern. In relation to this aspect of Braidotti's work, and in relation to Judith Butler's development of the concept of gender as performative, my major focus of critique is to question whether the directions they advocate for feminist analysis and action are actually reflecting uncritically, and unwittingly, key dimensions of the hyperreal world, rather than containing the subversive and critical import they contend.

   In the Introduction to *Nomadic Subjects* (1994a) Braidotti claims her 'project of nomadism' to be 'anti-essentialist'. Her characterisation of essentialism is different from the notion I am developing here. For example, she states that the embodiment of the subject is not to be understood as either a biological, or a sociological category, but rather as a point of overlapping between the physical, the symbolic, and the sociological. This understanding is, she claims, evidence of a 'radical rejection of essentialism' (p. 4). In the understanding I am favouring here, on the basis of an engagement with the work of Baudrillard, an essence is that which endures, has some kind of core that is identifiable, distinct from other essences, and hence has an origin and a finitude; it is irreversible. Thus, the concept of the nomadic embodied subject is not necessarily anti-essentialist simply by virtue of its defiance of either a biological or a sociological categorisation. Braidotti goes on, however, to argue that in feminist theory one:

> *speaks as* a woman, although the subject 'woman' is not a monolithic essence defined once and for all but rather the site of multiple, complex, and potentially contradictory sets of experiences, defined by overlapping variables such as class, race, age, lifestyle, sexual preference, and others.
> (Braidotti 1994a: 4)

Although she is intent on the importance of a critique of essentialism, we are faced with the same question of whether vestiges of essentialism remain in the enduring 'identity' of 'woman'. A critique of essentialism cannot function in half measures.

The most rigorous extant non-essentialist philosophy ever produced is arguably that articulated by Nagarjuna in India in the second century CE, where, through a method of critique, of systematic refutation of the positions and assertions of others, using their own criteria he arrives at the insight that 'all things are empty of any independent intrinsic nature' (Varela *et al*. 1991: 224). As Varela *et al.* comment, it is staggering that western philosophy often haphazardly revisits questions and problems of essentialism without reference to extant, non-western traditions and their roots in the work of Nagarjuna.

Braidotti develops and employs the notion of the nomadic subject as a response to the question of how feminism might redefine subjectivity within a poststructuralist metaphysics, 'after the decline of gender dualism' (1994a: 157). Her reference to the decline of gender dualism leads her to reject an end to sexual difference in the belief that 'de-sexualisation' would not be good for women. Any advent of so-called sexual neutrality would invariably incorporate women into the predominant masculine model and eradicate the feminine (see Braidotti 1991: 120–1).[9] Thus her view of the nomadic subject is sexually specific. My concern here is to focus attention on this 'decline of gender dualism' and to insist that this phenomenon is not simply one contained within debates between philosophers, but has an empirical politics, a history, and a trajectory. Analysing the structural conditions of this decline forces us to come to terms with the limitations of our philosophical intentions and our 'redefinitions'. It also prompts a reconsideration of the political and economic context in which particular formulations of subjectivity may or may not be subversive.

According to Braidotti the nomad is:

> a figuration for the kind of subject who has relinquished all idea, desire, or nostalgia for fixity. This figuration expresses the desire for an identity made of transitions, successive shifts, and coordinated changes, without and against an essential unity. The nomadic subject, however, is not altogether devoid of unity.
>
> (Braidotti 1994a: 22)

The nomad of this description has some uncanny similarities to the perfect, flexible corporate citizen of the transnational global economy. Braidotti sees the central issue as 'that of identity as a site of differences' (1994a: 157). These are precisely the terms in which Baudrillard analyses the totalising logic of sign value, whereby the identity of the sign is ascertained through a logic of difference. Differences proliferate in their positivity. Braidotti's vision of a 'feminism of difference' is that of 'an epistemological process of repossessing female subjectivity so as to redefine it in its positivity' (1991: 211). Is a (re)definition of 'female subjectivity' 'in its positivity' a subversive and challenging act which feminists should support, or is it concomitant with a global, totalising logic of economic value and representation that is happening anyway? The direction, or implication, of this critique of Braidotti's nomadic subject becomes more apparent in consideration of her use of the work of Deleuze.

In her major work, *Patterns of Dissonance* (1991), Braidotti presents an argument for the importance of psychoanalytic theory in contemporary philosophy, since the structuralist generation, particularly in France, has comprehensively critiqued the notion of the subject as the rational, conscious cogito of the Enlightenment. The poststructuralist generation is decidedly anti-Cartesian, and psychoanalytic theory provides us with a framework for understanding the role of unconscious processes in the formation of subjectivity. And at the heart of the discourse of psychoanalysis, according to Braidotti, is the 'decline of the paternal metaphor' (1991: 17). Here Braidotti, drawing to some extent on theorists such as Foucault and Lyotard, is referring to the progressive destabilisation of the paternal figure as the singular author of, and authority mediating, the meta-narratives of the modern era. This 'progressive decay' of the paternal figure, or metaphor, as the bearer of the Law, the decay accompanying the 'death of the subject', leads her to ask what sort of thought a 'fatherless society [can] have'. This question has particular salience for my own project here, and its relevance will become clearer in the next chapter. But to continue with Braidotti, she appears to divide the field of responses to this 'crisis of the subject' into two main branches: one which is 'nihilistic' and the other which is 'positive' in approach, viewing the crisis as an opening of possibilities for new constructions, new ways of thinking, and envisioning subjectivity as multiple, fluid, anti-essentialist, and no longer constrained within hierarchical relations. In this new era, she claims there is a connection between the 'affirmation of difference as a positive value' and aspects of psychoanalytic theory, in particular the critique of the primacy of rationality and its notion of the sexed and embodied nature of the subject (1991: 220). Psychoanalysis is a 'philosophy of desire', and this is what we need. Braidotti turns to Deleuze as one of those responding 'positively' to the crisis, and who, through his critical engagement with psychoanalytic theory, develops the concept of 'becoming woman' and 'becoming minority' which Braidotti finds useful and productive for her concept of the nomadic (feminist, female) subject.

Considering those contemporary philosophers who grapple with the problem of the representational structure of identity/difference, Braidotti is critical of Derrida's 'glorification' of the position of women, or the feminine, as the 'other', a stance which she characterises as a 'feminisation' of philosophy. Like Moore in her criticism of the 'pimps of postmodernism', Braidotti takes exception to the valorisation of women by male philosophers. Deleuze, on the other hand, takes a different stance, one which Braidotti is also critical of because of its 'de-sexualisation', but she argues that this is preferable to any form of romanticism of the subordinate feminine. Rather than valuing that which has been devalued as the feminine 'other', Deleuze

is concerned to 'overcome' the structural form of identity/difference by finding a way to express difference *in the positive*.

> Deleuze emphasises that since Hegel philosophy has been trying to
> express difference without negation, by using the Nietzschean term
> 'transmutation' to indicate the moment when the negative (or the
> reactive) is converted into the affirmative, in this way marking the
> triumph of positive forces and joy over the reactive forces of resentment.
> He argues that the affirmation of difference as pure positivity inevitably
> entails the abolition of the dialectic of negation, in favor of multiple,
> nomadic thought.
>
> (Braidotti 1991: 111)

Given Baudrillard's analysis of the contemporary era of sign value, we need to
pause and question the joyous embrace of the triumphant positive sign in all
its purity. Considering Baudrillard's work, yes indeed the 'affirmation of
difference as pure positivity' would entail the end of the dialectic, but his
work makes it clear that this has to be understood in terms of the complex
empirical phenomena that we might give in shorthand as political economy.
The significance of this concept of the end of the dialectic cannot only be
considered in terms of philosophers thinking it might be a good idea, and
therefore advocating it. The extent to which Braidotti's representation of
Deleuze's 'affirmation of difference' reflects the very object of Baudrillard's
critique is remarkable.

> Deleuze subverts this vision of one, steady central point of reference, a
> normative principle of rationality as the privileged viewpoint . . . he severs
> the thread which links the puppets to the master and lets them circulate
> freely in space, that is to say no longer activated by a central power but
> through the multiple effects of attraction and repulsion of spatial entities,
> bodies intersecting with each other.
>
> (Braidotti 1991: 111)

Again, we have to be extremely careful. Is the replacement of the phallocentric, hierarchically derived reference point with the free circulation of
those previously hostage to such a system, now disengaged from a centralised
form of power, necessarily the liberation assumed here? Is this severance a
liberating act, or one which indeed benefits the flotation of value, the circulation of capital, and the multiplicity of consumption? And if what is portrayed
in this quotation actually happens, which it arguably is doing, aren't we compelled to analyse it in terms of the complex intersecting forces of a global
transnational economy which constitute human beings as (hetero-, plural,
inherently contradictory) consumers and institute a logic of 'pure, positive,
difference'?

What in Baudrillard's terms is a characteristic of an order of hyperreal simulation, in Braidotti's interpretation of Deleuze is one of 'becoming'; 'becoming-woman' or 'becoming-minority', because the 'lines of escape' or the 'lines of deterritorialisation' are those of the minority position, the position of woman as 'other', of the nomad, the non-fixed. Braidotti is careful to clarify that Deleuze is not referring to 'empirical females' but to a position, or a mode of relation to the activity of thinking (1991: 116), a position that a person of any sex may assume. But it is Deleuze's concept of the positivity of desire that is in the forefront of Braidotti's interpretation of the liberatory potential of Deleuze's work. She refers to his new vision of a body-machine, a 'body-without-organs' where the body is reconceptualised as a material surface in constant transcendence, and not as a depth that can register, internally, social abstractions such as the Phallus. As a material surface where the codes of language interact, the body is no longer the embodiment of normalising forces in Foucault's sense. The concept of the 'body-without-organs' rather emphasises the 'positivity of desire', 'desire as production', which opens the possibility of the emergence of the 'non-oedipal woman' who is revolutionary, subversive – 'a new humanity which would function according to the model of free, positive desire' (1991: 117). It is important to ask the same questions of this 'new body', and of the 'positivity of desire': in what ways might this depiction be any different from the embodied consumer constructed and required by the dictates of hyperreal simulation?

Although Braidotti supports what she reads as Deleuze's 'quite remarkable concept of human consciousness moving beyond gender-dichotomies' (1991: 119), her concern with Deleuze's desexualised vision leads her to question whether women would indeed rediscover their bodies and their sexuality, their 'jouissance', in such a world. She embraces his work for the development of her concept of the nomadic subject, but rejects what she perceives as his annihilation of sexual difference, which, given that women have not achieved specificity and subject status, may well work to their annihilation.[10] Again, we see a concern that the goal of women achieving the status of subjecthood might be compromised. In this context of a concern with the neutralisation of sexual difference in the Deleuzian vision, Braidotti has one mention of Baudrillard. She refers to his analysis of the 'transsexual' as symptomatic of our era with its increasing blurring of sexual boundaries (an analysis I introduce below and revisit more fully in Chapter 4); but instead of engaging with this analysis as a potential critique of the Deleuzian vision, she dismisses Baudrillard as 'nihilistic'. So Deleuze responds 'positively' to the 'crisis of the (end of the) subject' and yet is criticised for his desexualised vision; Baudrillard responds with concern to the crisis and is criticised for his 'nihilism'. My reading is that Baudrillard's concern is not nihilistic, he is not concerned because it is the end of modernity, or because he can't see any future in a world without the dominance of the rational subject, or the paternal metaphor! An engagement with Baudrillard's ideas on this topic could have conceivably strengthened an appreciation of problems associated

embracing a sexually neutral vision. Baudrillard's critique of the hyper-
context in which gender duality is imploding is one which must be confronted in these debates. Once again, I want to argue that it is not sufficient to
dismiss Baudrillard's analysis as 'nihilistic', but rather it is important to
engage with his arguments and develop sound criticisms of their weaknesses.

Baudrillard develops a critique of the Deleuzian positivity of desire in the
context of his critique of the positivity of power in Foucault's writings. I want
to go on and discuss this analysis, but before I do it is useful to introduce the
work of Judith Butler, who, along with many other feminist poststructuralist
theorists, relies heavily on the work of Foucault, particularly his concept of
power.

Butler: Subverting Identity?

Judith Butler developed her theoretical discussion on the notion of gender as
performative in *Gender Trouble* (1990). Her book has the subtitle *Feminism and
the Subversion of Identity*, which clearly signals her intention to critique the
binary logic at the heart of 'identity'. Like Irigaray and Braidotti, Butler
addresses the problematic of the binary form that establishes identity through
a series of dichotomous exclusions, instituting a dominant term and subordinate term, locating women as the 'other' of a masculine identity.
Unlike Irigaray and Braidotti, however, Butler is not concerned to assert
the importance of the 'female subject', albeit constructed in different
terms. Butler is not arguing for the political necessity of a project of sexual
difference. In her second book on this theoretical discussion of the construction of gender, *Bodies That Matter. On the Discursive Limits of 'Sex'* (1993),
Butler addresses criticisms arising from her first book, one of which prompts
her to focus on the question of the place of materiality within a construction-
ist paradigm. Her response is directly critical of attempts to polarise the
material and the discursive, or socially constructed. She questions whether
recourse to 'matter' and the materiality of sex is not in fact reinscribing the
logic of exclusion that degrades the feminine (1993: 28–30). By insisting
on the excluded categories as 'irreducibles', through invoking the notion of
materiality, she asks if this does not in fact reproduce the very terms of the
violation feminists are seeking to redress (1993: 53–4). *De facto*, this critical
questioning problematises the inevitability of invoking the materiality of sex
in the quest for a redefinition of sexual difference and for the ontological
specificity of the feminine, or female sex. For all that Irigaray and Braidotti,
as only two examples of this line of feminist argument, insist that their
theoretical stance is not grounded in an assumption of the biological, anatomical nature of ontological difference, there is no way around the fact that this
must underpin their argument as a point of reference, whether expressed in
terms of the 'natural' or the culturally invested.[11] Butler refers to the 'internal
paradox' of this form of foundationalism that 'presumes, fixes and constrains
the very "subjects" that it hopes to represent and liberate' (1990: 148).

Butler's concern to subvert the order of 'identity', and hence 'gender identity', is premised on the assumption of the primacy of discursive acts in the construction of social reality, acts continually and relentlessly traversed by relations of power productive of the social. To argue that gender is performative is to argue that it is accomplished through repetitive discursive acts that reiterate and indeed *realise* (in the sense of make real) gender difference. To argue that the gendered body, as the site of the presumed materiality of sex, is performative is to suggest that it has no ontological status that precedes its representation, but rather that it is precisely constituted through the acts which create its apparently representable reality (1990: 136). According to Butler's analysis, this social reiteration of gender through the repetition of discursive acts serves to create the fiction of a 'natural' reference point which precedes and underpins the material realness of sexual difference. There is a parallel here with Baudrillard's analysis of both use value and the signified-referent being deployed as alibis providing the appearance of an unequivocal ontological anchoring point for an ideological apparatus focused on exchange and sign value to rest its case.

Hence Butler's critique of 'identity' is not undercut by a desire to reassert feminine specificity as a positive ontological presence. Furthermore, she specifically distances her analysis from an existentialist theory of the self as constituted through its acts. On the contrary, she brings the social and the discursive fully into play through her interest in 'the construction of each in and through the other' (1990: 142). Butler is arguing, intensely critically, that gender difference as embodied sexual difference is a 'truth effect' of socially intelligible performative acts that in turn regulate the entire field of gender. The question that arises at this point is whether Butler is presenting this critique as a universally applicable theorisation. Although her text is constantly referring to the local and the specific, her critique does indeed appear to tend towards the universalist. This, in my view, weakens her argument and limits the potential for her work to extend into a critical engagement with how it might be that the notion of gender as performative is in fact so readily intelligible in this historically specific moment. The motivating force of her discussion in *Gender Trouble* is to subvert '(gender) identity' through exposing the fiction of its 'natural' underpinnings. But surely the historically and culturally specific constructions of the naturalness of gender/sexual difference have to be the starting point? For example, Laqueur's (1990) theory, outlined earlier in this chapter, posits the replacement of a one-sex by a two-sex model in eighteenth-century Europe. My concern here is to emphasise the importance of tempering any suggestion of a 'subversion of gender identity' *in general* with an analysis that is resolutely grounded in a critique that is specific in terms of history and 'culture' or 'place'.

If Butler's analysis is couched in apparently universally applicable terms, there is a danger that her contemporary claim of subversion might in fact be historical. In other words, a subversive strategy designed to parody sexual difference with a view to undermining its anchoring in the ontological inevitability of anatomy is indeed subversive when the dominant structuring of gender difference does rely on such a natural reference. If, however, we accept Baudrillard's claim regarding the loss of the great 'natural' referent in the context of the contemporary ascendancy of sign value, then the sub-versive character of the exposure of the fictive nature of the 'natural' under-pinnings of gender difference at this precise historical juncture is less compelling. To claim that there is no 'true gender identity' might no longer be attacking the roots of the structural configuration of gender in the contemporary hyperreal era. Butler develops what she presents as a radical and subversive critique of Lacan (1993: Ch. 2) by arguing that the phallus is indeed transferable, claiming that this strategy of exposure of the transfer-ability of the phallus 'opens up anatomy – and sexual difference itself – as a site of proliferative resignifications' (1993: 89). But what if this is precisely what is happening in the hyperreal mode of signification? The fact that it might not *appear* to be happening, as reactionary discourses attempting to reassert the realness of the biological destiny of sex proliferate, does not mean that the structural conditions remain the same. In Baudrillard's terms we may well be witness to the frantic production of the 'real' in the hyperreal mode, as simulation, as the 'natural-real' loses its potency as a discursive construct.

If the categories of 'identity' and 'desire' are no longer 'naturalised' but are configured within a floating logic of difference, with no 'gold standard' of biology to render their 'truth', we need to rethink and carefully locate strategies that might be subversive of 'identity'. Butler is explicit in her aim to attempt to 'locate the political in the very signifying practices that establish, regulate and deregulate identity' (1990: 147), and, in agreement with this focus, my point is that there is a need to be rigorous in not allowing universalising assumptions to detract from this endeavour.

Another question relates to Butler's assumption, or conviction, that there is no 'outside' to, or standpoint other than, that of constructed identities. In Butler's view:

> The critical task of feminism is not to establish a point of view outside of constructed identities; that conceit is the construction of an epistemo-logical model that would disavow its own cultural location and, hence, promote itself as a global subject, a position that deploys precisely the imperialist strategies that feminism ought to criticise.
>
> (Butler 1990: 147)

If this statement is approached from the critical standpoint of symbolic exchange in Baudrillard's terms (and at the risk of reading Butler's statement in a way she did not intend), the series of points expressed here is turned on its head. Symbolic exchange, the symbolic, is barred or excluded by the binary logic of constructed identities: identity/difference. The symbolic is a social relation that is indeed not of the order of identity, that opens on to a critique of the construction of the linguistic subject, and which is contrary to the notion of a positive, irreversible presence. Certainly 'outside of constructed identities', the symbolic as a 'point of view' in fact reflects Butler's position as one 'promoting a global subject': that is, the assumption that the model of identity/difference is all-encompassing, has no possible 'outside', both disavows the cultural location of the imposition of this order and assumes a global subject. In other words, to presume there is no 'outside' is to imbue the order of 'identity' with a global, universal status that disavows its cultural and historical location. Perhaps this reflects a tension in Butler's work where on the one hand her express intention is the 'subversion of identity', and on the other she employs a notion of identity which has no 'outside'.[12] She attempts to reconcile this, however, with the possibility of subversion within the terms of the paternal law.

Fully consistently with the inevitability of remaining within 'constructed identities', Butler claims a parallel assumption of the inevitability of remaining within the terms of the paternal law. Again, there is no possibility of a position external to the law, and so subversion must be, can only be, enacted from within the terms of the law and through the possibilities that present themselves when the law 'turns against itself or spawns unexpected permutations of itself' (1990: 93). The paternal law that regulates the relative locations of masculine and feminine identities is not inevitable in any naturalistic sense, in Butler's terms. The inevitability that permeates Butler's analysis is not invoked by any sense of the natural, but rather is commensurate with her use of Foucaultian concepts of power as productive. The law is productive, and it is produced. Contrary to Kristeva, for example, whom Butler portrays as invoking a concept of a true (maternal) body beyond the law, pre-existing the law, Butler views the law as equally *produced* by the illusory assumption of the prior existence of that which it supposedly regulates.[13]

Butler is entirely consistent and unwavering in her commitment to Foucault's conceptualisation of power and to the ensuing implications of this concept for her feminist analysis of both how gender is constructed and reproduced, and what the possibilities for subversion might be. Power, in Foucault's terms, is inevitable. As Butler states, power 'encompasses both the juridical (prohibitive and regulatory) and the productive (inadvertently generative) functions of differential relations' (1990: 29). Power is productive of the 'subject', albeit this might be through prohibitions and exclusions, of 'sexuality', of 'gender norms', of material 'effects'. Performativity is the power of discourse to produce effects through reiteration (1993: 20). Her incorporation of this theorisation of power so fundamentally into her analysis leads Butler to the view that there is 'no recourse to a "person," a "sex,", or a "sexuality" that escapes the matrix of power and discursive relations that effectively produce and regulate the intelligibility of those concepts for us' (1990: 32). Given this, she asks 'what constitutes the possibility of effective inversion, subversion, or displacement *within the terms of constructed identity*' (p. 32, emphasis added). No possibility here of *reversion* in Baudrillard's meaning of this word. No possibility of an outside, no possibility of the symbolic, or of there being any historically or culturally meaningful specificity of this concept of power as productive.

The inevitability of power as productive of 'the subject' in turn creates 'the subject' as inevitable. As I have indicated, Butler is extremely meticulous in her concern to avoid a tendency to universalise, but there does appear to be a tension here. Her engagement with Haar's discussion of Nietzsche – '[t]he subject, the self, the individual, are just so many false concepts, since they transform into substances fictitious unities having at the start only a linguistic reality' (Haar cited in Butler 1990: 21) – is undercut in her later work with her repetitive reference to what appears to be 'the' inevitable 'subject'. And then again, the inevitable production of 'the subject' is in tension with her claim, in an interview with *Radical Philosophy* in 1994, that the notion of performativity contests the very notion of the subject (Butler 1994: 33). In *Bodies That Matter,* Butler emphasises the importance of the historicity of discourse and of the formation of norms. But there is still inevitably 'a subject' produced by such norms; for example, '[t]o think of "sex" as an imperative in this way means that a subject is addressed and produced by such a norm' (1993: 187). If Butler can state that it is precisely the historicity of norms that 'constitute the power of discourse to enact what it names' (p. 187), this apparently historically specific reference in turn appears to assume a universality of the relationship between discourse and the real.

This brief discussion of the work of Judith Butler has focused on one or two of its numerous critical aspects, in particular her placing arguments about the importance of 'sexual difference' for the project of feminism in a critical light pointing up the inevitable essentialism (strategic or otherwise) inherent in such a position. Her arguments for the importance of gender as performative raise a number of issues to question from the viewpoint of this engagement with the work of Baudrillard. These include the extent to which her theoretical directions are *reflecting* changes in the structuring of gender rather than *subverting* the status quo through her critique; the assumption of the inevitability of the production of 'the subject', of the unassailable dominance of the representational structure of signifier/signified, identity/difference, and hence of the centrality of psychoanalytic theory; and the inevitability of power.

Feminist Theory and the Identity Impasse

Feminist theorising on 'women's identity', the whole question of feminist debate on the notion of 'identity', appears to be in desperate need of an injection of some new ways of tackling the issues at stake. This is abundantly evident, for example, in the recent work of Allison Weir who, in her book *Sacrificial Logics. Feminist Theory and the Critique of Identity* (1996), reviews a number of theorists writing on the question of identity (Benjamin, Chodorow, Irigaray, Butler, Rose, Kristeva). Claiming to be presenting something new, and building on her analysis of Kristeva, Weir attempts to resolve the problem of the identity/difference dichotomy. Within this dichotomy, difference is understood to be meaningful only as an excluded term; she refers to this apparently inevitable process of exclusion as a 'sacrificial logic'. Weir argues that this exclusion does not in fact have to occur. On the contrary, she claims, 'identity' takes many forms, and does not have to be understood as that which excludes difference. 'Identity' can *include* differences, and indeed, this is the task of feminism: to articulate such a form of identity.[14] Weir is thus critical of those feminist theorists, including Irigaray and Butler, who, she argues, only view identity within an identity/difference structure and thus reinscribe the hegemony of this structure. According to Weir they fail to see that identity can include difference(s), and that such a (re)conceptualisation has emancipatory potential.

There are some profound problems here. First, continual juggling of the terms of the debate is beginning to lead to arguments which are going around in semantically moribund circles. Irigaray, Butler, and others (acknowledging the role of de Beauvoir's insights fifty years ago) are using the term 'identity' precisely to refer to the structure of a 'metaphysics of substance', whereby that which is asserted to exist (have presence, ontological positivity) takes its meaning within a dichotomous logic of exclusion. Thus 'identity' means same-as, identical to, in mathematical terms a relation of sameness according to specified criteria.[15] Given this working understanding of the term, how does it advance the debate to insist that 'identity includes differences'? Presumably this would meet with the response that 'identity that includes differences' is not 'identity' but something else, and it is precisely this something else that is structurally barred by the logic of identity/difference. Weir's insistence that the achievement of this something else, this identity that includes differences, is possible by just thinking about it differently speaks to the source of the second problem I wish to raise.

My impression of reading feminist theory texts on questions of 'female identity' or 'women's subjectivity' is that they are overwhelmingly dominated by a philosophical discussion that appears to assume that the task is one of looking critically at patriarchal, phallogocentric ways of *thinking* about gender and identity, and proposing 'new' ways of thinking and conceptualising. Kathy Ferguson, for example, proposes 'mobile subjectivity' for feminists (1993). There is indeed an enormous intellectual effort expended on proposing new ways of thinking about language, self, difference, subjectivity, identity, that might situate women, female subjectivity, in a more emancipated, or at least subversive, *subject* position. My concern is that this effort is going around in circles at least partly because very little consideration is being given to rigorous critical analysis of how the structuring of gender, identity, language, subjectivity, is actually taking place at this precise historical juncture. And even less consideration is given to situating these discussions, these ideas, in relation to such an analysis. For example, Weir (1996), in discussing Kristeva's 'critique and reformulation of linguistic theories', writes that Kristeva 'criticises the structuralist understanding of language solely in terms of structure or system or code, and argues instead for a theory of language as a *discursive practice of subjects*' (p. 153). In this 'argues for', is Weir saying that Kristeva is arguing in critical engagement with the structuralists, demonstrating where their theories are grounded on false or erroneous presuppositions and that Kristeva's theory better addresses the question of how language might be understood? Or is Weir suggesting that Kristeva is not engaging in a debate with any epistemological agendas whatsoever, but is taking more of an idealist view, i.e. that the structuralists might argue in these stated terms but she *prefers* her alternative view? Actually, neither of these views treats the problematic in a historically situated, critical manner (nor, possibly, reflects Kristeva's intent); both assume that a 'theory of language' is possible, is desirable. On the contrary, my view is rather that there is no such thing as 'a theory of language' in any absolute or universal sense. There are particular empirical manifestations of 'language(s)' all of which need to be encountered and theorised, critically, in their specificity. Another example from Weir: she states that, in Fuss's formulation, 'identity suppresses difference' and that she (Weir) wants to argue that this is not the case (1996: 110). My point is that it is not possible to 'argue' this in a vacuum – where and when is this 'not the case'? Whether or not it can be successfully argued to be the case is not simply a matter of reasoning, but one of having some kind of epistemological grounds for a theoretical engagement with the question of whether it can indeed be argued to be the case or not. My concern is that the confusion evident in these examples, and alluded to in the context of discussion of the work of Butler, is, currently, one of the most fundamental hindrances to feminist theory on 'gender', or 'sexual difference'.

In the earlier section of this chapter I suggested that Baudrillard's analysis of the role of the economic in structuring a coded binary logic confronts us with the argument that the structure of identity/difference cannot be understood only in semiological and psychoanalytic terms. In an interview with Judith Butler, Rosi Braidotti (1994b) rearticulates her view of the importance of temporal specificity in our theorising: '[w]hat matters especially to me is that we feminists find a way of accounting for the different matrices [of power] which we inhabit at different points in time' (p. 53). She refers to Irigaray's frequent claims that 'the phallogocentric regime cannot be separated from a material process of the male colonization of social space', and that 'the production of new subjects of desire requires a massive social reorganization and transformation of the material conditions of life' (p. 53). In agreement with this general sentiment, I would add that Baudrillard's analysis is indeed commensurate with such a claim. His approach, however, insists that we look critically at the assumptions embedded in at least three terms used here, *power*, *desire*, and *the subject*, because any assumption of their inevitability places them out of the field of vision precisely invoked here as important for a feminist critique.

Baudrillard: the Fictions of Power and Desire

> When one talks so much about power, it's because it can no longer be
> found anywhere.
>
> (FF: 60)

> This is the nature of desire and of the unconscious: the trash heap of
> political economy and the psychic metaphor of capital.
>
> (FF: 26)

Baudrillard's writing on the subject of power probably could not be more con-
troversial for feminism, or more of a challenge to feminist theory to rethink
its most fundamental premises. How relations of power produce particular
configurations of gender and gender relations (or sexual difference), and
how relations of power are implicated in the construction of the feminine
as barred from the position of desiring subject of language and economic
exchange, are pivotal questions for feminist theorising within a poststructuralist frame, where Foucault's concept of power as productive of the social has
been widely deployed. An engagement with Baudrillard's view invites what I
believe to be a very important critical distancing from the assumption that
the notion, or rather the *existence*, of power and of the desiring subject transcend history and culture. It is as if, from a feminist poststructuralist perspective, the suggestion that power, desire, the subject, have an origin and
an end (or worse, don't exist at all except as phantasmatic hallucinations of
a particular era in a particular culture) signifies the end of the social, the
end of the possibility of any sociality, the end of any analysis of oppressive
social relations, and is hence preposterous and absurd (or worse, politically
counter to any form of democratic, emancipatory social life). As if power
rules absolutely in the suggestion of its demise. In this formulation, *the
social* is predicated on the inevitability of *power* and power relations, and
the inevitability of a *subject* who has needs, who is an agent who exchanges
objects in an economic relation, who is a subject of language as a semiological
system of representation, and who has *desire(s)*, or *is desiring*, in a libidinal
economy. Baudrillard systematically challenges all of these assumptions; his
argument rather presents this formulation of power as an ideology of the
most extraordinary magnitude.

In Chapter 1 I discussed Baudrillard's critique of the linguistic subject and
the economic object, of the ideology of needs and utility. In this section we see
how his critique of the concepts of power and desire, particularly in the accep-
tations of Foucault and Deleuze, employ similar points of departure. A point
of discursive commonality across the feminist analyses discussed above
appears to be an emphasis on the 'positivity' of power and desire, and of
the subject who negotiates both power and desire; 'positivity' in the sense
of the 'productive' nature of power; the productivity of desire, power as 'productive' of the subject. Against an interpretation of power solely as repressive,

prohibitive, and restrictive, particularly in its juridical form, Foucault proposed a concept of power as productive of the social. Rather than a force held and exercised by groups and classes to be overthrown and seized, Foucault argues that power has to be understood at the micro-level of its productive operations. It is precisely this insistence on the singularity of production, the relentless and irreversible positivity of power as productive, that is at the heart of Baudrillard's critique of Foucault's view of power, and in more general terms his critique of power embraces both conceptualisations, and argues that they are, in turn, symptomatic of their respective eras.

To make important connections in Baudrillard's work it is worth returning to his discussion of the separation of life and death in *Symbolic Exchange and Death*. Throughout his entire work, Baudrillard is consistent in his rhetorics about power. Power can only be conceptualised as challenge, as symbolic reversion. Power in any other sense is a fiction, an ideological enterprise successfully (albeit temporarily) obscuring its emptiness through its pretence of irreversibility. In *Symbolic Exchange and Death*, Baudrillard writes: 'The emergence of survival can therefore be analysed as the fundamental operation in the birth of power' (SE&D: 129). The cost of erecting 'life' as a positive value that is opposed by death establishes the irreversible finality of death. This separation of life and death constructs life in terms of survival, with 'needs' to be met to sustain life which can be 'read in the operational terms of calculation and value' (SE&D: 131). Baudrillard is arguing that the emergence of this positivity of life that prohibits death is the fundamental bar that enables the 'birth of power'. But it is a fictional power, taking its meaning solely from this fixing of death as irreducibly separate from life. 'Power is established on death's borders' (SE&D: 130). As soon as death (or the object, the subject, the body, the word) is split off in a construct of exclusion in this way, it can no longer be symbolically exchanged. A social order predicated on such a system of exclusions is destined to cling relentlessly to 'life', 'identity', and to see no beyond of power.

In the early pages of *Forget Foucault*, Baudrillard is persuaded by what he reads as the 'mythic' quality of Foucault's texts; Foucault's writing enacts what it proclaims, and therefore is itself consciously productive of a 'truth effect'. Baudrillard's point is that those who follow Foucault without seeing this mythic character end up with the truth: the truth about power as productive, as everywhere constitutive of the social, power as:

> an irreversible principle of organization because it fabricates the real (always more and more of the real), effecting a quadrature, nomenclature, and dictature without appeal; nowhere does it cancel itself out, become entangled in itself, or mingle with death.
>
> (FF: 40)

Baudrillard comments on the perfection of Foucault's writing. His argument is that Foucault can only chronicle his analytics of power with such an exactitude because 'power' is, at this moment, over and finished with. Power inaugurated by the archetypal separation of life and death was integral to that great 'strategy of the real' with its natural referent, its grandiose polarisations of subject and object, the masculine and feminine, capital and labour. Baudrillard is categorical that this strategy has finished; the fantastic dialectics of 'power relations' that sustained this social order has crumbled. But of course, in blunt terms, Foucault doesn't see that power was never there in the first place.

To endorse a suggestion that 'power relations' are no longer operational in our social world, or even more problematic, that power, as the key signifier we have for understanding oppression, doesn't exist, appears to be an inconceivably heretical stance for a feminist to take. Worse, it simply has to be wrong. The objection is that it must be wrong because every day we see and hear of people, men and women, suffering the effects of what can only be understood to be abuses of power. But, following Baudrillard, this objection can be countered in two ways. First, a theoretical proposition that the structural logic of power has changed does not mean that this will automatically be reflected in empirical manifestations of that logic across the whole of social space. I made this same point in Chapter 1 in connection with the objection that in some instances economic value appears in fact to be calculated today in accordance with a logic of commodities (exchange value) and not sign value, arguing that Baudrillard's work has to be considered at the level of a structural critique that focuses on the main drivers of contemporary social life. To reiterate, Baudrillard makes the point that Marx analysed the logic of capital when 'capitalist industrial production was still largely a minority phenomenon' and that the 'theoretical decision is never made at the quantitative level, but at the level of a structural critique'. In relation to the question of power, Baudrillard does indeed develop an analysis suggesting that it is at precisely the moment that 'power relations' implode that we might witness their apparent intensification. Secondly, to counter the objection to questioning the *existence* of power: if it can be argued that conceptualising power as an irreversible 'force' constitutes an oppressive strategy in itself, one which is historically and culturally specific, and one which is integral to a larger cultural logic of which it forms a part, then there are surely grounds for feminist inquiry at least to explore this line of questioning.

Baudrillard's claim that power is 'finished' has to be considered in relation to his thesis of the ascendancy of sign value configured in accordance with a logic of difference, the loss of the relation of reference, and concurrent flotation of signs of the real in simulated, *hyperreal* form. Within such a view, the structural supports for power understood critically as a dialectic of force relations have volatilised. According to Baudrillard, Foucault does not theorise such a change; indeed, for Foucault the possibility of such a shift does not exist. Rather, Foucault's concept of power as an all-pervading, inescapable, capillary force, which modulates and produces the social, can be understood to *reflect* the fragmentation and disintegration of the social forms held together by the logic of a previous era. Foucault is adamant that his theory or discourse on power incorporates the possibility of resistance and transgression, but such a formulation of resistance is not of the order of reversion. Foucault's resistance is characterised more by a shift in the flow of the production of the social, along an alternative conduit, into a different network possibly. There is no annulment, nothing is lost or cancelled; there is simply the continued piling up of the positive production of the social with no 'waste'.

The end of the strategy of the real, of production, and the end of power as productive of the real: Baudrillard's claim is that 'power relations' have dissolved, or are neutralised within the hyperreal, re-emerging in simulated form. 'Power shares all the illusions of the real and of production' (FF: 45), thus power is everywhere precisely at the moment that it is nowhere. Scattered throughout a collection of interviews with Baudrillard, edited by Mike Gane (1993), are comments that help to piece together a more comprehensive picture of his argument regarding the end of power, the end of politics, the implosion of 'power relations' in the hyperreal mode. He talks about a time, one that he remembers, when there was indeed at least the appearance of a structural opposition of forces, when politics functioned in terms of distinctive oppositions (1993: 113), when there was a scene, or distinct arena, of politics configured in accordance with a history of power relations, and he particularly mentions relations of production and classes (1993: 119). Power was somehow locatable and it seemed to make sense to develop strategies for 'political action'. This was a time when an analysis in terms of dialectics as a critique of power relations had some credibility.

But with the decline of the real, we only have the *mise-en-scène* of power, which is itself a sign of its disappearance. Baudrillard writes of this disappearance in metaphoric language conveying his sense of the drama of this change, or 'peripateia' of power:

> [T]he substance of power, after a ceaseless expansion of several centuries, is brutally exploding and . . . the sphere of power is in the process of contracting from a star of the first magnitude to a red dwarf, and then to a black hole absorbing all the substance of the real and all the surrounding energies, now transmuted at once into a single pure sign – the sign of the social whose density crushes us.
>
> (FF: 51)

I read the word 'density' to conjure an image of a social order where the escalating accumulation of value, signs, life, identity, proliferating in their positivity is indeed a 'crushing' spectacle. In such a predicament, and employing the same imagery, Baudrillard talks of the weightlessness he experiences in a world where one is forced to operate without really having an adversary (Gane 1993: 93). Political relations that could be understood in terms of dialectics have finished, or only exist in simulated form, so rather than groups having political salience by virtue of their power relations with other groups, Baudrillard's structural critique suggests that such an analysis is no longer credible. The logic of sign value, the explosion of consumption, 'severs the thread' connecting the interdependent oppositions so that 'groups' now jostle endlessly for position through a calculus of their relative differences, advantages, disadvantages, costs, and benefits, devoid of any fixed reference. Baudrillard also uses imagery associated with cancerous growth to describe the characteristics of this shift in logic, whereby 'forms go their separate ways, meaninglessly, senselessly', to convey expansive, catastrophic growth without memory, or history (see, for example, Gane 1993: 113).

For Baudrillard, the form of power that instantiated the grand oppositions of modernity, to be played out in their dialectical struggles, was itself imaginary. Such a power performed its pretence of irreversibility in a structural order where this posturing could be contested, overthrown, power could be seized, albeit at great cost. But even so, as Baudrillard writes, power wins every time even though it changes hands as revolutions come and go. Hyperreal power is different; the logic of irreversibility is structurally integral to the premises of value and signification.[16] The hyperreal forms a totalising logic with no dialectical opposition structured into the equation; 'power relations' merely simulate an imaginary form of power from a previous era.

The secret of power, Baudrillard writes, is that it doesn't exist (FF: 51). Baudrillard's view is that power can only be understood as challenge. It is reversible, and in this sense none of the grand strategies of power will succeed in *being* power at the extreme of irreversibility. Power is something that is exchanged, and if power is not exchanged it simply disappears (FF: 43). At the limit, a challenge to the death in the face of power exerted and not exchanged reverts that power. For example, the power of the dominant over the subordinate vanishes when the subordinate challenges the dominator to death: if the master kills the slave, there is no more slave and hence no more master (the logic of power is annulled, another slave will not suffice). In a non-essentialist critique, the essence of the 'relation' is as much to be questioned as the essences of the subject and of the object. Baudrillard conveys a meaning of power which is not predicated on the terms of antagonistic forces, but rather which can only be understood as a reversible cycle of challenge and seduction. It now becomes clear how Baudrillard analyses Foucault's rendering of power as an aspect of his work to be 'forgotten', in the sense of not 'followed'. Foucault's lucid exposition of the microphysics of power might be read as a resurrection of power in a form that is readily intelligible to those in an era when the dialectics of 'power relations' have disintegrated. Baudrillard can't help but notice that Foucault's descriptions of the workings of power metaphorically overlay the dominant tropes of contemporary discourses. For example, he claims that for Foucault power operates like the genetic code with its ineluctable, immanent, positive generative inscription 'that yields only to infinitesimal mutations' (FF: 34).

> We see what benefit there is over the old finalist, dialectical, or repressive theories in supposing a total positivity, a teleonomy and a microphysics of power, but we must also see what we are getting into: a strange complicity with cybernetics which challenge precisely the earlier schemas.
>
> (FF: 35)

This leads into a discussion of Baudrillard's arguments on desire and his critical view on psychoanalysis, as he points out that the same comment (as that cited just above) could be made in relation to Deleuze's 'molecular topography of desire', claiming that the flows and connections of such a desire will no doubt soon converge with 'genetic simulations, microcellular drifts, and the random facilitations of code manipulators' (FF: 35). He notes that terms from microphysics and computer theory can be transferred today into discourses of desire as well as power (for example, 'particles', 'random elements', 'clusters', and so on). In fact, Baudrillard's arguments that position Foucault in relation to Marx on the question of power are paralleled in the position of Deleuze in relation to Freud on the question of desire.

Baudrillard claims that the similarities between Foucault's 'new' version of *power* and Deleuze's *desire* are not accidental. They can be readily understood within the social, historical milieu in which they took, or are taking, shape. According to Baudrillard, desire, in Deleuze's terms, is not to be understood through lack or interdiction, but through the positive deployment of flows and intensities; a positive dissemination, 'purged of all negativity'. Desire is 'a network, a rhizome, a contiguity diffracted ad infinitum' (FF: 17–18). Desire is productive, as power is productive, and in Baudrillard's analysis, the same concerns must be raised. Earlier, in the discussion of Braidotti's engagement with Deleuze's concept of desire, I raised a question about the nomadic desiring subject embraced by Braidotti as potentially emancipatory, asking whether this might rather be a concept of desire and subjectivity that is in fact complicit with the contemporary construct of value and consumerism. Baudrillard is very clear about it:

> This compulsion towards liquidity, flow, and an accelerated circulation of what is psychic, sexual, or pertaining to the body is the exact replica of the force which rules market value: capital must circulate; gravity and any fixed point must disappear; the chain of investments and reinvestments must never stop; value must radiate endlessly and in every direction.
>
> (FF: 25)

Rather than discovering the truth of the body through this productive, positive liberation of libidinal energy expressed and advocated in Deleuze's writing, it is, in Baudrillard's analysis, simply unearthing the 'psychic metaphor of capital'. Deleuze, through his critique of psychoanalysis, instantiates the axiomatic of desire in a parallel form to Foucault's instantiation of the inevitability of power in his critical distance from Marx. In *Forget Foucault*, Baudrillard's attention is understandably drawn to what he calls the convergence of 'the purified axioms of Marxism and psychoanalysis' in the catchword of the 'productivity of desire'. Desire annexed to production neatly eradicates seduction, meaning, again in a parallel form to power, that sexuality is everywhere at precisely the moment it is nowhere.

Desire in its positive, productive formulation functions differently from desire manifested through loss, or lack. It becomes 'negotiable' in terms of signs which are exchanged in terms of phallic values, 'indexed on a general phallic equivalent where each party operates in accordance with a contract and converts its own enjoyment into cash in terms of a phallic accumulation: a perfect situation for a political economy of desire' (SE&D: 103).

The implications of Baudrillard's arguments regarding the positioning of 'the feminine' in relation to contemporary discourses on 'sexuality' and 'desire', as these are explored in *Symbolic Exchange and Death*, will be discussed in Chapter 5 in conjunction with his book *Seduction*. My main purpose here is to foreground the critique of the productivity of desire in Deleuze, with its implications for feminist engagement with this theoretical notion. Further to this purpose, it is useful at this point to outline Baudrillard's related thoughts on psychoanalysis, and 'the subject' of psychoanalytic theory.

Baudrillard refers to the place of psychoanalysis in contemporary theory in three interviews in Mike Gane's collection (1993), conducted around 1983–5. Another mention in a 1991 interview shows how his view shows no signs of weakening, and given the analysis of desire discussed above, this is not surprising. 'Psychoanalysis has become useless, a burden' was Baudrillard's claim in 1984, and he goes on to say that in its more recent, Lacanian-inspired renditions, psychoanalysis has spun itself into a 'delirium of conceptual production' satisfying 'a sort of dizziness for explanations' (Gane 1993: 45); and later he refers to an escalating technical sophistication of the unconscious resulting in 'a kind of ecstasy of psychoanalysis' (Gane 1993: 83). His observations lead him to express the view that for all this, psychoanalysis in France has lost its glamour and fascination: 'the word "psychoanalysis" has very rapidly and strikingly lost its impact. It no longer has at all that authority and omnipotence that it once had' (1993: 59); indeed, 'there has been an extraordinary winding-down', it has 'fallen flat', it 'doesn't interest us anymore . . . [t]hat's for sure' (p. 83). Baudrillard acknowledges that the theoretical schools continue to produce their analyses and that the practitioners continue to practise, but his view is that, although the subtlety increases, the dubiousness of the point of it all increases at a parallel rate. As Sylvere Lotringer observed (Gane 1993: 101), Baudrillard could have written a parallel to his *Mirror of Production*, as a *Mirror of Desire*. He didn't develop his critique of Freudian psychoanalysis in a text devoted to such a project, because he felt it would be useless to engage in such a 'frontal attack'. The ideology of desire has to fall into its own trap; its demise has to run its own course. The view expressed in these interviews needs to be understood through his critical analysis of the discourse on the unconscious and 'the lost object' as this critique appears in a number of references in *Symbolic Exchange and Death*, and to a lesser extent in *Forget Foucault*.

I have referred a number of times to 'the strategy of the real', a phrase that Baudrillard himself uses, postulating an historical social process whereby 'reality' is produced through a dichotomous separation of subject and object, and of the subject/object (referent) and its representation. An *identity* of the subject and of the object is made meaningful through a series of exclusions. Thus 'reality' cannot be divorced from its excluded imaginary, which is attached to it like a shadow; hence the conscious subject is 'real' with its inevitable unconscious, its fascination with the imaginary. Baudrillard argues that the 'strategy of the real' produces the positivity of the object and the conscious subject, but it equally produces the phantasm of the irreversible unconscious cast in terms of repression, and the forever missing 'lost object'. This is the dual structure of this strategy, of 'reality', a strategy which is itself the phantasm of psychoanalysis.

Although a social order of economic exchange structurally excludes or bars symbolic exchange as an organising principle, the assumption of an irreversible logic of the economic, as pure positivity, is ceaselessly haunted by symbolic reversion. Psychoanalysis, in complete contrast to empiricist forms of psychology, gravitates towards this haunting. But although psycho-analysis, in its nascent form, was attracted to the shadow side of a metaphysics of presence, or substance, Baudrillard argues that it has ended up by repelling the symbolic. It 'fends it off'. It is not, however, just a matter of excluding the symbolic. At the same time as the symbolic is repelled, psychoanalysis seeks to contain it by circumscribing it within an individual unconscious, and by doing so reduces it to the obsessional fear of castration, under the Law of the Father (SE&D: 1). Baudrillard portrays a view of the entire movement of western history being compulsively drawn to a realism, a fascination with the real, that is predicated on this rather pitiful figure of castration.[17] A preoccupation with castration in psychoanalytic theory ostensibly concerns itself with restoring the 'reality' of castration (and with it the 'grounds of the real') through a 'conscious' recognition of the imaginary, of unconscious pro-cesses. But in Baudrillard's analysis this 'eyeing up the void' does not actually result in a recognition of castration, does not lead to a de-essentialising of a determined resolve to fetishise the real or to gain insight into our role in believing we can say it all, believing we can represent the real in its phantasised totality. On the contrary, this preoccupation with castration in psychoanalysis leads to establishing a plethora of phallic alibis which are then dismissed one by one in elaborate deconstructive flourishes, again osten-sibly to uncover the 'truth' of castration, but which in fact lead over and over again to a denial of castration (see SE&D: 110).

Earlier in this chapter I referred to the way meanings circulate within societies of symbolic exchange, how signs already reversed and sacrificed cannot be understood within a logic of representation and/or accumulation.

Such signs, or symbols, have no 'unconscious', no underside. Exchange takes place with no 'hallucination of reality' and therefore with no phantasmatic imaginary. Baudrillard refers to an excerpt from a 1969 text by Ortigues (*Oedipe Africain*) to demonstrate the absurdity of attempting to understand 'individual subjectivity' in a tribal social world in terms of the oedipal complex. In a society of people where life and death are reciprocally exchanged, to 'kill one's father' is simply not possible. It is worth quoting at least a part of the citation:

> In a society under the sway of ancestral law, it is impossible for the individual to kill the father, since, according to the customs of the Ancients, the father is always already dead and always still living . . . To take the father's death upon oneself or to individualise the moral consciousness by reducing paternal authority to that of a mortal, a substitutable person separable from the ancestral altar and from 'custom', would be to leave the group, to remove oneself from the basis of tribal society.
>
> (cited in SE&D: 135)

Baudrillard's point is that in such a society the collective movement of exchanges cannot be understood to be articulated through the Law of the Father, or in terms of the individual psychical reality principle. The very postulation of a modern, private, individualised unconscious fails to become meaningful where no bar splits life from death, subject from object, subject/object from sign. With this western, and modern, exclusion of death in the assertion of the presence of life, of the subject, of consciousness, the unconscious becomes a kind of accumulation of death not exchanged. Furthermore, Baudrillard adds the observation that desire 'invests' the very separation of life and death. Death becomes the object of a 'perverse desire' of a 'subject' subjected to the imperatives of a conscious ego.

We can now make more sense of Baudrillard's rendition of the unconscious as 'the psychic metaphor of capital'; as capital is the surplus not symbolically exchanged but rendered positive in its cumulative productive logic, so the unconscious is the psychic 'site' for the piling up of that which is not reversed, which enables the production of the present but finite subject haunted by its own death. As the strategy of the real flips into the hyperreal, as capital floats free from its anchoring points of reference in use value and some kind of standard of exchange value, as the dialectic implodes and value is coded into the sign in its continually shifting differential relations, Baudrillard ironically notes that Foucault had a point in not wanting to talk of 'repression': an anachronistic simulation model, no doubt. Baudrillard concludes that Foucault's 'microphysics of power' is best 'forgotten', dropped because it leads nowhere and is a mere reflection on, or echo of, an ending or a disappearing. Baudrillard then goes on to speculate on the finality of sexuality — what if it too were disappearing?

> While psychoanalysis seemingly inaugurates the millenium [*sic*] of sex and desire, it is perhaps what orchestrates it in full view before it disappears altogether. In a certain way psychoanalysis puts an end to the unconscious and desire, just as Marxism put an end to the class struggle, because it hypostatizes them and buries them in their theoretical project.
>
> (FF: 14)

A strategy of the real produces the struggle for liberation; the emancipatory struggles of the repressed, the oppressed, the dominated, exploited, subjugated are inevitably concomitant. But with the end of the dialectic of oppositional forces in the hyperreality of sign value, all 'values' are liberated. Those categories excluded from the order of identity through a phallic social 'politics' (including, of course, women) are now 'liberated terms' no longer subjugated as the necessary 'other', assuming their positive identities, which now circulate in their manifold differences. They are 'liberated' not in the sense of made free, or emancipated from a position of subjugation within a dialectic of exploitation and oppression, but 'liberated' from the structural logic of that very dialectic. Gender/ sexual difference becomes a simulation model; a difference no longer to be understood in terms of the grand oppositions but simulated to appear so. As Baudrillard argues in *Symbolic Exchange and Death*, power is only absolute if it is able to diffract into various equivalents (SE&D: 69). Even in its totalising singularity, the matrix of sign value is still a binary of 1/0. But it is no longer a model of oppositional struggle; it rather sets up a combinatory of neutral distinctions. The appearance or simulation of an oppositional struggle strengthens the monopoly. To make his point, Baudrillard comments on the example of the existence of the *two* towers of the World Trade Centre in New York. Why two? 'The fact that they are two identical towers "signifies" the end of all competition, the end of every original reference' (SE&D: 69). Simulation processes dominate, in Baudrillard's analysis; the simulation of a dominant term.

Baudrillard's uncompromising analysis of the contemporary world points at the fictions of power and desire, and the illusion of any form of positive 'identity'. In the next chapter I examine in greater depth Baudrillard's notion of simulation and its implications for the current feminist enthusiasm for, and critiques of, discourses of 'difference'. Implications of the implosion of the 'political' are also discussed along with a brief consideration of Baudrillard's writing on 'the silent masses', and critics' concerns about the disappearance of 'social class'. In Chapter 4 I will turn again to consider the specific question of contemporary gender/sexual difference as a simulation model.

3 Simulated 'Difference', Simulated 'Politics'

> A mistake concerning strategy is a serious matter. All the movements
> which only bet on liberation, emancipation, the resurrection of the sub-
> ject of history, of the group, of speech as a raising of consciousness . . . do
> not see that they are acting in accordance with the system, whose impera-
> tive today is the over-production and regeneration of meaning and
> speech.
>
> (SSM: 109)

This chapter addresses Baudrillard's analysis of the structural erasure of
'otherness', and the implosion of the 'political' in a hyperreal world of simulated difference. In Chapter 2 we saw how the concerns of feminist theorists
such as Irigaray and Braidotti to critique the 'otherness of sameness' seemed
to pivot around the desire for a feminine subject that would not be caught up
in the dualism of identity/difference, that would attain a subject status that is
autonomous, or at least somehow severed from the relation of the dominant/
subordinate term. Problems emerged, however, in the attempt to recast
this subject position. I raised concerns about the inevitable essentialism of
Irigaray's philosophy, and Braidotti's apparent embracing of such an
essentialism.[1] Fuss (1989) deems essentialism to be neither 'good' nor 'bad'
but rather 'strategic', endorsing Spivak's advocacy of a 'strategic use of posi-
tivist essentialism' in subaltern studies, a position which Spivak later retracts
(Spivak 1989). Unlike Fuss's, my concern with essentialism in Chapter 2 is
expressly related to a critique of the essentialist premise inherent in the
logic of economic value, and contemporarily sign value, in its axiological
and semiological permutations. Indeed, a concern with the problems that
accompany the fiction of essence is a primary underpinning of the analysis
presented in this volume.

Kirby (1997) is concerned to establish the view that feminists cannot or
should not attempt to 'dissociate ourselves' from essentialism. She considers
that the debates on the problems of essentialism within feminist theory
over the last decade or so lead to this inevitable conclusion. In the course
of her discussion, Kirby refers to Toril Moi's (1985) critique of the essentialism of which the work of Irigaray is redolent. Kirby insists that Moi's 'fervid

desire to remain unsullied by essentialism' means that Moi 'forgets that essentialism is the condition of possibility for any political axiology' (p. 71). There is a 'strategic mistake' (to use Baudrillard's words) evident in this conclusion. Endorsing a discourse of 'identity' for the purpose of 'strategic essentialism' confuses an important distinction: one's passionate advocacy of a particular political action or challenge is incumbent on one's situatedness, position, locatedness, which is not to be confused with 'identity'. To be positioned as women, to suffer as women, to act and challenge patriarchal structures from this positioning as 'women', does not necessarily mean that we *are* women, in terms of essence and 'identity'.

Concerns were also raised in Chapter 2 regarding the very different approach to the problem of the 'otherness of sameness' developed by Butler, questioning whether elements of her analysis are not complicit with, and uncritically reflective of, precisely what would be expected in terms of hyperreality as analysed by Baudrillard, but not engaged by Butler. The same questions were raised in relation to Braidotti's embracing of the Deleuzian-inspired 'nomadic subject'.

Why might it be that feminist efforts to articulate the irreducible nature of alterity, or 'otherness', remain in the domain of rather esoteric philosophy, failing to animate our social and political projects? Clearly there is no single answer, and certainly some suggestions have been advanced by feminist theorists, but, placing this question alongside a reading of Baudrillard's structural critique of simulation in the contemporary hyperreal world, it is arguable that the feminist analysis of the problem has not gone far enough. Gunew and Yeatman (1993) directly state their intent to shift feminist debates away from a preoccupation with binary oppositions that 'invariably absorbs alterity', and merely juggles the terms, but that does not contribute to 'changing the power structures behind such construction' (p. xiii). In sympathy with this intent, I believe that Baudrillard's analysis has something important to offer in terms of a critical understanding of these 'power structures'.

I begin this chapter with a brief review of feminist concerns with the question of 'difference' over the recent few decades, which complement and parallel the concerns with subjectivity and identity discussed in Chapter 2, and I then move on to consider Baudrillard's analysis of the contemporary structural form he calls 'simulation'. The implications of his analysis of simulation for understandings of the simulated nature of 'difference', the structural eradication of 'otherness' or 'alterity', and the implosion of the dialectics of the political will be explored mainly through his works *Simulations* (SIM), *In the Shadow of the Silent Majorities* (SSM), and *The Transparency of Evil* (TE). Consideration will also be given to Baudrillard's critics, who raise numerous concerns in relation to Baudrillard's analysis of simulation, the media, the end of the 'social' and 'politics', particularly the implications for understandings of social class and systemic processes of exploitation. On the basis of this analysis, I will return again to the specific question of 'sexual difference' in Chapter 4.

Feminism(s) and 'Difference'

The dichotomous coupling of identity/difference means the focus on the 'one' brings with it the inevitability of the 'other'. As noted by Edward Said (1989), anthropological reflections on 'otherness' and 'difference' invariably invoke that 'secret sharer', identity and identarian thought; one could say in parallel that feminist reflections on identity implicate their twin concern, that of 'difference'. Feminist inquiry into the logic of 'sexual difference' has witnessed considerable attention paid in the Anglo-American context to the dilemma of advocating a politics of equality, or a politics of difference. Intractable contradictions are evident whichever way it goes, when the male is the norm against which both sameness and difference are registered. Equality for women with men (sameness) where men remain the standard of reference does not resolve the problem, and nor does women's 'difference' from men when men remain the standard of reference against which the different feminine is rendered inferior or otherwise. Hence the theoretical endeavour to critique the structural bar that creates the dichotomous construction. This theoretical critique, however, has revolved more consistently around a feminist concern to articulate 'difference' differently, as discussed in Chapter 2, and in doing so tends to return to identarian thinking with its essentialist underpinnings and insistence on the importance of the 'female subject'.

Baudrillard's challenge is to push this critique of the structural bar further. Feminist attempts to reconceptualise 'alterity' and 'otherness' will continue to fall on barren ground without a more fully developed theoretical critique of the structural conditions of their erasure. In fact Baudrillard's analysis makes the case that the ground has shifted. As introduced in earlier chapters, the advent of the structural law of value, sign value, at heart hyperreal and simulated, is propelled by a logic of difference. Identity/difference, where 'difference' is the negative (−) of identity, is no longer the structuring polarity; our attention must turn to the proliferation of differences structured in accordance with the precession of the model. In other words, the contradictions accompanying the form man/woman (politics of identity or difference) can no longer be considered the key drivers of sexual politics. The need now is to rethink the stakes of a gender politics configured in accordance with a logic of simulation. This is also the case for the other 'axes of difference' which have become central to feminist inquiry and activism since the late 1980s.

As ('white, western, middle-class') feminist concerns with the political positioning of the feminine as 'other' matured during the 1970s and 1980s, problems with the exclusions performed through positing a unitary category of 'women' came increasingly into focus. These problems were palpable in the form of active opposition from those groups of 'women' who did not recognise themselves in the abstraction of 'women' articulated by 'white, western, middle-class' feminism. Numerous feminist texts published in the late 1980s and early 1990s claim the importance of responding to this challenge and addressing the issues involved in the fact that 'women' do not form a homogeneous group. By 1996 Zinn and Dill were able to state that '[m]any feminists now contend that difference occupies centre stage as *the* project of women's studies today' (1996: 322).

Lennon and Whitford (1994) introduce their edited book on feminist epistemology, *Knowing the Difference*, with a similar acknowledgement that the problem of differences within the category 'women' has come to occupy the 'centre stage' of feminist theorising. They claim that feminists who were committed to the articulation of what was 'other' in relation to masculine thought have 'had to confront the challenge of other "others" for whom they constituted a new hegemony and in relation to whom they themselves stood in positions of power and domination' (1994: 3). They refer to the different experiences and perspectives of women 'depending on variables such as class, country, age, colour or sexuality' and also to their differing positioning within power relationships (p. 3). Lennon and Whitford go on to discuss the way this critique of the unitary term 'women' has also led to the notion of a lack of unity within each individual 'woman'. This concept accompanied the poststructuralist turn in feminist theorising and has led authors like Fuss (1989) and Weir (1996) to write of 'differences within identity'.

Gunew and Yeatman (1993) begin the introduction to their edited book, *Feminism and the Politics of Difference*, with the statement that '[i]n its third decade, a dominant area of debate in second-wave feminism concerns being able to deal with differences among women without losing the impetus that derives from being a coherent movement for social change' (p. xiii). Fraser and Nicholson (1990) refer to the 'growing interest among feminists in modes of theorizing which are attentive to differences' (p. 33); Braidotti talks about the 'shift in feminist theory towards difference' (1989: 91). Di Stephano (1990) refers to the view that 'the totalising fiction of "woman" . . . runs roughshod over multiple differences among women' (p. 65). Susan Bordo (1990) provides a good example of the impetus in the turn to 'difference' in feminism; she begins her chapter:

> Recently I heard a feminist historian claim that there were absolutely no common areas of experience between the wife of a plantation owner in the pre-Civil War South and the female slaves her husband owned. Gender, she argued, is so thoroughly fragmented by race, class, historical particularity, and individual difference, as to self-destruct as an analytical category. The 'bonds of woman-hood,' she insisted, is a feminist fantasy, born out of the ethnocentrism of white, middle-class academics.
>
> (Bordo 1990: 133)

In 1987 Teresa de Lauretis was concerned that one of the limits of 'sexual differences' is that they universalise sex opposition, which 'makes it very difficult . . . to articulate the differences of women from Woman, that is the differences among women, or perhaps more exactly the differences *within women*' (1987: 2). And again in 1990, de Lauretis refers to the 'third moment in feminist theory', its current, whereby the subject is reconceptualised as 'shifting and multiply organized across variable axes of difference' (1990: 116). Eisenstein and Jardine published an edited book in 1990 with the title *The Future of Difference*, and Eisenstein's introduction briefly summarises the history of American feminism with respect to 'difference', claiming that a shift in emphasis from one on equality (eliminating gender differences) to one on valuing the difference of women from men (womancentred or gynocentric feminism) was an important backdrop to the development of new views on differences among women (1990: xix). Charles (1996) charts a similar history.

Nancy Fraser (1992) also tracks the trajectory of debates on 'difference' in the Anglo-American context as a prelude to 'revaluing' French feminist theories on 'difference, agency and culture'. She refers to the issues that have emerged from these debates as 'an explosive mix of contested concepts and practical conundrums' (p. 6), where every attempt to grapple with one problem seems to spawn numerous others (for example, 'difference' in the singular being potentially hegemonic and exclusive, yet the plural 'differences' glossing over the power relations constituting differences differently).

Feminist analyses of the philosophical and political issues inherent in responding to the 'shattering' of the illusion of a universalist sisterhood of mainly North American, British, and Australasian feminism have been diverse and comprehensive. At the same time, many of these feminist analyses raise varied critical questions relentlessly in response to an unease with any uncritical embracing of 'difference' or 'differences', questions and concerns that are consistent with the critique of 'difference' developed by Baudrillard (discussed below). To cite Donna Haraway:

> We risk lapsing into boundless difference and giving up on the confusing task of making partial, real connection. Some differences are playful; some are poles of world historical systems of domination. Epistemology is about knowing the difference.
>
> (Haraway 1991: 160–1)

Susan Strickland (1994) develops a critique of a 'postmodern' version of difference, paying close attention to the way difference reduced to a form of depoliticised diversity is 'consumerist' in its logic. Butler and Scott (1992) ask 'how can "colour," "ethnicity," "gender," and "class," be read as more than attributes that must be added to a subject in order to complete its description?' and 'to what extent does the theorization of the subject and its epistemic postures through the categories of race, postcolonialism, gender, class compel a full critique of identity politics and/or the situated or encumbered subject?' (p. xv). Spivak (1989) wants to critique and reject universalism, but finds 'multiplicity' to be a problematic alternative. Kirby (1997) worries that 'postmodern concessions to cultural diversity' are sustained through an inclusive logic that recognises 'difference' but within an homogenising framework (p. 153). De Lauretis (1990) is concerned that the articulation of differences as parallel axes seemingly on co-equal terms does not provide the conceptual tools necessary to grasp the constant intersection of these different axes, and how they are mutually implicated in one another.

While Gunew and Yeatman (1993) claim that poststructuralist theory offers a means to do precisely this, they are alert to what they perceive as 'the dangers inherent in certain methods of accommodating differences' (p. xxiv). Bordo (1990) is cautious that any incitement to attend to difference might become a dogma, with its implications for a 'correct' perspective on 'race, class and gender' (p. 139); Di Stephano is concerned to distinguish between an 'imposed myth of difference' and 'crucial and as yet subjugated arenas of difference' (1990: 65). Di Stephano goes on to argue that 'difference' appeals to essentialised identities as much as 'identity' does, and that this critique seems to be stuck in a 'vicious discursive circle' (1990: 73). Crosby (1992) also questions whether 'feminisms which "deal with the differences between us" break out of this vicious circle in which women are self-evident and history mirrors the present' (p. 133). Robyn Wiegman (1995), particularly interested in the project of theorising race and gender, attempts a reframing of questions of 'difference', suggesting that the contemporary cultural moment is one of resistance to political organisation based too rigidly in identity claims. This very fact, she argues, is leading to a diversification of critical positions concerned to 'de-essentialize identity' (p. 5). Most importantly, Wiegman's intention is to situate 'difference', that is, to understand how differences are specifically produced contextually and contingently.

These kinds of critical question point to a frustration with the limits of the debate as it is currently framed. Generally, authors are emphatic about the importance of the 'irreducibility' of 'difference', of absolute alterity, or 'otherness', and yet there appears to be a relationship between the problematics revealed through the critical questions raised, and the unsatisfactory quality of an emphasis on alterity that fails to materialise on its discursive articulation. In terms of Baudrillard's analysis, it is structurally occluded.

This occlusion is apparent in the following paragraph by Braidotti (1991), which, in my view, reveals a number of the points where Baudrillard's critique becomes salient to this discussion. Braidotti is introducing her approach to her topic of analysis for her book *Patterns of Dissonance*:

> It will indeed be a question of differences: differences between men and women, differences among women, differences within the woman that 'I' is. The difference that is thus marked and enacted is such that it would

disqualify any attempt at synthesising the referents. Like weaving parallel lines which will never meet as one; like the contours of two bodies in a film by Marguerite Duras, hermetically empathic; like 'pure', that is, irreducible and fertile difference. A sign of infinite possibilities of difference.

(Braidotti 1991: 13)

'Difference' in Simulation

Turning to the consideration of 'difference(s)', the first point of importance, foregrounded through a reading of Baudrillard's work, is that 'difference' cannot be understood to transcend history and culture. The analysis of the structural interweaving of political economy and signification that is so central to Baudrillard's insights enables a number of distinctions to be made. 'Difference' in the context of symbolic exchange is closer to the irreducibility sought by a number of feminist authors. Baudrillard refers to this as 'otherness', where that which is 'other' is neither opposed nor comparable. 'Difference' within the coded form of identity/difference instantiating the (linguistic) 'subject' and the (economic) 'object' is of an entirely different order. In this case, comparability, that imperative of the economic, is central to the construct 'difference'. As outlined in Chapter 2 (see n. 15 there), the 'identity/difference' formula is premised on an abstract mathematical concept reliant on the notion of criteria. Accordingly, an element, any element, is 'identified' and is then used to construct the criterion for identity across a set. In the note mentioned, I used the example of apples. To continue with this example, if an apple has identity 'apple' modulo^2 its genetic belonging to the apple genus, apples may have a whole range of 'differences' in terms of other criteria of size, shape, taste, crispness, and so on. To extrapolate to the issues at hand in this discussion, women have the identity 'woman' modulo some defining characteristic abstracted to form a set, but some are black, white, Asian, Arabic, Jewish, and so on. Thus the 'identity' that includes 'differences' inevitably postulates some kind of 'essence' (even albeit a 'performative' essence), and in accordance with this formulation excludes or bars 'otherness'.

In the hyperreal mode, the signifier, released from its anchoring in the referent, becomes the *sign*, in Baudrillard's terms. As the 'natural' status of the real that precedes its representation is no longer the reference point for 'reality', the sign itself becomes the real. The implosion of the Sr and Sd, or referent, discussed in Chapter 1, is paralleled by the eradication of use value as the underpinning motif of value, and the installing of sign value, where, in axiological terms, value is not anchored to any prior standard of equivalence. The sign is real. The value of the sign (as object of consumption) is accomplished through its differentiation from other signs. The logic of difference that structures the spheres of value and meaning in the hyperreal mode is still coded in terms of identity/difference. But dislocated from the referent, reality follows the model of value and meaning instigated by the logic of the sign. 'Difference' in this formulation is thus still predicated on the mathematical relation of identity modulo criteria, but the differences that inevitably result from the criterion of identity lose their negativity and become fully positivised as signs. From another angle, differences are no longer subordinate to equivalence; being the same isn't better! Being 'different' is just as good! In fact the more value associated with difference, the better.

Hyperreality could indeed be perfectly characterised as 'a sign of infinite possibilities of difference', to pick up Braidotti's words, quoted above. And the notion of parallel lines that weave but 'never meet as one' is evocative of an image used by Baudrillard to conjure precisely the exclusion of the 'otherness' of symbolic exchange with the advent of economic value, especially in its form of sign value: freeways on an American landscape where motorists travel at speed criss-crossing and interweaving, but never meeting (except catastrophically). Nothing is exchanged or transformed, difference is fully recognised and valued, in fact it is paradigmatic. Identities and differences all remain intact, 'hermetically empathic'.

Baudrillard begins *Simulations* with a citation from Ecclesiastes: 'The simulacrum is never that which conceals the truth — it is the truth which conceals that there is none. The simulacrum is true' (Ecclesiastes, cited in SIM: 1). Within the order of a semiology of representation, reality is deemed to have an ontological priority of some sort, definitely antecedent. Within the order of simulation, signs *are* the real, concealing the truth that there is none — no real, no truth. Reality and truth emanate from signs. The precession of the model figures the real; identities and differences are modulated in accordance with the model and proliferate indefinitely. This precession of the model is at the heart of Baudrillard's notion of simulation. The hyperreal overturns any distinction between the real and the imaginary, and leaves 'room only for the orbital recurrence of models and the simulated generation of difference' (SIM: 4). 'Orbital' is a spatial metaphor that conveys a sense of floating in a vacuous space with no other gravitational point of reference than the preceding model, and 'simulated generation of difference' refers to the modelled (modulo, modulated, modal) quality of the resulting difference.

Baudrillard describes how simulation is not about feigning. Understood as feigning, or as a form of pretence, simulation maintains the principle of representation and the distinction between truth and falsity: 'the reality principle'. To evoke the difference, Baudrillard uses the example of illness. If one simulates paralysis (in the sense of feigning) there is the appearance or pretence of paralysis, but the 'reality' of normality. If, however, paralysis is simulated — i.e. actually produced — then the relation of truth and falsity, real and appearance, implodes (and the limit of a medicine reliant on such a distinction is revealed). It is in this sense that simulation as an order of the real obliterates the 'relation': the sign is the reality, and there is no falsity to be unmasked.

There is no simulation versus truth: the simulated and the true are one and the same thing.

Referring to the status of the image, Baudrillard argues that reality configured in terms of a relation of truth and appearance means the image can be a reflection of a basic reality, can mask, pervert, or distort a basic reality, or it can mask the absence of a basic reality. But when reality is configured in terms of simulation, the image bears no relation whatsoever to any reality: it is its own pure simulation (SIM: 11). Thus Baudrillard makes it clear that within an order of representation, simulation is interpreted as false representation, whereas within an order of simulation 'the whole edifice of representation (is) itself a simulacrum' (SIM: 11).

Clearly this implosion has serious implications for those social forms predicated on the salience of an unalienable distinction between truth and falsity, reality and appearance. In the western context, the social forms Baudrillard discusses include, among others, science, medicine, the law, and the authenticity of 'culture' (I will extrapolate to consider the simulation of sex/gender and the parodic transgender challenge to its 'truth' in Chapter 4). In addressing the question of why it might be that we see the 'panic-stricken' production of 'realness' at precisely the moment of its demise, Baudrillard analyses the sustaining of power in the 'strategy of the real'. Hopefully this will become clearer as I discuss his examples. In brief, the forms of power which are invested in the social institutions of modernity require the binary distinctions of truth and falsity, reality and appearance; these forms of power are predicated on reality staying where it was. This provides considerable momentum for the continued staging of the signs of the natural, the true, the real, the authentic, albeit in simulated form. Furthermore, 'when the real is no longer what it used to be, nostalgia assumes its full meaning' (SIM: 12), and the 'truth' of (the memory of) 'lived experience' takes on a renewed intensity.

Baudrillard incites his readers to organise a fake hold-up of a bank:

> Be sure to check that your weapons are harmless, and take the most trustworthy hostage, so that no life is in danger (otherwise you risk committing an offence). Demand ransom, and arrange it so that the operation creates the most commotion possible – in brief, stay close to the 'truth', so as to test the reaction of the apparatus to a perfect simulation.
>
> (SIM: 39)

But the reaction will be such that the simulation cannot succeed. In the same way as it becomes impossible to discover some absolute real, so too it is impossible to stage an illusion. In the case of the fake hold-up, the matrix of signs will combine the artificial and the real to such an extent (a police officer will really shoot someone on sight, a bank customer will really have a heart attack) that the illusory is absorbed into the real – 'you will unwittingly find yourself immediately in the real' (SIM: 39). The point here is that the established order on which the law is built trends towards reducing everything to some reality; in this way attempts at simulation are 'devoured'. Transgression is much less threatening to the established order, where obedience and transgression are opposed. Simulation of an offence, Baudrillard observes, will either receive some light form of punishment because it had 'no consequences' or be punished as an offence wasting police time. Both of these retain the distinction of the simulated and the real, albeit in a relation of equivalence. His point is that such an offence will never be recognised and punished *as simulation*. To do so is to recognise the abolition of this relation, which power cannot respond to, and which in turn reveals the law itself as a simulation. For power to circulate between the poles of policing obedience and sanctioning wrong-doing, the law has to be based on the difference between the truth of identifiable transgression and identifiable obedience.

This rejection of simulation is evident in the medical sphere. It seems to me that this is most clearly apparent with conditions such as chronic pain and fatigue, where alleged symptoms defy the medical production of their evidence in the tissues or systems of the organism. Medical diagnosis is reliant on the identification of the diseased organ or damaged system within the body, as this is revealed through tests, scans, laparoscopes, and so on. Where no such evidence is revealed, the symptoms must be feigned in the sense of not real: 'there's nothing wrong'. To allow the simulation of symptoms throws the epistemology and ontology of the medical paradigm into turmoil. It effectively disables the distinction on which medicine rests: between real, identifiable disease as causative of symptoms, and wellness where there is an absence of such disease. It is important to note that such conditions are experienced by women in far greater numbers than by men, suggesting such challenges to the medical mode of representation are gendered.

The master-narrative of 'science' (biomedical, physical, or social) traditionally assumes a syntax of 'subject knows object', science 'ostensibly masters the object' (SIM: 17), and again, simulation threatens the poles through which power secures its stakes. Baudrillard points out that even with the critique of objectivity, even when the singularity of objectivity is broken (he uses the metaphor of breaking a mirror into many pieces), and science 'effaces itself before its object' now dispersed into multiple fragments, nothing in fact changes. To 'bow down before "differences"' (SIM: 17) and to institute a shift from mastery by the subject of science to the sovereignty of the object, now challenged to 'speak' in its 'own voice', be a 'subject', is simply a symptom of a different form of the confinement of the scientific object. It merely means, in a way, that we have all become scientific objects; along with all events and phenomena. Baudrillard uses the example of ethnology, which could possibly more broadly be referred to as anthropology, claiming that as soon as it collapses in its traditional form, its place is taken by an 'anti-ethnology', 'whose task is to reinject fictional difference and Savagery everywhere' (SIM: 18). Again, there is not only a retention of and nostalgia for, but indeed a frenzied proliferation of, signs of the real and of 'difference': 'reality' and 'difference' in simulation.

Thus Baudrillard is analysing a social dynamic where power is no longer reliant on an ideological masking of the truth of social relations, but rather on concealing the fact that the real is no longer real, of 'saving the reality principle' (SIM: 25). This process of concealment he calls a strategy of deterrence. Before discussing in more detail the question of 'cultural difference' in the hyperreal mode, I will continue with examining this 'strategy of deterrence' and the displacement of causality by the principle of manipulation, as these are central to an understanding of simulation.

'Deterrence' is the term Baudrillard uses to connote a process ensuring that the fiction of political stakes continues to animate the social. Unlike surveillance, or ideology, deterrence is void of any notion of agent, class, manipulator, interest; it operates precisely to activate these concepts in simulated form to conjure their (apparent) reality (who can say they are not real when they are simulated?). Referring to power, Baudrillard writes:

> When it is threatened today by simulation (the threat of vanishing in the play of signs), power risks the real, risks crisis, it gambles on remanufacturing artificial, social, economic, political stakes.
>
> (SIM: 44)

In Baudrillard's analysis, power 'for some time now produces nothing but signs of its resemblance' (SIM: 45). The political dynamic as a stake is empty, finished, appearing in simulated form in a logic of social demand. Here Baudrillard is referring to a demand for signs of power, signs of meaningful political social relations. 'True' power was a relation of force with stakes and strategy, but Baudrillard argues that these things are now nothing more than an object of social demand, and so, like anything else in the logic of consumption, are subject to the law of supply and demand rather than to violence and death (which doesn't mean there is no violence and death!). 'Power is no longer present except to conceal that there is none' (SIM: 46). Simulated power, simulated political stakes, 'deter' the collapse of power. Baudrillard suggests that the only strategy against this collapse or 'defection' is to 'reinject realness and referentiality everywhere' (SIM: 42). It is this analysis that enables Baudrillard to refer elsewhere (FS: 57–8) to the apparent discovery by those on the political 'left' of the subversive nature of the claim that 'everything is political', that the political was not confined to the level of governance of nation-states but that sport, fashion, household arrangements were all to be affirmed as 'political'. Again, at precisely the moment when the 'political' implodes, it is 'found' everywhere.

As discussed in Chapter 1, Baudrillard argues that the hyperreal world of simulation is an order of totalitarian control far greater than any social form previously known. The implosion of dialectical polarity with the ascendancy of sign value, in addition to annihilating political stakes, reconstitutes the operational construct of 'causality' in a simulated mode. The notion of cause and effect is similarly reliant on the poles of subject/object, active/passive, positivity/negativity. The notion of one thing/element/force causing/impacting on/transforming another relies on the prior separation of that affected, or changed, from its changing agent. Such separation implies a distance, in turn implying contingency: some thing, or act, may intervene and change the course of events, since there is a 'causal relationship'. In social terms there can even be struggle and resistance. With the collapse of the poles sustaining this causal structure, Baudrillard argues that its fundamental dimensions have shifted. Rather than a relation of cause and effect, the precession of simulacra ensures that the real is generalised from the model; the real proliferates from the modulation of differences in accordance with the model. Reality is coded. The best example is perhaps found in the dominant discourses about genetics.

'The operation of simulation is nuclear and genetic' (SIM: 3). DNA cannot be described as 'causal'; rather it codes, or programmes. The shape of things to come is encoded in the form itself. There is no 'causal relationship', no determination, but rather an informing. The significance of this concept of 'information' will become clearer when we consider Baudrillard's analysis of the media, but first, I will discuss 'cultural difference'.

'Cultural Difference'

Where the Other was, there the Same has come to be.

(TE: 125)

Without the Other as mirror, as reflecting surface, consciousness of self is threatened with irradiation in the void.

(TE: 122)

We are engaged in an orgy of discovery, exploration and 'invention' of the Other. An orgy of differences.

(TE: 124)

Baudrillard develops his most sustained discussion of the erasure of 'Otherness' and the proliferation of 'difference' in *The Transparency of Evil* (TE). His critique distinguishes 'difference' from a form of otherness that is radical, in which there is no scale of values upon which otherness can be registered. Baudrillard is emphatic that not only is otherness not the same as difference, but difference is what destroys otherness. Differences are indeed differentiated along a single scale of values. In an interview with *Le Journal des Psychologues* he says that difference is diversification, 'it is the spectre of modality', making it distinct from alterity in a way he describes there as 'absolute' (Gane 1993:

173). The 'hell of the same' (the void in the second quotation cited at the beginning of this section) is deflected by the hyperreal 'melodrama of difference' (both being chapter titles in TE). Simulation of a spectacular, ever-proliferating display of 'difference' is entirely consistent with the logic of sign value. Baudrillard claims that otherness can now be considered to be subject to the law of the market, and in fact, as a rare item, is highly valued. The 'Other' is no longer to be conquered, exterminated, hated, excluded, or seduced but rather now to be understood, liberated, recognised, valued, 'coddled', resurrected as 'different'.

This distinction between a form of 'otherness' that is indeed structurally irreducible, neither comparable nor opposable, and a form of 'difference' that is precisely predicated on establishing criteria against which difference is ascertained,[3] is central to the critique offered here of feminist insistence on 'irreducible difference'. For this feminist proclamation to be meaningful we need some kind of structural critique of the social, political, economic, and semiotic structuring of difference and otherness. Baudrillard's analysis shifts the ground considerably. It makes additional questions pertinent; for example, what is at stake contemporarily in insisting on the importance of 'irreducible difference'? His work suggests that this kind of question has to be addressed through a critique of the political economy of the sign. At least.

With reference to Baudrillard's 'melodrama of difference', the word 'melodrama' has the sense of 'decidedly overdone'. A dictionary definition is: 'sensational dramatic piece with crude appeals to emotions and usually happy ending'. The 'usually happy ending' is rather ironic given its humanist appeal, and the 'happy ending' of cultural hybridity would see the end of the apparent anachronism of racism, a form of discrimination Baudrillard analyses as precisely prescribed by 'difference' (I will elaborate on this below). Baudrillard uses the term 'melodrama' in conjunction with 'psycho-drama' and 'sociodrama' to critique contemporary discourses and practices of 'otherness', both of which conjure the centrality of simulation to the scene of 'cultural difference', and metaphorically depict the simulated and drama-tised absence of the other, with its 'melodramatic' undertones of crude emotionality.

Baudrillard's argument that racism is an artefact of the institution of difference is integrally related to the structure of differentiation and the axio-logical and semiological form of its logic. To differentiate in the hyperreal mode of simulation is to discriminate: to establish differences that, generated from the model, are nothing more than more of the same. Racism, Baudrillard argues, does not exist 'so long as the other remains Other' (TE: 129). When the Other is foreign, strange, 'other', for example, within the order of the symbolic in Baudrillard's critical terms, there is no scale of equivalence or difference against which discrimination can be performed. Encounter and transformation are fully open and reversible, in all forms (including the agonistic encounter of violence and death). Racism becomes possible when 'the other becomes merely different' as then the other becomes 'dangerously similar'. This is the moment, according to Baudrillard, when 'the inclination to keep the other at a distance comes into being' (TE: 129). The intolerable introjection of difference in the case of the construction of 'the subject' as 'different', or traversed by a multiplicity of 'differences', means the other must be exorcised: the differences of the other must be made materially manifest. The inevitability of a fluctuation, oscillation, vacillation of differences in a differential system means the 'happy ending' will always be illusory. 'Difference' (of others) is fetishised as the icon that keeps 'the subject' different.

As the biological bases of racism are exposed as pure fallacy in theoretical and genetic terms, and as the principles of democracy have advanced since the Enlightenment, racism should have declined. Logically, as Baudrillard claims in his book *The Perfect Crime* (PC), this should have been the case, yet he observes that as cultures become increasingly hybrid, racism actually grows stronger (PC: 131–2). He analyses this contra-indication in terms of the increasing fetishisation of difference and the loss of the encounter with the Other, and in the erosion of the singularity of cultures *qua* increasing simulation of differentiation. The 'relation' within the order of 'cultural difference' is phobic, according to Baudrillard: a kind of reflex that is fundamentally irrational in terms of the logic of the system. The 'other' is idealised, and:

> because it is an ideal other, this relationship is an exponential one: nothing can stop it, since the whole trend of our culture is towards a fanatically pursued differential construction, a perpetual extrapolation of the same from the other.
>
> (PC: 132)

'Autistic culture by dint of fake altruism', he adds, recapturing the cultural imperative of the western hyperreal 'culture' to recognise, value, liberate, and understand difference. On the other hand, racism can equally result from the opposite sentiment; that of a desperate attempt to manifest the other as an evil to be overwhelmed. Either way, both the benevolence of the humanitarian and the hatred of the racist seek out the 'other' for reasons symptomatic of the fetishisation of difference.

As the increasingly cult-like dedication to differences escalates with its concurrent impulse to increasing homogeneity,[4] another 'other' emerges. Baudrillard comments on the figure of the alien as a 'monstrous metaphor' for the 'viral Other', which is, in his words, 'the compound form of all the varieties of otherness done to death by our system' (TE: 130). I remember thinking recently how there must be some significance to the outpouring of 'alien' movies (on television especially) and wondered if this was the final frontier of 'otherness' to be 'done to death' (what else is left?). I recall also being disturbed, as I watched one such movie, to reflect on my accepting ut question the imperative of exterminating the aliens who (that?) were to invade and transform human society in evil ways. Baudrillard emphasises that this metaphor of alien 'Other' seizes on what he describes as a 'viral and automatic' form of racism that perpetuates itself in a way that cannot be countered by a humanism of difference. Viral in the sense of self-generating and invisibly infecting, reconstructing: a 'virus of difference', played out through minute variations in the order of signs.

Such a form of monstrous otherness is also the product of what Baudrillard calls an 'obsessional differentiation' (TE: 130), emanating from the compulsion of the 'self' (same) to manifest signs of 'difference' in the form of the 'other'. The problematic structure of this self(same)–other(different) dynamic, Baudrillard argues, demonstrates the weakness of those 'dialectical' theories of otherness which 'aspire to promote the proper use of otherness' (TE: 130). Racism, especially in its current viral and immanent form, makes it clear that there is no such thing as the 'proper use of difference'. This point links again with my concerns about the emptiness of feminist claims for the importance of 'irreducible differences' in the absence of a structural critique.

'Difference', as analysed by Baudrillard, is illusory. The splitting of terms into same/different within a binary dichotomous logic is attended by the problematics analysed in detail in Chapter 1: in particular, the problem of articulating their relation. The embracing of a discourse of 'cultural difference' can also be analysed from the standpoint of this critique. Articulating a satisfactory 'politics' of 'difference' will necessarily escape us. Baudrillard refers to a 'humanitarian ecumenism', and insists that it is a 'cul-de-sac'. In *The Perfect Crime* he calls it the 'dead end of difference' (PC: 122). He gives the example of what was a recent event in France at the time of writing *The Transparency of Evil*, when a considerable commotion was generated by North African schoolgirls wearing headscarves for religious reasons. Observing the range of rational arguments attempting to support the allowance of this practice to embrace 'cultural difference', he comments that these arguments were 'nothing but hypocritical attempts to get rid of the simple fact that no solution is to be found in any moral or political theory of difference' (TE: 131). His view is that 'we' (French, the west) 'are the ones who brought difference to the four corners of the earth: that it should now be returned to us in unrecognisable, Islamic, fundamentalist and irreducible forms is no bad thing'. Again, the incommensurate character of the 'irreducibility' of 'otherness' cannot be encompassed in a 'politics of difference'.

An example of the problems of attempting to articulate a 'politics of difference' which is closer to home for me comes from a recent review of a women's studies programme at a university in New Zealand, where the review panel recommended consideration of a joint appointment between women's studies and Maori studies.[5] A 'politics of difference' in this context was described as having the fundamental axiom:

> that major stakeholders in New Zealand society are differently positioned, and that this difference of positioning means that these

stakeholders will hold different perspectives on the nature of reality and what should be done about it. These differences include: gender differ- ence; Maori/Pakeha[6] difference; the multicultural differences of immi- grant identity and ethnicity; differences of sexuality; class difference; and differences of stage in the human life cycle. A politics of difference means that different stakeholders are aware of such differences and are prepared to enter democratic processes of deliberation where these differ- ences can be discussed and negotiated in ways which produce policies which have credibility with all and respond to real issues or problems.

And further:

Difference of this kind needs to be both welcomed and articulated . . . Students need to be educated to understand that difference of this kind cannot be 'resolved' for this would involve the imposition of one perspec- tive on another.

(University of Otago 1998: 19)

This is arguably a domesticated and manageable formula for dealing with 'difference' that reveals the void of 'politics' in this context. We are all differ- ent, we can learn about these differences, we can discuss and negotiate these differences and through this democratic process produce policies that are acceptable to all. This implies that there must be a universal that transcends the differences and which is ultimately productive of a point of agreement. And yet they (differences) cannot be 'resolved' (so how do we reach agreement on policies that obtain credibility: the cul-de-sac of 'ecumenical humanism'?). But that's OK (parallel lines that never meet as one). We can all be happy about such differences, as they line up equally beside one another in a non- hierarchical plurality. 'Otherness', 'alterity': *degree zero* (an expression Baudrillard uses to refer to household pets; derived from physics, it means the lowest absolute temperature where atoms stop their random movements). Elsewhere Baudrillard writes that such a vision of plurality is precisely about differences being exchanged as positive qualities, again commensurate with his critique of sign value (IE: 46).

Baudrillard writes that the radical Other is intolerable to the west, which is reliant on its eradication. But contemporarily the Other can be neither exter- minated nor accepted, so what is promoted is the negotiable other, the other of difference. He calls this a subtler form of extermination, and one involving all the 'humanist virtues of modernity' (TE: 133).

What happens to the Other that does not become 'different' in confronta- tion with the west, where those of the west are not the other for the Other? Baudrillard writes of the Alakuluf of Tierra del Fuego, who never sought to understand those from the west, never spoke to them, never negotiated with them. The Alakuluf were the people; there were no others. Those from the west were not 'different' but unintelligible. Baudrillard relates how, even after three centuries of contact, the Alakuluf had not adopted any form of western technology. Even though members of the Alakuluf would be slaughtered, it was as if the whites did not exist. 'They would perish without ever allowing the Whites the privilege of recognising them as different' (TE: 134). Baudrillard interprets their extermination as it is reflected in the three stages of how they were named or how they named themselves. First they were simply people, 'Men' (as translated from Baudrillard's French into English). Secondly the whites referred to them as 'foreigners', using the word they used originally for the whites, and the people came to call themselves by that name. Finally they called themselves by the word 'Alakuluf', meaning 'give, give', which was the only word they used in the presence of the whites. Thus in Baudrillard's analysis they were themselves, then strangers to themselves, and finally absent from themselves (TE: 135). Latouche is another author who, following a different route, arrived at similar conclusions:

> The inability of Third World societies to 'reflect on their own experience and to invent appropriate solutions to their own problems' does not come from their congenital inferiority nor from a backwardness, but results from the destruction by the West of their own coherence.
>
> (Latouche 1982: 38)

Latouche continues to comment how the west has 'invented destructive material and moral forms capable of ensuring its domination over every other society, and finally to impose on them its supreme value: economic development'.[7]

An Indian group in North America, the Seminoles, have retained their independence in fierce and defiant rejection of the economic values of the west. Their story is extraordinary (see Caufield 1998). In the mid-1970s the federal government was about to pay them a sizeable monetary compensation for the seizure of their aboriginal lands last century (comprising three-quarters of the state of Florida). The Seminoles sought the help of a lawyer to refuse the compensation. 'We do not believe in accepting money for the land because the land is not ours to sell. It belongs to everybody.' The government was going to compel them to accept the money. This group has continued to live in their traditional ways (against incredible odds), and has absolutely refused to get involved with the federal government. This group has struggled since this time to find exactly the right place where they can hold their Green Corn Dance, so crucial to the cycle of existence, the existence of their culture. Their story is one of refusal of obtaining this land in any way that is complicit with the economic values of the west, values they can see would eradicate their culture. 'The Indian way will die with the end of the world. If they kill the Indian way, prematurely, the world will die with it' (Bobby Billie, quoted in Caufield 1998: 70).

Baudrillard too questions whether the eradication of the kind of singularity of the Alakuluf (and the Seminoles as a different kind of example) will not itself prove fatal to the west. Possibly it is the west that is so singular and will become virally contaminated with the 'foreignness' it tried to exterminate, and will one day itself disappear. In fact, Baudrillard does not draw what might appear to be such a clear and absolute distinction between those (few) non-western cultures, like the Alakuluf (and the Seminole), that have not recognised the west, and those that have entered the gamble with 'difference'. The universal vision of differences, a way for the democratic west to exonerate its past, is met with indifference by the different others. His suggestion is that the west, with its universalising vision, is not the only partner to manipulate otherness for profit. Those members of non-western cultures who adopt a western 'lifestyle' to varying degrees do so in ways, he proposes, that never really embrace it as their own, and in some ways it often remains an object of their contempt, derision and amusement. Baudrillard wonders if 'we' (westerners) take 'them' far more seriously than 'they' take 'us'. In an interview with Nicole Czechowski he makes the remark that 'it is the Africans who despise us! Their contempt for the way we live and die is much greater than ours for them!' (Gane 1993: 194).

Cultural artefacts and performances are sold for tourist consumption, which, we learn from the media, can't be tacky replicas; tourists are discerning and want the real thing – authentic Thai, Maori, Indian, etc. culture. This packaging of cultural experiences and things, referred to in one newspaper article as 'indigenous tourism',[8] can be interpreted both as a form of cultural impoverishment captured and regurgitated in simulated, hyperreal form, and at the same time as a parodic pandering to the superficiality of the west's construction of 'difference': a smart entrepreneurial response to the panicked desire for signs of the real and of difference. This is one example of an important point of tension in Baudrillard's analysis. It is here that we see the vulnerability of the western edifice of representation, 'political power', and economic value predicated on the barring of a symbolic it can never erase, while simultaneously we are aware of the relentless and totalitarian nature of its structure. The totalising quality of the structure of simulation ensures that all attempts to realise 'cultural authenticity' will be recaptured through a strategy of deterrence: the system is your friend, cultural difference is valued. As Spivak noted in an interview with Ellen Rooney (1989), the concern that 'Little India' in a US city is more Indian than India can be analysed in terms of Baudrillard's concept of hyperreality: more real than real. The logic of sign value can be considered to be fundamentally 'anti-culture' by virtue of its structural eradication, or barring of the symbolic, although, of course, this barring is a mythical construct, albeit with deadly consequences. In this sense, the west is a deculturing force that has swept the globe, a process that has been referred to by Latouche (1989) as 'the westernisation of the world'.

Latouche (1989) claims that when one cultural group invades and overwhelms another, there tends to be a period of deculturation followed by some form of acculturation. As the two cultural forms interact the vanquished acquires some new cultural forms as it lives 'with' the dominating cultural group (and to some extent, vice-versa). What is unique about westernisation, Latouche argues, is that the process of deculturation is not followed by a process of acculturation. One cannot 'acculture' to, or with, a non-culture. In non-western or pre-western processes of conquest the period of deculturation may well be fraught with anguish and malaise, but this cannot be compared to the loss of meaning that follows conquest by the west; he describes this loss of meaning as the 'source of the only misery which is truly intolerable' (Latouche 1989: 72).

> This process ends up with an alienation, the invaded culture cannot understand itself by its own categories but has to use those of the invaders. It no longer has its own desires, but only the desires of the other. This identification with the other occurs only at the imaginary level, the 'material basis' does not follow, cannot follow. Fragmented by its insertion in a foreign cultural context, and judged with the criteria of a foreign civilisation, the aggressed culture is already wretched before it has actually been destroyed. Underdevelopment pre-exists in the imaginary before it has been cruelly inscribed in the flesh of Third World people.
>
> (Latouche 1982: 42)

While Latouche analyses uncompromisingly the cultural devastation that has accompanied the 'westernisation of the world', Baudrillard's viewpoint is that, at the term of this process, it is actually, from another angle, the west that is now the most vulnerable:

> contrary to the apparent facts which suggest that all cultures are penetrable by the West – that is, corruptible by the universal – it is the West which is eminently penetrable. The other cultures (including those of Eastern Europe), even when they give the impression of selling themselves, of prostituting themselves to material goods or Western ideologies, in fact remain impenetrable behind the mask of prostitution. They can be wiped out physically and morally, but not penetrated. This alienness is linked to their complicity with themselves. The West, for its part, is alien to itself, and anyone can just walk right in.
>
> (IE: 48)

Accordingly, as Baudrillard observes, it would be a kind of naïve arrogance on the part of the west to assume that it is resented by its 'others' for its power and wealth.

Baudrillard is clear that, in his analysis, the power of the postcolonised (the indigenous peoples subjugated by the western economic-semiologic order) is not in the reappropriation of their lands, their privileges, their autonomy (that is obviously a victory for the west), but rather in their capacity to infect the west with that which it does not understand and cannot encompass: the symbolic power of culture that destabilises any pretence to the universal and the coded instantiation of the real. To link again with the New Zealand example cited above, casting Maori within a discourse of 'difference' (and for that matter 'Maori development') furthers the demise of their symbolic power.

In this context, I want to respond briefly to the criticism that this analysis casts 'the west' as a singular, homogeneous construct, disavowing its diversity of culture. To posit a 'reality' through a process of critique is not simultaneously to exclude all other possible facets; in other words, to suggest, for example, that the west is a deculturing force is not to say that this is *all* it is. 'The west' is only singular in such resolute and absolute terms from one angle, according to one set of problems and issues; on another 'cut' such a homogeneous construction is not only a travesty but simply wrong. The 'west' can be a singular, coherent construct while considering the logic of simulation and sign value,[9] and simultaneously comprise such a disparate mix of cultural groups that it ceases to be a meaningful categorisation. The validity of the latter does not erase the validity of the former. In fact, to focus on the latter at the exclusion of the former is actively to obscure the commonality inherent in the problem of 'the west'. Latouche (1989) makes the point that 'If the West is indeed the anticultural machine [already discussed] . . . then no society and no individual can be wholly *Western*' (p. 53). In this vein, it is arguable that the 'west' decultured itself throughout the Industrial Revolution, through local processes of abstraction and universalisation in the establishment of nation-states, through the process of mass consumption.

Moreover, it is precisely through the residual cultural elements of western peoples' lives (in all their diversity) that the symbolic continually haunts the logic of the hyperreal system.[10] To continue with the viral imagery engaged above, an 'infection' of the west by its 'others' has the capacity to transform the west precisely because the west is equally a diverse and complex mix of cultures with their origins in forms of symbolic exchange. Whether this 'infection' in fact happens/is happening is an open question. Baudrillard both points to the persuasiveness, from his point of view, of its eventuality and at the same time chronicles examples around the world of the logic of western consumerism objectifying, assimilating, overwhelming, exterminating, and resurrecting in simulated form its cultural 'others'. In both *Symbolic Exchange and Death* and *Simulations*, Baudrillard comments on what he sees as the paradoxes clearly reflected in the western practice of demarcating the topographical space of the Other. Indian reservations and animal reserves apparently serve to protect life but rather, he suggests, merely hide the fact that the Indians and animals are dead, and further, that we are actually all 'dead' (SE&D: 19). The cordoning off of the Tasaday Indians in their 'virgin forest' establishes them as the simulation model for all Indians 'before ethnology'. Protected to death, they mask the process whereby they, as object of western science, generalise ethnology in its universal truth, rendering us all Tasaday (SIM: 16). Certainly, to master the universal conceptualisation of difference is to be anthropologically superior (TE: 133).

Latouche echoes this observation with the claim that the 'success' of the anti-culture of the west 'depends on the uncontrollable mimetic spread of deculturating fashions and practices. It universalizes loss of meaning and the society of the void' (Latouche 1989: 73). Baudrillard refers also to fashion as the site where the promiscuity of the exchange of signs is at its height. He notes how 'all cultures, all sign systems, are exchanged and combined in fashion, they contaminate each other, bind ephemeral equilibria, where the machinery breaks down, where there is nowhere any meaning. Fashion is the pure speculative stage in the order of signs' (SE&D: 92). Reference to a 'void' in connection with the social links us to consideration of Baudrillard's analysis of the mass, the media, the 'end of the social', and the 'silent majorities'.

The End of the Media in Implosive Simulation

In both *Simulations* and *In the Shadow of the Silent Majorities* (SSM), Baudrillard emphasises the media as a site that is particularly salient to his theoretical confrontation with hyperreality. Central to his argument that the media's status as a medium has disappeared is the concept of 'implosion'. 'Explosion' has a connotation of pressure, force, energy, outward movement with intensity, spectacle, noise, commotion, and release. 'Implosion' is an inward movement of collapse, falling away, disintegrating in on itself, dissipation, enervation, disappearance, and silence. One key attribute of the implosive metaphor that Baudrillard employs is the merging or coming together of two poles as a result of the implosive collapse; two poles kept apart by a substantive 'relation'. Signifier/signified becomes sign; reality/appearance becomes simulation; cause/effect becomes information, not in a revolutionary transformation but through a collapse that goes unnoticed. The 'mediation' of reality, whereby a form of 'communication' about 'it' ('reality') is mediated through a technology called a medium, is predicated on the separation of the 'message' from the medium. The medium – television, newspaper, radio – is assumed to transmit the message (emit, transmit, receive, decode). Baudrillard uses Marshall McLuhan's expression 'the medium is the message' for his own purposes; it describes exactly what happens with the emergence of the media (which is no longer the media) in simulated form as the relation message–medium implodes. The one becomes the other. The separation of 'reality' from its mediated presentation implodes. Thus the media becomes a site where the strategy of deterrence, the 'manipulation' through information, and the simulated nature of the real are readily analysable.

Foucault's vision of the society of surveillance, modelled on the panopticon, has, according to Baudrillard, come and gone. The panoptic metaphor is contingent on perspective, whereby poles of interest and control remain, even though the technology enlists the subject in his or her own control and monitoring. It depends on the opposition of seeing and being seen; there is an exteriority, and a 'relation'. In the order of simulation, that deemed to be real is produced through its coded inevitability, like the genetic code. Baudrillard writes about the shift from a system of surveillance to a system of deterrence, where the distinction between acting and being acted upon (active/passive) is abolished. It is no longer a question of submitting to the model or the code: you *are* the model, the code. In his book *Simulations*, Baudrillard refers to a US family, the Louds, who were televised as they went about their lives, to illustrate this strategy of deterrence in a more obvious example (there has been a parallel case in Australia: a television show called *Sylvania Waters*, which was also broadcast in New Zealand and the UK). Baudrillard's view is that the Louds were subjected to a 'manipulative truth' by the television medium. Their lives are not mediated by television. Television does not produce a version, or interpretation of their lives. It *is* their lives. Baudrillard's point is that, by extension, we are all Louds.

> [W]e are all Louds, doomed not to invasion, to pressure, to violence and to blackmail by the media and the models, but to their induction, to their infiltration, to their illegible violence.
>
> (SIM: 55)

The social does not subject us to a system of surveillance, there is no violence of a 'relation' of control, but rather we are 'in-formed'. He writes of this as a slow and imperceptible process: a 'secret virulence', a 'chain reaction', a 'slow implosion' (SIM: 54). One cannot isolate an instance of the gaze, or the model, or the process of control, of power. The medium itself cannot be isolated as a conduit of images and messages from one pole to another. The presence of such a (non)medium is, in Baudrillard's words, 'viral', 'endemic', 'chronic', 'an alarming presence' (SIM:54); constitutive rather than rendering of 'effects'.

'TV manipulates us': this assertion has been criticised for its assumption that people are mere cultural dupes who are indoctrinated by television, simply soaking up messages, images, information, as uncritical, non-discriminating sponges. Research in 'media studies' and 'cultural studies' into 'audience reception' has shown otherwise; people interact with television, criticise what they see or hear, enact various 'resistant' strategies, ignore it. They do everything except simply absorb it passively.[11] Read against Baudrillard's analysis, this is a non-critique. The manipulative presence of television is understood in a very different way by Baudrillard (see also Cook 1994, for a discussion on this point). In a simulated reality, there is no message to soak up; there is no 'relation' whereby one can be a 'passive' member of an 'audience'. In fact, the findings of the research in media and cultural studies precisely endorse his interpretation. Of course people actively engage with television, and do all the things they've been found to do by the empirical researchers. *This is your life!*

I will come back to this question of Baudrillard's analysis of what this engagement means below. To continue with television as pure simulacrum, Baudrillard suggests that we need to think of the media as if they were a sort of genetic code, 'in outer orbit', a code which 'controls the mutation of the real into the hyperreal, just as the other, micromolecular code controls the passage of the signal from a representative sphere of meaning to the genetic sphere of the programmed signal' (SIM: 55). Even to use the concept of 'signal', 'message', or 'impulse' is still rendering the process of control as one involving a vector of some sort, an inscription, a coding and decoding. Baudrillard's point is that this seems to be the only way we can make a process of control intelligible; somehow the eradication of a relation, and hence of subject–object, makes the process syntactically impossible to convey in familiar, recognisable terms. He writes:

> it is no longer even a 'dimension', or perhaps it is the fourth (that which is defined, however, in Einsteinian relativity, by the absorption of the distinct poles of space and time). In fact, this whole process only makes sense to us in the negative form. But nothing separates one pole from the other, the initial from the terminal: there is just a sort of contraction into each other, a fantastic telescoping, a collapsing of the two traditional poles into one another: an implosion – an absorption of the radiating model of causality, of the differential mode of determination, with its positive and negative electricity – an implosion of meaning. This is where simulation begins.
>
> (SIM: 57)

When the distinction between poles implodes, simulation becomes a form of manipulation that is absolute in character. It is not a question of passivity, but the non-distinction between active and passive. It is no longer a matter of who or what is doing what to whom.

To return to the strategy of deterrence, Baudrillard characterises deterrence as precisely the annihilation of stakes (SIM: 60). It is not about a subject who deters, or a passive receptor who is deterred. There is no adversary, no antagonistic cause. In this sense deterrence as described by Baudrillard is neutral; it works by neutralising stakes. It simply does not recognise opposition or defiance, and opposing forces are neutralised by an 'implosive violence' that 'involves' rather than confronts. Because the strategic stakes are elsewhere, the 'politics' of struggle can only be understood as a simulacrum. Baudrillard claims that the 'political stake is dead' and '[o]nly simulacra of conflict and carefully circumscribed stakes remain' (SIM: 62). The two fundamental modes of deterrence are, he claims, the absorption of every principle of meaning, and the impossibility of any deployment of the real.

Social exchange becomes 'cyberneticised', to use an expression Baudrillard used in *Symbolic Exchange and Death*, conveying a sense of an exchange that is programmed and informed according to ones and zeros, the digital binary matrix. The loss of referentiality transforms the mode of sociality into a continuous circulation of coded questions and decodable responses. The cycle of question–response reactualises the models circumscribing the questions. In this sense, the digitality of the 'test' is the ontological horizon of hyperreality. To function in the hyperreal world (and here functionality is survival) is to be a 'reader' or 'decoder/recoder' of signs. We are constantly being prompted to respond to a dizzying circulation of signs. As Baudrillard observes, the formula for exchange is for everything to be presented in a series, in a line-up of products which immediately tests the consumer to buy or not to buy, select, not select, this item, yes, no, that item, yes, no. You are obliged to make decisions. 'This approximates our general attitude towards the world around us to that of a *reading*, and to a selective deciphering. We live less like users than readers and selectors, reading cells' (SIM: 121).[12] Simultaneously we are constantly selected and tested: television ratings, consumer preferences registered against purchase patterns, polls, surveys on and on, in a 'circular operation of experimental modification'. Tests test tests in the attempt to circumscribe the social fully; nothing 'other' is allowed to remain.

The hegemony of the binary scansion must, logically, abolish the singular or unitary system. The real is that which is always already reproduced (SIM: 146), and the logic of that reproduction is regulated in accordance with the binary code. Baudrillard argues that any such unitary system must acquire a binary regulation if it is to survive. Duopoly is more stable and will survive longer than monopoly, and hence the simulated fragmentation into endless series, the flotation of multiple differences. In Baudrillard's terms, in the hyperreal context, 'power is absolute only if it is capable of diffraction into various equivalents'. The simulation of opposition between two political parties creates a more impermeable political system than rule by a single party: with two there is scope for this one rather than that one. (I am reminded of a friend explaining to me that she learnt in her child-rearing class that when a child is doing something that you want to stop, don't say 'no', but rather ask the child whether he or she would like to do *x* or *y*, two alternative activities. It works!)

The Dispersion of Meaning without a 'Social'

[I]f the social is both destroyed by what produces it (the media, information) and reabsorbed by what it produces (the masses), it follows that its definition is empty, and that this term which serves as universal alibi for every discourse, no longer analyses anything, no longer designates anything.

(SSM: 66)

'Information' is not about 'meaning' and 'communication'. In fact, in Baudrillard's analysis, information destroys both. Parallel to the increased production of signs of the real on the disappearance of referentiality, we see the increased production of signs of meaning coinciding with its radical loss. Information *stages* communication, and in the process absorbs, or 'devours', communication and the social (SSM: 97). The proliferating phenomenon of mediatised 'phone-in' and 'talk-back' could be considered paradigmatic of the rather frenzied demand to stage participation; participation in the construction and circulation of (apparent) meaning – a simulacrum of meaning that hides the truth that there is none.

It is crucial at this point to discuss Baudrillard's work on the 'silent majorities', the 'mass(es)', and the vexed question of the 'social'. In his book *In the Shadow of the Silent Majorities*, Baudrillard wonders whether the 'social' has never existed, whether it has really existed and in fact exists more and more, or whether it existed once, but not any more. I will try and convey what I consider is important in his theoretical encounter with these ideas. His arguments have received considerable criticism through to outright rejection, and I will discuss some of these views in the following section.

In Baudrillard's analysis, the 'social' (if it can be said to 'exist' or have existed, or even if not) is an invention of the west that accompanied the emergence of the entire edifice of 'political economy' and 'semiology' (discussed in Chapter 1), and which intensified with the virulent expansion of consumerism in the latter half of the twentieth century. The one hypothesis that we can be sure he rules out is that there has always, everywhere been and will be what can be called a 'social'. The 'social' is necessarily that which is contrary to the logic of symbolic exchange. It is predicated, amongst other things, on the essentialising abstractions of the linguistic subject and the economic object, and the necessity, therefore, of articulating their 'relation'. 'The social', as this term appears in institutional, media, and academic discourses, tends to refer to a realm or sphere that is distinct and separate from the economic, reducing it ('the social') to a kind of residual left-over, that which remains 'outside' of the hegemonic economic.

Baudrillard argues that there has always been an historical resistance to 'the social'; he mentions things like resistance to work, medicine, schooling, security, information (SSM: 41). In fact, he contemplates that maybe resistance to the social has, contrary to appearances, progressed at greater speed than the social itself. He points to societies, or cultures, that could never be understood in terms of the 'social', 'societies without the social', in the same way as 'there were societies without history' (SSM: 67). The crucial issue here is that networks of symbolic ties cannot be understood in terms of the social; 'they were precisely never "relational" nor "social"' (SSM: 67). That which we call 'society', or the 'social', establishes the assumed rationality of the economic and the semiological, which excludes the symbolic.

Baudrillard pushes this still further: 'ultimately, things have never functioned socially, but symbolically, magically, irrationally'. He considers the example of the 'contract'; all this 'sound and fury' as if it is the case that a contract is exchanged between distinct agencies according to the law. Within the symbolic there are only ever stakes and defiances, processes of exchange, challenge, and seduction that simply do not proceed via a 'social relation'. Baudrillard writes that defiance is not a dialectic between opposing poles, it is not a confrontation between poles, or terms, in an extended structure. Defiance is:

> a process of extermination of the structural position of each term, of the subject position of each of the antagonists, and in particular of the one who hurls the challenge: because of this it even abandons any contractual position which might give rise to a 'relation'.
>
> (SSM: 69)

The contemporary insistence by Maori in Aotearoa, or New Zealand, on the necessity that the Crown honour the Treaty of Waitangi[13] is accompanied by the earnest endeavours of the Crown's representatives actively to do so. There is every indication that the Pakeha, for whom the Treaty is a contract, sincerely believe that Maori wholly embrace the gravity of this 'social contract' in its entirely 'Pakeha' and colonising terms. For Maori, their insistence that the Pakeha 'honour the Treaty' can be understood as a challenge to the Pakeha to *be* the agent, or term (in Baudrillard's sense), of the contract signed by those representatives of the Crown in 1840. With respect to the preceding discussion of defiance as a process of extermination of the structural position of each term, the outcome of this challenge, for Maori, remains to be seen, as the Treaty also cedes sovereignty to the British Crown, and some Maori indeed challenge this transfer of sovereignty.

Hyperreality creates a gravitational vacuum for the 'social'. The anchoring points that secured a social framework have vaporised, as we have seen in Baudrillard's analysis (utility, exchange value, the real, representation, the 'relation', meaning). A 'meaningful' social has to be simulated, and it requires a population (distinct from a 'people' or 'demos'), a socially constituted body. Baudrillard's term the 'silent majorities' or 'masses' is a way of characterising what he perceives to be the predominant trend that emerges as human beings encounter a hyperreal world. The word 'mass' works as a pun on the electrical meaning of 'earth'; the mass absorbs the social, everything flows through it, leaving no trace. The 'silence' comes from this capacity for absorption that neutralises and disperses all meaning, all simulated meaning. Baudrillard is careful to make it clear that his use of the concept of 'mass' cannot be likened to 'the mass of workers' or 'the peasant masses'. He reserves the concept of 'mass' to refer to the abstract, nameless kind of residue left once the social has been removed: 'The mass is without attribute, predicate, quality, reference . . . It has no sociological "reality". It has nothing to do with any *real* population, body or specific social aggregate' (SSM: 5). In this sense, the mass is not a social entity made up of one plus one plus one, etc., in an aggregation of actual individuals or people. In fact:

> there is no polarity between one and the other in the mass. This is what causes that vacuum and inwardly collapsing effect in all those systems which survive on the separation and distinction of poles. This is what makes the circulation of meaning within the mass impossible: it is instantly dispersed, like atoms in a void.
>
> (SSM: 6)

Baudrillard also uses the imagery of the mass functioning like a black hole in which everything, again, disappears without trace, an 'implosive sphere, in which all dimensions curve back on themselves and "involve" to the point of annihilation, leaving in their stead only a sphere of potential engulfment' (SSM: 9).

The 'silent majorities' do not respond to the simulation of the social and of the meaningful with the seriousness and responsibility required to sustain the appearance of a credible politics. According to Baudrillard, there is no longer 'any social signified to give force to a political signifier' (SSM: 19). Rather than playing the game and responding to this imperative to produce meaning, to produce rational communication, the masses 'scandalously resist', and take the hyperlogic of the play of signs to its most banal. Baudrillard interprets this as a powerful strategy that systematically disables attempts to produce meaning. He confronts simulation with the masses' fascination for the orbital circulation of models; in other words, with simulation's own logic. Surveys, polls, referenda, tests remain the only way in which the silent majority makes its appearance, but in terms of a simulated mode of apparition, not in terms of a sociality where meaning flows from one pole to another. The masses cannot be represented; they are no longer a referent; they do not belong to the order of representation (SSM: 20). The silent mass refuses to be spoken for as well as to speak. And yet the demand is that they speak, that they participate.

Baudrillard refers to an earlier phase where power was secured through the passive apathy of the mass of people. But as the logic of the structural order has changed, this very inertia is precisely a definitive challenge to power, which seeks to promote participation and speech at any cost. 'Everywhere the masses are encouraged to speak, they are urged to live socially, electorally, organisationally, sexually, in participation, in festival, in free speech' (SSM: 23). But the mass absorbs all efforts to engage in this fabricated sociality, dispersing the signs of politics, sexuality, festivity, talk in a meaningless void; more information produces more mass.[14]

Post-1929, the need to produce demand for goods, to produce consumers, was such that it became more costly than the production of goods themselves.

Baudrillard argues that it is now the production of demand for meaning which has become crucial for the system (SSM: 27). Meaning is mass-produced in ever-increasing quantities; it is creating the demand that is in crisis. Baudrillard's point is that, without a demand for meaning, 'power' is revealed as nothing but an 'empty simulacrum'. But the mass does not participate in this charade; rather, 'inundated by flows and tests' it precisely conducts these flows (information, news, norms, fashion), all flows, any flows; 'it forms a mass or earth' (SSM: 28). The masses, by their inertia and refusal to 'participate' in the simulation of power, challenge power to *be* power, which it cannot do (see the discussion on Baudrillard's critique of power in Chapter 2). Baudrillard wonders if manipulation really has never existed, as the simulation of power is matched by an inverse simulation through which the masses absorb and conduct its efforts and effects. The 'involving' hyper-conformity of the masses equally absorbs the 'involving' strategy inherent in the hyperreal logic of simulation. Maybe, Baudrillard suggests, the genuine stake today is about this confrontation between the 'silent majorities and the 'social' imposed on them (SSM: 47), if 'confrontation' is the right word. In this sense, the 'social' does not exist for 'the masses', or 'the silent majorities'. It is only conceptually meaningful for those nostalgic for power (politicians, those in government agencies, socialist groups, activists, academics of the 'left', and on the 'right' those holding recurrent concerns for the fate of the family and other perennial 'values'), for whom those not assimilated into the smooth functionality of hyperreal life present evidence of the existence of the 'social' (the never-employed, gangs, drug and alcohol abusers, glue sniffers, skinheads, 'solo mothers', pregnant teenagers, and so on). On the contrary, in terms of Baudrillard's analysis, such 'evidence' points rather to the virulent disruption and tearing of simulated life, and hence to the impossibility of totally neutralising the symbolic, the 'Other', through the logic of sign value, and equally the impossibility of its total exclusion.

The era of the transpolitical is better characterised through a metaphor of the hostage and the terrorist. In *Fatal Strategies*, Baudrillard argues that any suggestion of a 'circuit' of dominating and dominated, or exploiter and exploited, has been replaced by one more like that of the terrorist and the hostage (FS: 39). Rather than alienation it is terror that modulates the 'political' sphere, and indeed every sphere. The grip of blackmail and scandal, indeed the prospect of blackmail and scandal, serve to render action hostage to manipulation. 'We are all hostages, and we are all terrorists' (FS: 39). This 'relation' is precisely no relation. There is no exchange; a form of banality that witnesses the 'historical loss of the scene of exchange' (FS: 49).

To return to the quotation cited at the opening of this section, 'the social no longer designates anything'; but not only is it superfluous, it also conceals that which it cannot eradicate – 'defiance, death, seduction, ritual, repetition' (SSM: 66). It conceals that it is an abstraction. Baudrillard also questions the term 'social relation', asking bluntly 'What is that?' What is the 'production of social relations'? He suggests that maybe the term 'social relation' *ratifies* the end of the social.

Baudrillard's Critics: Confusion and Dire Straits

Although Baudrillard said 'please follow me' (SV), and numerous critics (especially sociologists) took great satisfaction in saying 'no thank you', he continues on course, leaving behind him a veritable trail of sociological outrage in the English-language literature. If social analysts are incited to make allowance for the disappearance, implosion, or end of those concepts and modes of understanding that made an entire politics, and their own careers, meaningful, then it is not surprising that many will find reasons why this is an entirely preposterous suggestion.

Fuss (1989), not referring in any way to Baudrillard, wrote '[t]he fear is that once we have deconstructed identity, we will have nothing (nothing, that is, which is stable and secure) on which to base a politics' (p. 104). The 'fear' Fuss refers to here seems to reverberate through readings of Baudrillard's work, particularly of his writings on simulation, the media, the end of the 'social', and the end of 'politics'. My response to this is to suggest that Baudrillard might well want to say, via a phrase by Warren McCulloch (see von Foerster 1995), 'don't bite my finger, look where I'm pointing'. It would enhance the level of analysis considerably if the engagement with Baudrillard's writings focused more on the full composite of his arguments and their empirical manifestations, and less on what appear to be tangential issues or smoke-screens: for example, whether what he writes is problematic and not worth reading because it is old and has either all been said before or indeed all happened before, or whether what he writes is problematic because it is so new it is simply unrecognisable, because it fails to honour those well-worn and enduring sociological traditions that provide a basis for scholarly assessment of the value of an analysis. My concern here is to keep the focus fixed on the issues as much as possible.

I cannot help but wonder what it is that motivates the difference between a sympathetic reading of Baudrillard's analysis of simulation (see Chen 1987; Gane 1991a, Butler 1999), and one that is searing in its criticism (for example, Bauman 1992; Kellner 1989). Why one reader does and another does not find Baudrillard's ideas 'convincing' is not always clear. What makes the difference is not apparent from a reading of the texts. Difference of interpretation is sometimes, but not always, the case. Too frequently, the 'reasons' given for a refusal of Baudrillard's analysis are insufficient, lacking an engagement with the ideas at the heart of his argument. Such refusals certainly need to be revisited in the light of a comprehensive analysis of his entire works, and a review of empirical research on contemporary social, political, and economic trends globally. Equally, the salience of his analysis needs to be developed more coherently to provide a more substantial framework for discussion and debate.

Concerns about Baudrillard's concept of simulation revolve, at the most elementary level, around what is perceived as a loss of the 'real' material *real*. Bauman (1992) concludes a brief chapter on 'the world according to Baudrillard' with the statement that:

> [t]o many people, much in their lives is anything but simulation. To many, reality remains what it always used to be: tough, solid, resistant and harsh. They need to sink their teeth into some quite real bread before they abandon themselves to munching images.
>
> (Bauman 1992: 155)

Ignoring the sarcasm that permeates Bauman's writing on Baudrillard, it should be clear that the interpretation of Baudrillard's analytical concept of simulation in the context of 'hyperreality' developed in this volume is drastically different from Bauman's. There is nothing in Baudrillard's work that would in any way suggest that bread conceptualised in terms of simulation is not made of flour and water and is not dietetically nutritious, and so on. In my view, an interpretation such as Bauman's could only emerge from the most superficial reading by a reader who has an eye more firmly fixed on his own assumptions about the difference between 'reality' and 'simulation' than on engaging with what Baudrillard actually has to say. And it has to be said that this interpretation is not uncommon in the English-language literature. Kellner (1989), in similar vein, criticises Baudrillard's 'move to what I would call a *semiological idealism*' (p. 62). 'Simulation' is understood to refer to ephemeral and non-material forms of signs and images, which are assumed to be the 'primary constituents of social life'. Here Kellner (and less obviously Bauman) is retaining the distinction between the 'sign' (as a non-material, representational form) and the 'real' (solid, material, ontically prior things or experiences), where Baudrillard's analysis is explicitly constructing the concept of simulation to refer to the structural logic emergent from their implosion. This criticism, which recurs over and over again, is similar to that referred to in Chapter 1 in relation to Baudrillard's statement that the Gulf War will not happen. His concept of the precession of the model informing the structure of simulation is simply rendered unintelligible if viewed from a standpoint that ignores its major premise: the implosion of poles. If the issue is with this premise, then it would be more useful to debate his arguments regarding the premise than making trite comments about 'real bread'. Baudrillard himself refers to this concern in *Simulations*:

> Moralists about war, champions of war's most exalted values should not be greatly upset: a war is not any the less heinous for being a mere simu-lacrum – the flesh suffers just the same, and the dead ex-combatants count as much there as in other wars.
>
> (SIM: 70)

Emotion about the 'realness' of pain, suffering, bread, and water is displaced in contemplating Baudrillard's analysis of simulation. The issue is to do with stakes. To use a rather juvenile example that comes to mind for me, think of two children in a sandpit fighting over some toy. They bash each other pretty vigorously in the process, and scream and yell. The bruises are 'real', resulting from 'real' impact of 'real' little fists on skin, breaking 'real' blood vessels. But the agonistic point of the tussle is rendered completely meaningless if the said toy is whisked away, destined for another sandpit, another child altogether. In other words, the antagonists are not aware that the stakes are not what they thought they were, they are not fighting for a victory that can be won in the terms they believed, and, most importantly, this was 'known' beforehand. *But their hurt is just as real and just as 'material'.*

In the case of bread, the issue is about the structural logic of how it is produced. Items of consumption (including literal consumption) can be understood in terms of simulation where the reference point for their realness is the model from which, for example, a loaf of bread, is generated. Every single loaf of bread purchased in western consumer outlets is entirely simulated on the basis of models derived from intense market research that also model the consumers of these loaves. The preceding models pre-define entirely the whole production process, from the engineering of the strains of wheat, through the processing of the flour, the inclusion of food additives, the fermenting and baking process, the packaging, advertising, marketing, and merchandising right down to the point of sale and beyond into the customer's mouth. Presumably Baudrillard developed his analysis of simulation through the observation and analysis of such processes.[15]

MacCannell and MacCannell (1993) similarly misconstrue Baudrillard's notion of simulation, but in a different way. They claim that there are actually very few examples of consumer items that are 'simulated', but they are using the term in the sense of fake. MacCannell and MacCannell draw a distinction between fake or simulated items and the real thing (fake marble, fake gold, against real marble, real gold) in their analysis of the dynamics of social class differentiation in 'postmodernity' (which is discussed below). As seen earlier in this chapter, Baudrillard's notion of simulation is specifically distinguished from that of fake; indeed, in Baudrillard's analysis a real marble bathroom floor is just as simulated as a fake one. MacCannell and MacCannell go on to make the rather extraordinary observation that Baudrillard's 'problems with "reality"' are grounded in an 'unacknowledged nostalgia for a kind of naïve positivism – the suggestion that human kind once lived in "objective reality"' (p. 131). Given Baudrillard's lengthy and detailed critical, historical analysis of the problematics surrounding the construction of 'objective reality' (discussed in Chapter 1 of this volume), and his sustained discussion of symbolic exchange which cannot be understood in these terms, this is an example of the kinds of bizarre claim that traverse the literature on Baudrillard.

The argument the MacCannells make regarding the status of the 'real' is that 'technically'(?) 'the real is only that which cannot be assimilated symbolically' (1993: 131). As soon as any concept or event is 'symbolically appropriated' it has a technical status that is different from 'the real'. This conceptualisation, again, assumes language to be a symbolic system of representation, cross-culturally, transhistorically, and as such it is an inappropriate construct to make sense of Baudrillard's concept of simulation. An example the MacCannells use makes the point clearly. With respect to the medical example of psychosomatic symptoms that Baudrillard employs, they claim that this presents a convincing case that medical symptoms can be effectively simulated, in the sense of a person really becoming ill. Missing the point, however, they go on to argue that his discussion stops short of considering 'the reality of mental and other illnesses', which exclude 'symbolic appropriation'. In other words, 'real' illness is outside the order of discourse, and they give an illustration by stating that for the schizophrenic, 'acting normal' cannot be simulated. Baudrillard's proposal regarding the medical *exclusion* of simulation as an explanation for the 'reality' of the psychosomatic symptoms is precisely argued to capture the problematics of the medical paradigm's assumption that 'real' illness is that which 'objectively' registers itself observable in its truth against that which is feigned. Who is nostalgic for 'objective reality' now?

Ontological concerns flow into issues surrounding Baudrillard's analysis of the media. Baudrillard has been criticised for conceptualising the media as external and hostile 'demi-gods' (Kellner 1989: 70), and yet on the other hand has been read as portraying the relationship between the 'body and society' (the individual and technologies of media and telecommunications) as one transformed into a seamless kind of symbiosis (see Rojek 1993: 112–13), whereby bodies themselves become monitoring screens. According to Kellner (1989), Baudrillard has to be criticised for his 'formalist subordination', for privileging the form of the media over its content, meaning, and use. Kellner's concern is that Baudrillard tends to abstract the form and effects of media from their context of production, meaning, and engagement, and by doing so is 'erasing political economy' (p. 73). Once again, for Anglo-American social scientists who valorise what they perceive as their own style of measured, sober, scholarly academic writing against Baudrillard's 'rhetorics', 'allegories', 'poetics', and 'exaggerations' to make such blatant kinds of ill-considered and clearly unsubstantiated judgement strikes me as a rather bold and uncharacteristic move. Baudrillard's work is a critique of the entire edifice of 'political economy'. To evaluate his work on the media in terms of his 'erasing political economy' is simply failing to engage with the issues explicit in his work. Similar problems are evident in Kellner's insistence that Baudrillard is guilty of 'media essentialism', and 'technological determinism' (p. 74).

If there is one thing I would have thought it impossible to claim in relation to Baudrillard's work, it would be that his 'sociology' is 'bluntly ahistorical'

(Rojek 1993: 120). As acknowledged by a number of other authors (see Poster 1994: 76; Goshorn 1994: 287), Baudrillard does not perform any analysis in an historical vacuum. Gunew (1990) exemplifies the process of reconstructing Baudrillard's argumentation to have him do exactly this. After appearing to endorse Hartsock's reference to 'postmodernism's universalising tendency to create a transcendent and omnipotent theorizer outside time, space and power relations' (p. 22), Gunew later claims that Baudrillard 'perceives the communicative act as an endlessly circular one in which sender and receiver assign power to each other, culminating in the formation of the silent majority' (p. 23). Baudrillard does not 'perceive the communicative act', period. Any analysis Baudrillard makes of any 'communicative act' is always historically and culturally specific. It would be consistent with his analysis to reject the notion that such a thing as a 'communicative act' can be said to exist outside of historically and culturally specific contexts. The very construct of a 'sender' and 'receiver' has been analysed by Baudrillard critically, and contextually; by contrast, in Gunew's reading the 'sender and receiver' appear as givens.

Kellner (1989) makes another curious claim regarding Baudrillard's analysis of the media, which deserves attention. On the basis of a quite lengthy quotation from Baudrillard's *For a Critique of the Political Economy of the Sign*, Kellner claims that Baudrillard is 'technophobic' and that he is 'nostalgic for face-to-face conversation which he privileges (as authentic communication) over debased and abstracted media communication', ignoring the fact that face-to-face communication can be 'just as manipulative, distorted, reified . . . as media communications' (p. 67). In the passage quoted from PES, Baudrillard's critique of the mass media focuses on their fabrication of 'non-communication', meaning that there is no opportunity for reciprocal exchange of 'response', and hence of 'responsibility' in the sense not of 'a psychological or moral responsibility, but a personal, mutual correlation in exchange'. Baudrillard is arguing that it is this unilateral nature of the 'communication' that is 'the real abstraction of the media'. Reading this argument as evidence of 'technophobia', with Baudrillard problematically valorising face-to-face communication over a technologically mediated mass form, can be countered by an alternative reading which draws out more consistently the key point about the non-reciprocity of the 'exchange'.

To illustrate by way of example, a New Zealand-made documentary was screened recently with the title *Girl Talk*. In it a diverse range of women and girls was 'observed' and filmed by the documentary crew as these women and girls engaged in various conversations, particularly about 'personal' and intimate topics. The method of filming achieved a kind of 'fly-on-the-wall' effect, and it was obvious that the conversations were not scripted. In one segment of this documentary a woman of middle age, whose ethnicity may have been that of one of the Pacific Island nations, talked to two other workmates (New Zealanders of European descent) about her feelings about 'sex' (this appeared to have been their designated topic).

During the course of the conversation she, very hesitantly, not very articulately, revealed that she didn't like sex very much, because she found it painful, and that her first experience of sex had been when she was raped as a very young woman. This was the first time that this woman had voiced this to any other person. The violence of the abstraction of the mass media conveyed by Baudrillard is, in my view, made abundantly evident in this example. This *exposure* of something so intimate and personal is broadcast to the mass audience in a way that provides no reciprocal exchange for that woman. What is important is the mutual presence of human beings to one another, for this kind of reciprocal exchange and 'responsibility' to take place. Such exchange could equally happen through telepresence, where mutual presence can be accomplished through technological means. My point is that it is not the technology itself, in isolation, that is the object of Baudrillard's critique, but the simulated, mass-mediated non-communication. The fact that Baudrillard develops a critical engagement with the significance of 'tele' technologies elsewhere (see SEDN: 164–5) is immaterial in relation to this point.

Baudrillard's concept of the 'masses', or 'the silent majorities', is anathema to those social theorists for whom the notion of the power of the collective is integral to political action. Where action at the level of the social group, or class, is understood as the key principle of social change through the formation of a movement to confront and overturn oppressive social structures, the notion of an inert 'mass' is received as entirely contrary to radical social theory. Kellner (1989) comments on Baudrillard's 'contempt' for the masses (p. 69); the masses who 'passively consume' are hardly the agents of revolutionary class action. From this perspective it is possibly understandable that commentators like Bauman would be scathing in their response to Baudrillard's claim that the silence of the masses is indeed their best strategy to confound the system. If the politics of the system is theorised in terms of some form of a dialectics of historical materialism (albeit postindustrial), then Baudrillard's 'bovine immobility' of the masses (Bauman 1992: 153) can indeed be read as a conceptualisation that opposes change, secures the status quo, and apart from anything else appears profoundly disrespectful. However, if the 'dialectics of historical materialism' are found to be no longer operative, or merely simulated, as Baudrillard's work argues, then such a scathing response reveals a failure to address the issues at stake.

Kellner (1989) criticises Baudrillard for claiming to speak for the masses (p. 206). On the contrary, my reading is that the critics cited above convey their indignation precisely on behalf of the masses, indicating that they assume such a speaking position themselves. Baudrillard does not in fact construct the masses as a social class, a group, an aggregate of individuals who can speak and be spoken for. As we have seen, in accordance with his analysis of the implosive force of simulation, the 'silent majorities' do not constitute a social entity or movement caught in an oppositional dialectic. It makes no sense to talk of 'contempt' for the masses in Baudrillard's formulation. The 'silent mass', as an epiphenomenon produced by the hyperreal 'system', on the contrary has Baudrillard's unambiguous encouragement to be subversive by not 'playing the game' or by flipping the game into the vortex of its own hyperlogic; 'playing dead' as Sylvere Lotringer put it in conversation with Baudrillard (Lotringer in Gane 1993: 114). Baudrillard himself acknowledged in an interview with Salvatore Mele and Mark Titmarsh in 1984 (Gane 1993) that his earlier thinking on the passivity of the masses appeared to compel the masses into silence and alienation in a way that had a pejorative undertone. Since then he has endeavoured to refine this rather simplistic picture, and in *The Silent Majorities* this silence is conveyed as a source of power and a strategy that effectively derails the media's insistence that the silent majorities demand meaning and participate in its circulation: '[a]nd at the moment, the masses, instead of being manipulated by the media, actually utilize the media in order to disappear' (Baudrillard in Gane 1993: 87–8).[16] Later in the same interview, Baudrillard is clear that:

> [t]he mass is a form, a kind of inertia, a power of inertia . . . Quite simply, there is no need to set up a definition of the masses as millions of assembled individuals. The mass is something else. It's a mode of circulation and inertia. In this sense it is the event of the modern world.
> (Baudrillard in Gane 1993: 90)

Turner (1993) claims that, in sociological terms, the notion of the 'mass society' has already been thoroughly critiqued, and has come and gone. Baudrillard's notion of 'the masses' is not, however, one that can be narrowly encompassed by the patterns of mass production and consumption referred to by Turner. Contemporary shifts to niche production, targeted marketing, right down to the personalised production of goods and services, and the marketing of 'experience', are equally commensurate with Baudrillard's notion of 'the masses', and indeed with the logic of the proliferation of pre-modelled differences. Furthermore, the masses definitely do not engage in processes of consumption (mass, niche, targeted, or otherwise) in accordance with the dictates of economic theory, rationally balancing purchasing behaviours and ends. Baudrillard suggests that the mass systematically confounds this phantasmatic order of things (see SSM: 45).

Those critics most firmly committed to the centrality of 'class struggle', to the materiality of production, and to the political significance of the exploitation of labour for capital gain will inevitably distinguish 'infra-structure' from 'superstructure'. They will therefore be predisposed to view Baudrillard as one of those 'ludic postmodernists' who revel in the frivolous, counter-revolutionary pastime of theorising the determining characteristics of superstructural semiotics. This view is a useful foil to a brief discussion of what Baudrillard does have to say about social class and exploitation (I have discussed his critique of 'production' in Chapter 1).

Teresa Ebert begins her book *Ludic Feminism and After* (1996) with one of the questions motivating her work: 'why the dominant feminist theory in the postmodern moment – ludic feminism – has largely abandoned the problems of labor and exploitation and ignored their relation to gender, sexuality, difference, desire, and subjectivity' (p. ix). This has to be a very good question. If we accept that postmodernity is at least partially characterised by a structural dislocation of the determining relation of infrastructure–superstructure, then we can make a distinction between those forms of post-modern theory that simply reflect uncritically the dislocated realm of significations and those that seek to understand this dislocation, critically.[17] 'Postmodern theory' that simply (or often very complicatedly) indulges in forms of self-referential analyses of signs and meanings (structurally the possibilities are infinite) is the appropriate target for Ebert's question. Whether or not this is the 'dominant' form of feminist theory is another question. I think not. But there is a sense in which this concern for feminism's, or feminist theory's, apparent abandonment of the problems of 'labour and exploitation' needs to be considered. Surprising as it may seem, the work in the present volume has some points in common with the concern expressed in Ebert's question, but takes a very different track.

If Marx were alive today, would he critique the existing social order in terms of a dialectics of class struggle and the exploitation of labour? If we are concerned about the huge numbers of women and children working in horrendous conditions for very low pay in numerous western as well as non-western countries around the world, is an analysis developed to understand the dynamics of early capitalism going to be appropriate, or do all the concepts need to be critically reworked as conditions change? What would it mean if in fact a dialectical relationship was no longer the best way of conceptualising the political dynamic at play in constructing this reality? If we are concerned about the 'new poor' of the 'Fourth World', whose labour no one seems to want to exploit, what theoretical understandings become valuable to develop an understanding of their structural location? It is increasingly arguable that the production of wealth is less and less reliant on the exploitation of any form of labour, and that vast numbers of people in the Third and Fourth Worlds are simply redundant, in the real sense of totally superfluous to the economic system, with no prospect of their 'labour' having any value. In *America* (AM), Baudrillard observes how:

> entire social groups are being laid waste from the inside . . . Society has forgotten them and now they are forgetting themselves. They fall out of all reckoning, zombies condemned to obliteration, consigned to statistical graphs of endangered species. This is the Fourth World. Entire sectors of our modern societies, entire countries in the Third World now fall into this Fourth World desert zone.
>
> (AM: 112)

Many other commentators are making the same observations, from critical social theorists to multinational company directors (see Arnoux and Grace

1997). Elsewhere Baudrillard refers to the unemployed as a sort of inert 'artificial satellite' that has faded out of circulation (TE: 33–4).

Baudrillard claims that the political demarcation of importance contemporarily is best understood in terms of a simple but striking binary model: the A and the Non-A categories. 'Thus, the old bogey of the duel between antagonistic classes is conjured away in a statistical dichotomy: there are still two terms but they are no longer in conflict – they turn into the two poles of a social dynamic' (PES: 59). This social dynamic renders As and Non-As different but not locked into and determined by a contradictory social relationship. As and Non-As are differentiated on the basis of consumption, but Baudrillard argues that this source of difference veils the 'true political strategy'. It *appears* that a whole new conception of class strategy is organised around consumption: the possession of cultural and material goods and experiences by the As. But he argues that this appearance serves the political effect of *consigning the Non-As to consumption*. In other words, the formal barrier between As and Non-As is indeed traceable in statistical terms through patterns and quanta of consumption (though not always), but the distinction that matters is that between those who consume as a result of (usufruct of) their privilege and those who are 'consecrated to consumption'.

The political pre-eminence and superiority of the As are not to be measured by its higher-level material benefits, but by the very fact that its pre-eminence is precisely *not* predominantly established through consumerist signs of prestige and abundance. Its superiority lies elsewhere, 'in the real sphere of decision, direction, political and economic power, manipulation of signs and men [*sic*]' (PES: 62). Baudrillard refers to this process of committing the Non-As to consumption as the route to social status, power, and prestige as a kind of 'amorals for the slaves': consumption cannot be the route to responsibility and power. The source of wealth has shifted from control of the means of production to a mastery of the process of signification. Production of sign value simply cannot be understood in terms of the 'capitalist mode of production' (nor, presumably, can the 'means of production' be 'seized'). The shift from the significance of the ownership of the means of production to that of the apparent control of the code is a shift Baudrillard claims is equal in importance to the Industrial Revolution (MOP: 122). Thus, to use Baudrillard's words, only a critique of the political economy of the sign can analyse the current mode of domination (PES: 120), and that includes the transnational economic transactions that lead to the exploitation of women's labour in the Third World.

Baudrillard writes that 'economic exploitation based on the monopoly of capital, and "cultural" domination based on the monopoly of the code, engender one another ceaselessly' (PES: 125). This can be understood in terms of the interpenetration of the structure of the sign and the object, or commodity form, analysed in Chapter 1. It is only because of this interpenetration that the commodity, or consumer object, can take on the effect of signification (PES: 146). In fact, according to Baudrillard, 'consumption . . .

defines precisely the stage where the commodity is immediately produced as a sign, as sign value, and where signs (culture) are produced as commodities' (PES: 147). As Mark Poster writes in his introduction to Baudrillard's *Mirror of Production*, 'for Baudrillard . . . it is the investment of things with value; it is the placing of a sign on a thing and the logic of this process of signification that is the true essence of capital' (MOP: 5).

Given this concern of Baudrillard's to rethink the theoretical concepts needed to critique the structures of social differentiation, and the logics that sustain their reproduction, it comes as a surprise to read, for example, MacCannell and MacCannell's (1993) claim that 'central to his [Baudrillard's] theory is his claim that *social class* analysis is not necessary to understand post-modernity' (p. 124). It should be clear from the above that this is a reduction-ist reading that simplifies and distorts Baudrillard's analysis; it is not a matter of 'not necessary'. 'Where', they ask, 'is the field of battle, if not between classes?' A good question. But their response again falls short, bordering on the trite: '[i]t is, according to Baudrillard, the common struggle of all humanity, no matter what class, against the tyranny of signifiers; for liberation from the prison house of signs' (p. 125).

One of the MacCannells' major concerns is an entirely legitimate one couched in a way that implies some degree of acceptance of Baudrillard's analysis of structural transformations since the era of early capitalism: they seek stronger efforts to locate 'new sites of exploitation that are generative of postmodern class structures' (MacCannell and MacCannell 1993: 125). Their claim is that Baudrillard has failed in this regard, and until this (and other) work 'is initiated as a self-conscious collective effort, Baudrillard's terse pronouncements will hang in the air like bullets fired in a guerrilla celebration of the end of gravity, spent and frozen at the height of their vertical trajectory' (p. 125). (Baudrillard's colourful language seems to give Anglo-American writers a licence to indulge in their own colourful rhetorics, which they appear to enjoy, whilst condemning him for it.)

First, in Baudrillard's terms, the issues at stake are precisely not to be analysed in terms of 'class structures' in the Marxist sense of 'class'. The MacCannells do not mention Baudrillard's analysis of the differentiation of As and Non-As, even though they cite *For a Critique of the Political Economy of the Sign*. Secondly, Baudrillard does indeed identify 'new sites of exploitation': the shift from exploitation of labour power to the exploitation of consump-tion power. The individual as consumer is a new kind of 'slave' to be exploited to the limit. Hence the point he insists on, which many critics tend to over-look: consumption must be defined '*not only structurally as a system of exchange and of signs, but strategically as a mechanism of power*' (PES: 85). Baudrillard uses the word 'slave' advisedly. The mobilisation of 'needs', 'pleasures', 'cravings' to the end of 'competitive exploitation' has to be understood in the context of his entire critique, evident from his earliest works (SO and CS): the con-struction of the private individual as productive force. In an interview with Philippe Petit (1997), Baudrillard refers to the 'consumption strike' as the

'last resistance to enforced free circulation' (p. 61). In possibly more sociological terms, the exploitation of the consumer can be analysed empirically.

For instance, consumers are paying many times over for pharmaceuticals
through inflated prices that the pharmaceutical lobby attempts to justify,
erroneously, in terms of research and development costs, according to
Washington economist and American consumer rights advocate James
Love. US government trade protection policies enable pharmaceutical com-
panies to inflate their prices on the overseas market. According to Love, the
cancer drug Taxol was developed with US taxpayer funding but is now
being sold by a drug company for twelve times more than it costs to produce.
Love claims that the US government has made it difficult for dozens of
countries to accept a generic form of Taxol, which would make this life-
saving drug more affordable for cancer patients.[18]

More generally, the New Zealand case is illustrative of global trends. Over
the last fifteen years the 'cost of living' with respect to communications,
energy, housing, transport, health, recreation, and education expenditure
by New Zealand households has increased about three-fold. However, the
majority of 'customers' are not of a view that their 'quality of life' has
increased in similar proportion, and a number of social indicators point at
significant declines in the provision of services included in 'standards of
living' like health and education (Arnoux 1998c).

Baudrillard's work provides the backdrop for critical theorising of contemporary processes of domination and exploitation, which have their foundations in analyses of economic structures and systematic processes of social
differentiation. His approach, however, is not premised on enduring sociological concepts of dialectics, social class, and 'power relations' that have
their origins in a prior era of political economy. He is concerned to engage
critically with the assumptions that might make such concepts appear indis-
pensable. When asked in an interview in 1988 if 'economic power relations
are determining, all the same', Baudrillard replied 'I no longer believe that
there are objective power relations nor objective strategies of this kind. In a
way, they themselves have lost their own reality principle' (Baudrillard in
Gane 1993: 150). If politics once functioned in terms of distinctive oppositions, it is no longer the case. 'It is no longer the dialectic of the two terms
that organizes things, but the fact that the forms each go their separate
ways, meaninglessly, senselessly' (Baudrillard in Gane 1993: 113).

To return to the quotation that opened this chapter, Baudrillard recognises
that where the strategy of a 'system' is one of oppression and repression, then
it makes sense for resistance to be found in the liberating claim of subjecthood. But he writes that:

> this reflects rather the system's previous phase, and even if we are still
> confronted with it, it is no longer the strategic terrain: the system's
> current argument is the maximization of the word and the maximal pro-
> duction of simulated meaning. Thus the strategic resistance is that of a

refusal of meaning and a refusal of the word – or of the hyperconformist simulation of the very mechanisms of the system, which is a form of refusal and of non-reception.

(SSM: 108)

In this chapter I have considered Baudrillard's arguments regarding 'difference' and 'politics' as simulacra. Baudrillard's analysis opens hitherto unexplored directions for addressing the kinds of conundrum confronting feminist concerns with 'difference', in particular those 'other' axes of difference from that of gender. It is clear from an engagement with Baudrillard's work that the feminist concern with 'irreducible difference' lacks substance without a critical analysis of simulation. The sociological critiques of Baudrillard's work on simulation and his construct of the 'silent majorities', or 'the masses', that have been discussed in this chapter are clearly limited in their attachment to concepts useful for analysing a previous phase of political economy. At times these sociological responses represent a non-critique, missing what he is pointing at and in doing so missing an opportunity to be politically effective. Even more than thirty years after Baudrillard first started publishing his analysis, this aspect of his 'challenge' has still not been addressed by the majority of English-language commentators on his work, or by those insisting on the importance of returning to a focus on materialism (work, labour, relations of production, political economy, 'race, gender, class').

In the course of the discussion in this chapter, references to implosion evoke a metaphor of engulfment displacing the oppositional tension of polarised terms. The implications of this shift will be explored in the next chapter through Baudrillard's focus on the phenomenon of 'trans', specifically the implications of transgenderism for feminism and the deconstruction of gender/sex difference.

4 Hyperreal Genders

Perhaps genders/sexes could function more like language, motivated but arbitrary signs carrying desire as words do meaning but remaining only signs for our manipulation, not essential realities in themselves.

(Nataf 1996: 56)

The importance of analysing discourses of 'difference' in their historical and cultural contexts extends of course to analysis of sex/gender difference. In the hyperreal west, 'difference' is implicated in the very nexus of simulation, and hence, as with questions of 'cultural difference', consideration of the historically specific structural logic of simulation is vital to a critique of the construction of sex/gender difference in our contemporary era.

This chapter will focus on a contentious strand of theorising and activism that claims transgenderism is, at least potentially, a transgressive force that destabilises and challenges the gender binary, male/female, as the paradigm of 'sex difference'. To the extent that transgender discourses rely on the transgressive assumptions of gender as 'performativity', this focus serves to highlight a concern raised in Chapter 2, where I questioned whether Judith Butler's concept of gender as 'performance', or 'performativity', does in fact hold the subversive import she contends, or whether it is rather more complicit with the structural imperatives of simulation. This chapter extends that discussion. Judith Butler (1990) was writing her important work on conceptualising gender as 'performance', or 'performativity', at the same moment Baudrillard was writing the *Transparency of Evil* (TE), in which he critically situates the hegemonic 'performance principle' as paradigmatic of hyperreality. Both works were published in the same year (1990). In the *Transparency of Evil* Baudrillard also develops his analysis of the contemporary phenomenon of 'trans', within which he includes a discussion of 'transsexuality'. I will first develop some background to feminist and transgender theorising on the critical portent of transsexuality, or transgenderism, for feminist theory and politics. Then I will discuss how Baudrillard's work, with particular focus on Part One of the *Transparency of Evil*, and *The Ecstasy of Communication* (EC), forces a reconsideration of the assumptions underpinning this argument.

Posttranssexual

Transgender writer Susan Stryker (1998), in her introduction to 'The transgender issue' of the journal *GLQ*, draws attention to the rapid evolution of discourses on transsexuality and transgenderism during the 1990s in the context of debates around 'queer' and the implications of these various terminologies for feminism and for lesbian and gay politics. My concern here is to acknowledge how this complex and turbulent context makes it foolhardy to attempt any singular and coherent rendition of the current thinking on transgenderism, and, rather than engaging in these debates as such, to draw attention to the key issues framing them.

In 1991 Sandy Stone's 'posttranssexual manifesto' presented a powerful counter-argument to Janice Raymond's *The Transsexual Empire* (1979), a 'radical feminist' demolition of the male-to-female transsexual's assumption of femininity or the identification of 'woman'. Although only just over a decade later, Stone's essay is written in a milieu where critiques of 'identity', philosophically and politically, have greater familiarity for, and impact on, feminist theorising. Thus she is able to suggest that the discursive positioning of the transsexual, far from being conservative, reactionary, and anti-feminist, has the potential to disrupt the accepted discourses of the gender binary: an argument that would have been less meaningful or convincing even twelve years earlier.

Against medicalised constitutions of transsexuality as a 'third gender', Stone's intention is to foreground the practices of 'inscription and reading'. Such foregrounding, she claims, enables her to constitute transsexuals as a *genre*: 'a set of embodied texts whose potential for *productive* disruption of structured sexualities and spectra of desire has yet to be explored' (1991: 296). The transgressive and disruptive 'potential' of transsexuality, according to Stone, lies in its being outside the gender binary, as neither one sex nor the other. Stone's manifesto, therefore, is to exhort transsexuals not to *pass*, that is, not to transit from one sex to (passing as) the other sex (hence her call for the *post*transsexual). 'Passing' exonerates the 'naturalness' of sex difference: if it cannot be 'really' achieved, it has to be feigned. Stone claims that passing 'means the denial of mixture' (1991: 296). She writes that living a life 'grounded in the intertexual possibilities of the transsexual body' (p. 297) is foreclosed by passing. Indeed, the act of passing, Stone argues, is 'the essence of transsexualism', and so she acknowledges what she calls the inconceivable nature of her request that transsexuals forgo passing. This incitement to 'post'transsexuality Stone implies is the 'groundwork for the next transformation'.

Nowhere in feminist theorising (except possibly media studies) is Baudrillard's observation that we have all become 'readers' more evident than in discussions on transgenderism or queer theory. Judith Halberstam, in her discussion of the making of female masculinity (1994), writes '[c]reating gender as fiction demands that we learn how to read it'.

In order to find our way into a posttranssexual era, we must educate ourselves as readers of gender fiction, we must learn how to take pleasure in
gender and how to become an audience for the multiple performances of
gender we witness every day.

(Halberstam 1994: 226)

Halberstam (1994) explores what she describes as the 'costs of misreading or
refusing to read another person's gender' (p. 216). With reference to Stone
('are we entering a posttranssexual era?'), she also echoes Butler with her
emphasis on the fictionality of gender as a critical deconstruction of the
'naturalness' of gender, or sex difference. Gender is no longer to be rendered
fixed and factual, to be 'known' in its dichotomous biological anchorage of sex
difference, but rather to be articulated as fluid and fictional, to be 'read' in the
circulation of signs performatively reiterated in a kind of democracy of interpretation. The contribution of numerous transgender activists to the 'ruptur-
ing' of the binary of 'man' or 'woman' is exemplified by Stryker's depiction of
this rupture as spawning a 'wild profusion of gendered subject positions . . .
like an archipelago of identities rising from the sea' (1998: 148). 'Gender flex-
ibility' has the edge. 'Movement is all' (Halberstam 1994: 226). Thus the
development of transgenderism in accordance with the recent writings of a
number of transgender authors (including Kate Bornstein, Sandy Stone,
Susan Stryker) is about gender 'fluidity and ambiguity' against the 'illusion'
of being rigidly one gender or the other. The artificiality of the signs of gender
renders femininity and masculinity constructible and malleable. For
Bornstein this is expressed in terms of her view of her 'identity':

My identity as a transsexual lesbian whose female lover is becoming a
man is manifest in my fashion statement; both my identity and fashion
are based on collage. You know – a little bit from here, a little bit
from there? Sort of a cut-and-paste thing.

(Bornstein 1994: 3)

For Robin Maltz (1998) 'stone femme' refers to a 'femme' who not only
desires 'stone butch masculinity', but also 'knows how to resignify a stone
butch body from a female one to a masculine one' (p. 277). This denaturalising process of resignification is argued to be radical and transgressive, as
masculinity is not only *performed* by male impersonators and stone butches,
but simultaneously critiqued as the privileged gender of males ('born male
bodied' people). Shifting signs of gender have to be read through layers of
signification where meaning depends on the context (Maltz 1998: 279).

Kate Bornstein embodies the figuration of transgenderism through staging
the 'performance' of trans. She is a North American performance artist, actor,
and writer of books and plays. Although her writing does not follow academic
conventions, nor is she located within academia, Bornstein's work contributes to theorising on transgender experience and politics. She advocates

colourfully, powerfully, and polemically the importance of gender fluidity, against the oppressive nature of a dichotomous gender regime that polices the certainty that every human being must be one or the other sex. 'Please, assume no gender' she implores in *Gender Outlaw* (1994). The 'glorious transgender revolution' will lead us all from the darkness (and implicitly boredom) of rigid and blindly assumed gender fixation on either male or female to a 'gender enlightenment' where we can realise that we are all already transgendered. Bornstein writes with humour ('real gender freedom begins with fun') and a self-reflexivity that gives her writing less a sense of a manifesto and more a sense of a challenge. Indeed, the intent of her work, and by implication her performances, appears to be to challenge the reader/viewer to reflect on previously unshakeable assumptions about the inevitability of sex difference and 'being' one or the other. In a similar vein, Jacqui Gabb writes of the photographed bodies in the works of Del LaGrace, which, Gabb claims, 'transgress the boundaries of gender in a spectacular display that disrupts the binary logic of "the sexes"' (Gabb 1998: 297); a visual performativity of 'born female bodied' people performing masculinity, depicted in supposedly erotic interactions with one another. 'Sex' is 'liberated' from its assumed biologically unalterable status, hence the performativity of 'gender' is no longer subordinated to the dictates of 'sex'. Freedom at last: 'once the gendered notions of feminine and masculine are freed from their sexualised origins, they can refer to any-*body*' (Gabb 1998: 303).

Gender Outlaw is precisely about being outside the 'laws' of gender, 'laws' that naturalise, enshrine, and perpetuate male privilege. Like Stone, Bornstein writes of what she experiences as the oppressiveness of the 'either/or' gender system, and transsexualism (where it involves passing in the sense of a switch from being perceived as one gender to being perceived entirely as the other) does not present the radical critique of gender that is needed. Stryker (1998), on the other hand, argues for the use of 'transgender' as:

> an umbrella term for a wide variety of bodily effects that disrupt or denaturalise heteronormatively constructed linkages between an individual's anatomy at birth, a nonconsensually assigned gender category, psychical identifications with sexed body images and/or gendered subject positions, and the performance of specifically gendered social, sexual, or kinship functions.
>
> (Stryker 1998: 149)

This construction of 'transgender' is therefore inclusive of 'transsexuality', which, Stryker claims, can be 'queer' in the above sense of transgressive. Stryker (1998) is critical of interpretations of Stone's 'posttranssexualism' whereby the 'post' refers to a beyond of sex reassignment surgery. Rather, she emphasises Stone's concern to foreground the importance of individual transsexuals' speaking their personal history of 'bodily inscription' in a way that is 'politically productive' (p. 152). She is wary of any construction of 'transgender' that could become 'yet another version of the morality tale that condemns cutting the flesh' (p. 153).

Julia Epstein and Kristina Straub write, in their introduction to their 1991 edited collection on the cultural politics of gender ambiguity, that the tensions generated by transgender claims mean that the reception of these ideas by those broadly on the political 'left' of critical theory have been mixed and troubled. Ambiguities of gender and sexuality, they claim, are 'alternatively and sometimes simultaneously celebrated as liberatory strategies breaking with dominant ideologies and warned against as a recuperative, conservative cultural mechanism' (1991: 5). An example, possibly, of the latter is Jeffreys' (1997) 'lesbian feminist' critique, where she argues that transsexuality is a violation of human rights. Her concern is to analyse what she views as the implications of transgender activism for lesbian and gay politics, critiquing the 'postmodern legitimation' of transsexuality through queer theory in particular. Echoing Raymond nearly two decades earlier, she insists transsexualism is 'deeply reactionary' and in fact, rather than being socially transformative, prevents the disruption and elimination of gender roles, so important to feminism. Even with the emergence of transgender discourses, Jeffreys still considers male-to-female transsexuality to be based on a fantasy about women which is fundamentally conservative. It is Jeffreys' contention that transgenderists do not really challenge gender stereotypes, and, contrary to the claims made by transgendered, pro-feminist activists, she is of the view that '[t]ransgenderists would find it difficult to abandon gender because their life's project would then lose all meaning' (1997: 58). Her argument in relation to human rights relates to what she calls the 'mutilation of healthy bodies' perpetuated with the sanction of medical institutions: 'transsexual surgery and hormone treatment should be seen as state sanctioned violence' (p. 59). In addition, Jeffreys' contribution specifically addresses her concern about male-to-female transsexual lesbians, and the question of whether they can 'really' be lesbians. I do not want to pursue questions that inevitably emerge regarding the problematics of contributions such as Jeffreys', but rather to illustrate the 'heat' generated by the claims of transgender theorising for some feminists.

My concern is to develop a critical engagement that is not couched within a framework where transgenderism is either liberatory or conservative in relation to gender norms, but rather to examine the political, semiological, and axiological ground on which such notions of transgression may or may not be meaningful. The critique I want to develop derives from Baudrillard's work on simulation, sign value, and beyond to the contemporary phenomenon of a 'fractal' logic that exceeds value altogether, discussed below. The dynamics described by the transgenderists as transgressive and liberatory reflect uncritically precisely what is happening with the simulation of gender, and accord almost perfectly with the contemporary hegemonic structuration that is rewriting (since we must 'read') all discourses on 'liberation'.

Performativity

Stone's posttranssexual manifesto (1991) was published one year after Butler's *Gender Trouble* (1990). Stone acknowledges the impact of Donna Haraway's writing on her work but does not cite Butler; possibly the publishing schedules overlapped. Butler's work is recognised by many as developing an in-depth and scholarly backdrop to important ideas influencing trans-gender and queer theorising.[1] In Chapter 2, Butler's emphasis on performativity was introduced to engage with her use of the work of Foucault. Baudrillard's critique of Foucault's construct of 'power' was discussed, and provided a starting point to query aspects of Butler's subversion of 'identity'. In the present chapter, the notion of 'performativity' is both central to the kinds of theorising discussed above, and also a key feature of Baudrillard's critique of the contemporary ascendancy of 'trans', which itself trans-verses numerous discourses from sexuality to economics, from aesthetics to globalisation, from fashion to politics. I will revisit Butler's examination of issues surrounding performativity in so far as these provide points of intersection with Baudrillard's critique of 'trans', to propose another angle from which to view these discursive practices. In the light of Baudrillard's critique of the political economy of contemporary processes of signification, Butler's viewpoint is arguably complicit with these processes.

As Butler restates in an interview with *Radical Philosophy* in 1994, she views 'performativity' as 'that aspect of discourse that has the capacity to produce what it names' (p. 33). The social and psychic production of gendered selves is evident in reiterative discursive acts, and not predicated on the prior existence of any 'natural sex'. Butler's idea, or argument, regarding the 'transferability' of the phallus was introduced in Chapter 2. Conceptualising gender in performative terms means that sexual difference, 'anatomy itself', is opened up as a 'site of proliferative resignifications' (Butler 1993: 89). The extent to which the anatomical exceeds its signification is only an appearance, according to Butler, an appearance that provides the illusion that a referent precedes the articulation of sex. But the anatomical, inevitably caught up in the very signifying chain by which sexual difference is discursively negotiated, cannot be understood as somehow 'given', somehow 'outside', or extra-discursive.

> The body posited as prior to the sign, is always posited or signified as prior. This signification produces as an effect of its own procedure the very body that it nevertheless and simultaneously claims to discover as that which precedes its own action. If the body signified as prior to signification is an effect of signification, then the mimetic or representational status of language, which claims that signs follow bodies as their necessary mirrors, is not mimetic at all. On the contrary, it is productive, constitutive, one might even argue performative, inasmuch as this

signifying act delimits and contours the body that it then claims to find prior to any and all signification.

(Butler 1993: 30)

The process of defining 'performative' appears to be circular: it is defined by reference to its being 'productive' and yet here 'productive' is elaborated in terms of 'performative'. It is not clear in the above quotation what 'performative' adds to 'productive'. Understanding sex/gender as performative/productive, Butler's concern is to develop insights into how (gender) identities and subjectivities might be performatively avowed, while at the same time repudiating an exclusionary framework whereby identity is purchased at the expense of a profound refusal and rejection of an abjected and subordinated other. Butler is careful to avoid any *a priori* inclusionary theoretical premise that might attempt to 'appropriate difference' into a prefigured assumption of unity (1993: 116). She refers in this context to the oppressive and totalising humanism of an Hegelian synthesis wherein difference merely exemplifies divergent features of the singular, with the imperialism this implies. Nor is it a matter of simply honouring unproblematically a plurality of identifications that might constitute the subject, as these identifications are not constituted independently, are not 'analytically discrete'; they are not only 'imbricated in one another', they also provide mutual conditions of possibility. Butler concludes that an 'economy of difference' is needed whereby 'the matrices, the crossroads at which various identifications are formed and displaced' effectively contest, or 'force a reworking' of, the possibility of a logic of exclusion (1993: 118).

What exactly this 'economy of difference', that is predicated neither on a logic of exclusion nor on one of equivalence, might comprise remains unclear. According to Butler, within such a framework, shifting identifications will not mean the repudiation of one for another, but rather the embracing of a more expansive set of connections. It appears that Butler's formulation would have subjects constituted through movement across identificatory positions as they shift and slide around a web of precariously bounded nodes of 'identity' with high connectivity.

Butler is clear that her text seeks to recast performativity 'as a specific modality of power as discourse' (1993: 187), where the specific performative instance derives its power from the historical norms preceding it and constituting its context of inevitably anticipated reiteration. The politics of resignification involve, therefore, a movement against existing norms, opening sites previously naturalised and uncontested to new possibilities of signification. In *Bodies That Matter* Butler discusses representations of bodies that 'contest the norms that govern the intelligibility of sex' (p. 139). Notions of masculinity and femininity can be 'queered' to produce gendered subjects whose divergence from the norm constitutes a radical critique, and parodic subversion of the assumed ontological referent, male or female. This analysis rests to some extent on Butler's discussion of Žižek's engagement with Lacan and

Derrida. I do not want to pursue this engagement here, except to reflect on Butler's point regarding the 'performative' as that discursive event where the sign *is* the referent. The relationship between language and the real, according to this account, is fixed and universal (Butler 1993: 207); the 'real' is the impossible 'outside' of discourse, instituting a permanent, yet unsatisfiable, desire for a referent that eludes representation (the 'sublime object of ideology' in Žižek's words). Discourse becomes a vector of power when, in its performative instance, it simply *is* a referent; when the divide between signifier and referent is 'overcome' and discourse can precipitate that which it names. Here, the performative is a specific mode of discourse within an ontological understanding of reality as that which of necessity exceeds signification. This ahistorically construed ontological paradigm is informed by psychoanalytic theory. In a more recent publication, *Excitable Speech* (1997), Butler considers that in fact no term can 'fully or exhaustively perform its referent', and that rather the signifying term always 'gestures toward a referent it cannot capture' (p. 108). Furthermore, it is precisely this lack of capture that enables resignifications, rearticulations. It is questionable whether this tension between discourse as constructive, or productive of effects, and discourse as that which attempts but never captures that which it signifies, is really resolved in the course of Butler's discussion in *Bodies That Matter*. It is clear that Butler is uneasy with the implications of an inevitable split of language and reality. Baudrillard's approach to such questions is to insist on analysing critically the historically (and culturally) specific context in which they are meaningful.

In Baudrillard's analysis, this relation of language and world is far from fixed and universal. Rather than postulating a 'performative' ahistorically embedded within a universally applicable relation of discourse and world, Baudrillard's analysis singles out an historically defined performative as integral to the structure of simulation in contemporary hyperreality. A collapse, or implosion, of the poles of the sign (signifier/signified) precisely registers the loss of the referent (itself a phantasmatic formulation of a previous era, or 'episteme' in Foucault's terms), and institutes the precession of the *model* of reality, and the logic of simulation. 'Performativity', far from being a universally analysable mode of discourse, is itself the dominant logic of discourse in an era where the relation of language and world is structured in accordance with sign value. 'Performativity' is paradigmatic of the idealism of simulation. 'Identity' is no longer premised on the abjected as the necessarily excluded term. Furthermore, Baudrillard writes of the 'performance principle' as precisely the modality of production in the hyperreal order. In *The Transparency of Evil* he refers to the construct of 'communication' in these terms. Communication is now about creating speech ('making people speak') rather than a matter of speaking; information is about 'making people know' rather than about knowledge; participation is about mechanistically inducing response, engagement (TE: 46): about operations rather than actions.

At the conclusion of an interview with *Radical Philosophy* (1994), Butler states:

> I am in favour of opening up certain kinds of practices, be they sexual or gender practices, as sites of contestation or rearticulation. In one sense, that is enough for me. I see that as part of a democratic culture.
>
> (Butler 1994: 39)

That which Butler advocates as democratic, Baudrillard observes happening within the operational, functional logic of the hyperreal. 'Everywhere the active verb has given way to the factive, and actions themselves have less importance than the fact that they are produced, induced, solicited, mediaized or technicized' (TE: 46). Not only is the era of the factitious about 'performing what it names' but the very process of performing takes precedence over the resulting naming; the 'cult of performance'. In this vein, the performative rules when the process, as Baudrillard observes, of 'getting' people to do things, 'getting' people to want things, 'getting' something to be worth something, 'getting' people to know, to participate, 'getting' people to enjoy, takes primacy. Kristeva (1998) is also critical of what she calls the contemporary 'performance-culture' of consumer society, analysing its role in what she argues to be a marginalising of political revolt.

According to Butler, the performative constructs reality through the apparent 'politics' of its movement across chains of meaning in a veritable sea of floating signifiers (that are also referents, that is that do not refer to anything outside themselves), and, through processes of resignification, all vectors of power can be inclusively identified. It is not that the material is ontologically distinct from language, but that the sign *is* the real. In Baudrillard's analysis, this exemplifies the positivity of a semiological and axiological structure predicated not on the bar separating the signifier and signified (signifier/signified), but on the bar that excludes the symbolic (sign/symbolic).[2] This distinction is one Butler never entertains; the symbolic in Baudrillard's sense does not figure in her work, and thus her analysis of the logic of exclusion is only understood in terms of semiotics and never in terms of seduction and the accursed share (see Chapter 5).

Where Butler, through her discussion of Žižek, employs the notion of the real as 'unsymbolisable' (see, for example, 1993: 207) we are left with the question, what *is* symbolisable? If the real is unsymbolisable, then presumably to talk of language as symbolising anything does not make much sense; something, it would appear, Butler would agree with (see, for example, 1993: 68, 207). Indeed, she questions whether Žižek's argument that 'the real itself offers no support for a direct symbolisation of it' can possibly have the rhetorical status it claims. Of necessity it undermines itself at the metatheoretical level and seems to invoke the real in a sense as resistance to symbolisation (1993: 207). Maybe it is not so much that the real is unsymbolisable, but that to understand language as representational (or symbolising in this sense) is inevitably ideological in the sense Baudrillard employs this term. This is a subtle difference, but a significant one because the inevitability of psychoanalytic assumptions of the Law of the Father, and of castration, with its logics of exclusion, follows close behind Butler's formulation; a formulation that never strays far from this inevitability. Baudrillard, on the contrary, considers simulation to be in less accord with a paternal, phallic law of identity/difference, where the terms are constituted in a dialectical tension of positivity and negativity, and more in accordance with a kind of 'maternal law', characterised by an implosive collapse, engulfment, and the displacement of any oppositional term; a fusional logic even more difficult to oppose. Negativity is excluded at a systemically higher level of abstraction (sign/symbolic), and to attempt to build a radical and progressive politics on the opportunities for positive, present, inclusive identities currently on offer is, Baudrillard claims, a mistake. He comes back to this observation over and over again, as will become apparent later in this chapter.

Butler (1993) discusses the 'lesbian resignification of the phallus' which she deems feminist and potentially subversive for the way it disrupts the assumed naturalised and inevitable link to a male body. Through rendering the idealised 'phallus' *trans*ferable, this link, and its privilege, are aggressively 'reterritorialised'. Butler does question whether denaturalising gender or heterosexuality will in fact subvert their normative power, and she is careful to distinguish 'performance' from 'performativity', questioning whether there may be a difference between the embodying or performing of gender norms and the performative use of discourse. Connections between Butler's theoretical questions and transgender arguments are clear when we consider Stryker's claim (1998) that:

> '[t]ransgender phenomena' emerge from and bear witness to the epistemological rift between gender signifiers and their signifieds. In doing so, they disrupt and denaturalise Western modernity's 'normal' reality, specifically the fiction of a unitary psychosocial gender that is rooted biologically in corporeal substance.
>
> (Stryker 1998: 147)

How this 'epistemological rift' is understood in Stryker's work is not entirely clear. It appears, in tune with Butler, to be assumed to result from a political discursive act of wresting the signifier from its inevitable signified, whereas in Baudrillard's analysis, this 'rift' is a structural inevitability at the heart of the contemporary flotation of signification and value.

Suzanna Danuta Walters (1996) is critical of the 'motif of performance' in the work of Butler and others whose writings might fall in the broad field of 'queer theory'. Her concern resonates with Baudrillard's work; she comments that 'performance' is 'the perfect trope for our funky times, producing a sense of enticing activity amid the depressing ruins of late capitalism' (1996: 855).

That the pastiche quality of the 'cut and paste sort of thing' that Bornstein refers to speaks directly to our postmodern times is, in Walters' terms, no coincidence. Most importantly, she laments that the importance of the specific historical, social, and political conditions that make some configurations of power possible and others delimited are too often glossed over. Walters calls for 'substantive engagement with complex sociopolitical realities' if we are really to understand the material conditions within which the 'performative' is so compelling, and whereby questions of gender and power can be addressed more satisfactorily. Walters too is concerned about the ahistorical implications of an analysis that fails to situate its object socially, culturally, economically. If we are now to be 'readers of texts', shouldn't we be concerned to reflect on why this turn to 'performativity' appears so inevitable? As Laqueur (1990) analysed the shift from a one-sex to a two-sex model (sex as difference) with reference to the historical conditions of possibility for these models, should we not analyse the contemporary multi and 'trans' sex model also in these terms? Baudrillard's thesis is that the 'indistinguishability and substitution of the sexes' is a necessary consequence of the modern theory of sex as difference (IE: 108).

Ki Namaste (1994) is concerned to critique what she perceives as Butler's 'negation of transgender identity' in *Bodies That Matter*. There is possibly a point in common with Walters in Namaste's specific focus on questions regarding the kind of research methodology employed by analysts such as Butler. In contrast to 'readers' of 'texts' who appear not to have a research method as such, she places 'social scientists' who, she claims, devote far more attention to the question of processes of research and ensure they make these processes available to the reader for scrutiny. Without wishing to engage with the merits or otherwise of these critics' concerns, it is clear that they point toward a need to situate historically, socially, politically, and economically the kinds of analysis developed within queer and/or transgender theory. Baudrillard's analysis provides some critical insights into the contemporary context within which an enthusiasm for the performative, the fluid, the multiple, the 'trans' might be understood. Through a discussion of his work, the boundaries and illusory character of the supposedly liberatory and transgressive agendas of 'queer' and 'trans' acquire some relief.

The Ecstasy of 'Trans'

> This is the era of the Transsexual, where the conflicts linked to difference
> – and even the biological and anatomical signs of difference – survive
> long after the real otherness of the sexes has disappeared.
>
> (PC: 117)

An early reference in Baudrillard's works to the phenomenon of 'trans' was to the 'transpolitical' in *Shadow of the Silent Majorities*, published in 1978. *Fatal Strategies* (FS), first published in 1983, contains a section on 'figures of the transpolitical'. Thus by the time Baudrillard wrote *The Transparency of Evil* (first published in 1990), these ideas had been maturing for some time, and can be considered to be integral to the coherence of his analysis across the books written during these decades. I will return to *Fatal Strategies* along with another earlier work, *Seduction*, in Chapter 5.

The Transparency of Evil opens with Baudrillard's observation that our current predicament could be described as 'after the orgy'. This depiction evokes a sense of extravagant and committed energy expended with earnest ebullience and intensity, in all directions at once, from which one emerges having 'done it', and wondering what to do next now that it is in fact 'over'. This allegory refers to the explosive moment of modernity when 'liberation' in every sphere was the passionate and energising motivation for political action: '[p]olitical liberation, sexual liberation, liberation of the forces of production, liberation of the forces of destruction, women's liberation, children's liberation, liberation of unconscious drives, liberation of art' (TE: 3). 'After the orgy' does not necessarily mean that the 'goals' of liberation have been achieved in their own liberal or radical, transformative terms. It can rather be understood to refer to the entry into a world structured in accordance with the logic of sign value, where all values, all signifiers, are indeed 'liberated' to produce more of the same, *ad infinitum*, in a boundless, hyperrealised consumerist world. All signifiers are 'liberated' in the sense of no longer being caught up in the oppressive dialectics of 'race, gender, class', but the fact that this means we are now wandering around in the 'depressing ruins of late capitalism' (to use Walters' phrase), rather than blissfully enjoying some other fantasised form of 'freedom', testifies to the poverty of the understandings on which such politics of liberation were premised, and to their illusory character.

If 'liberation' was the political goal, and if everything has been 'liberated' (albeit in a manner not recognised as 'liberation' by advocates and protagonists of the multitude of causes – as Baudrillard himself writes, 'not in the way we expected'), the preferred action now appears to be to simulate a continuing orgy through simulated liberatory agendas. Baudrillard refers to this simulated liberatory movement as one which is in fact 'accelerating in a void' (TE: 3): its goals are behind it, having already been achieved, so it is on a fast track to nowhere in a sort of meaningless orbital circuit, nostalgic for the times when there were 'real' opponents and 'real' power relations. Having overshot the finalities of modernity (remember Foucault and the finalities of 'man'), through what Baudrillard elsewhere has referred to as a 'hypertelic process' (Gane 1993: 163), we have moved into a state he characterises through the repetitive use of the prefix 'trans': transpolitical, transsexual, transeconomic, transaesthetic.

What to do after the orgy? '[W]e can only "hyper-realize" them [utopias] through interminable simulation. We live amid the interminable reproduction of ideals, phantasies, images and dreams which are now behind us, yet which we must continue to reproduce in a sort of inescapable indifference'

(TE: 4). This indifference results from the radical indeterminacy that accompanies the 'liberated' state; '[e]verywhere what has been liberated has been liberated so that it can enter a state of pure circulation, so that it can go into orbit' (TE: 4). The tensions and contradictions which were understood to traverse and constitute relative social positions meant subjects-in-process were always somewhere, relative to something or someone else/others. Positions could be challenged and overwhelmed. 'Politics' meant something. But in a social (that is probably, therefore, no longer a social) where all such positions lose their dialectical relationality and float with a kind of weightlessness 'free' from any bearings, these tensions and contradictions have vaporised, leaving an indifference to the very simulations of conflict and tension endlessly fabricated.

'Trans' literally means moving across, or through, being in a state that is neither here nor there, or is both here and there, in between, but importantly moving. 'Trans' is about confusion of boundaries, contagion across boundaries, promiscuity between states, a loss of specificity in the movement from, to, across, through. The loss of the referent, the flotation of the signifier and of economic value, the liberation of all 'values' in accordance with the structural law of sign value have, Baudrillard argues, precipitated what he calls a fractal stage of value. Following his analysis of the natural, commodity, and structural stages of value, the fractal stage, rather than being governed by a code (whereby value develops by reference to a set of models), has no point of reference at all. '[V]alue radiates in all directions, occupying all interstices, without reference to anything whatsoever, by virtue of pure contiguity' (TE: 5). To convey what is distinctive about the fractal stage of value, Baudrillard refers to 'an epidemic of value' (distinct from a 'law of value' and its Marxian antecedents), processes of growth and proliferation that are characterised as a 'metastasis of value', a 'dispersal of value', 'radiating' in all directions. In fact, he writes, it is not really any longer a matter of 'value' at all, since this kind of fractal chain reaction defies valuation in any cumulative classical or neo-classical economic sense.

The pattern of the fractal, which Baudrillard metaphorically denotes as 'a new particle in the microphysics of simulacra' (TE: 5), is self-replicating: an endless repetition of the self-same. Baudrillard's imagery of a fractal logic refers to the process of self-reproduction (into the void rather than towards some end and new beginning) which inevitably results from the liberation of all value from any point of reference. In other words, if actions, signs, and things in the world are released from any reference point of meaning (ideas, concepts, origins, aims), and the latter disappear but the actions, signs, and things continue, having no point of reference they circulate in a kind of orbital dispersal. With no relationality, fractal repetition becomes the metastatic mode of self-reproduction. In terms of actual human reproduction, Baudrillard wonders if we are not witnessing a reverse of the so-called 'sexual revolution' of the 1960s in the west. What was then a matter of more sex and less reproduction (sexual liberation through the birth-control pill) is increasingly now a matter of less sex and more reproduction: less sex both as 'ecstasy' replaces 'passion' (see below and Chapter 5), and as the imperatives of immune-system protection escalate, and more reproduction with the ascendancy of the logic of division of the One into two and the transmission of a code. Genetics, cloning, replacement body parts exemplify this logic, and the possible trajectory towards 'genetic substitution . . . to achieve the linear and sequential reproduction, cloning or parthenogenesis of little celibate machines' (TE: 7). Baudrillard claims that the body was once a metaphor for the soul, then for sex, but today it is no longer a metaphor for anything at all. Metaphor requires discrete fields and objects, and, with the confusion of boundaries, the possibility of metaphor is disappearing. The non-metaphorical body simply is itself – produced as sign, fully positivised presence – and as such it is:

> the locus of metastasis, of the machine-like connections between all its processes, of an endless programming devoid of any symbolic organisation or overarching purpose: the body is thus given over to the pure promiscuity of its relationship to itself – the same promiscuity that characterizes networks and integrated circuits.
>
> (TE: 7)

All those spheres that took their meaning and actions from the assumed 'naturalness' of the terms of their specificity exhibit a tendency towards 'trans': economics, sex, politics, aesthetics. Baudrillard refers to 'a general commutability' of terms, or the 'law of the confusion of categories', where everything is sexual, everything is political, everything is aesthetic – anything can be an object of desire – in other words, 'each category is generalised to the greatest possible extent, so that it eventually loses all specificity and is reabsorbed by all the other categories' (TE: 9).

Much earlier, Baudrillard commented on the way, in fashion in the hyperreal context, 'sex is lost as difference but generalised as reference' (SE&D: 97). It is this generalisation at all levels of a structural code that Baudrillard argued in his early work is at the heart of the ideological process (PES: 92). As fashion 'neutralises the opposition between the body and the costume' (SE&D: 97), so the increasing tendency for the body to be appropriated as a projection of self (PC: 124) neutralises the assumed character of the body as 'destiny', as given and unchangeable. Cosmetic surgery abounds to figure one's appearance or one's image exactly as one wants. The precession of the desired model of self/body simulates (sexed/transgendered) self. And furthermore, 'it is the body's resemblance to its model which becomes a source of eroticism' (PC: 124). The eroticism of the simulated body/self is inextricably connected to the generalisation of sex as reference rather than lived as difference in the sense of 'otherness'. Sex generalised as reference can be modelled and signified in all sorts of ways; a sort of heteroconsumerism of the signs of sex. And of course, in its 'liberation', 'sexuality' achieves an autonomy as 'an undifferentiated circulation of the signs of sex' (TE: 12).

Baudrillard's rendition of the significance, contemporarily, of the figure of 'transsexuality' does have some striking resonances with the transgender discourses and practices discussed above. According to authors like Stone, Bornstein, and Stryker, transgenderism is precisely not about 'passing' but is about disrupting those boundaries that would have sex fixed as one or the other in a tightly bounded, binary inevitability. Transgender is not about going from one to the other, but rather about situating oneself within all the ambiguities of the in-between or the moving between, the neither this nor that, or the both/and position, but with the emphasis on the fluid, the changing, and the sovereignty of the subject to enact the sexual configuration he/she wants. When he writes of his conviction that we are 'certainly in transition towards a transsexual state of affairs' in *The Transparency of Evil*, Baudrillard is explicit that he is not referring to any kind of liberatory revolution of life through sex (sexuality). Rather he is pointing to the confusion and contagion of categories that is more to do with indifference (in all senses of the word) in terms of the sexual. This indifference is commensurate with the fractal model of self-reproduction.

Transgender authors Halberstam (1994), Bornstein (1994), and Nataf (1996) agree that, in a posttranssexual era, the claims can equally be made that 'we are all transsexuals' and 'there are no transsexuals'. In other words, in accordance with their radical critique, if gender is 'really' fictional, and if the signs of sex can be resignified to 'queer' gender in a deconstructive move, then there is no 'real', 'natural' sex, so in this sense we are all transsexuals and equally there are no transsexuals. Where Baudrillard's analysis differs is in his insistence on a critical epistemology that lays no claim regarding whether gender is 'really' a fiction or not. It is rather a matter of analysing critically the construction of gender both as 'really' natural and as 'really' fictional. Baudrillard would agree 'we are all transsexuals'; he writes as much (TE: 21). But, crucially, his assertion does not claim the status of a radical critique of the gender binary. His statement inclines more towards a theorised observation of what is actually going on in the world: sex is made fictional through the flotation of signs of sex; through simulation '[t]he sexual body has now been assigned a kind of artificial fate' of transsexuality (TE: 20).

Baudrillard's use of the term 'transsexual' is explicitly not intended to invoke the medicalised meaning of 'wrong body' leading to sex reassignment surgery, but (and notably in accordance with transgender theorising) to refer to the attraction of 'playing' with the commutability of the signs of sex, with the lack of differentiation between the sexual poles, with the simulation of 'difference'. If 'sexuality' is underpinned by pleasure, by jouissance (and in psychoanalytic terms sexual desire cannot be divorced from the gendering of subjects), 'transsexuality' is underpinned by artifice (TE: 20): an eroticism engendered through the artifice of playing with the morphological or gestural signs of sex. Stone femme reads stone butch; the erotics of stone butch is precisely in its being read as such. The queer and transgender literatures are satiated with just this kind of eros, but possibly no more than any other discourses on sexuality contemporarily; hetero, homo, straight, queer makes little difference. Sexuality in the west is everywhere except in sex, Baudrillard has observed (SEDN: 5, with reference to Barthes), referring to the virulence of the signs of the 'trans'sexual crossing all spheres. As Baudrillard wrote in *Symbolic Exchange and Death*, 'sexuality impregnates all signification and this is because signs have, for their part, invested the entire sexual sphere' (SE&D: 97).

As today the body appears to be destined to become a prosthesis, Baudrillard views the increasing proliferation of the signs of 'transsexuality' as a 'logical enough' development. To speculate about the (apparently absurd) idea that we might one day want to have designer antlers or horse tails (never mind pigs' hearts) points to the suggestion that the commutability of the signs of sex is more about the confusion of categories than about gender or sex(uality) as this has been known, experienced, articulated in recent western history. Rather than asking whether transgenderism is or is not transgressive and liberatory, this argument strongly suggests that we need to wonder what it means to ask feminist kinds of question about transgenderism when it appears complicit with a structural logic of sign value constructing gender as a simulation model. Is transgenderism (and that we are all transsexuals) symptomatic of the simulation of gender/sex difference and the concomitant eradication of sexual 'otherness'? Transgender authors discourage 'passing' in favour of the 'realness' of the transgendered experience: it is what it is — no reference to sex difference, pure sign. In Baudrillard's terms this is simulation, which is not about feigning. Is transgenderism a deterrence obscuring the indifference of sexual 'difference', which is precisely about the loss of sexual 'otherness'?[3] Baudrillard observes that, unlike repression based on taboo, the 'conjuring away of desire through the overkill of its staging' seems to make everyone suffer equally. Maybe, as Baudrillard suggests, the outcome of every revolution is paradoxical.

> After the orgy, then, a masked ball. After the demise of desire, a pell-mell diffusion of erotic simulacra in every guise, of transsexual kitsch in all its glory. A postmodern pornography, if you will, where sexuality is lost in the theatrical excess of its ambiguity.
>
> (TE: 22)

We have all become transsexuals, according to Baudrillard, in much the same way as we became 'transpoliticals'; we cannot *not* traffic in signs even if we do so wearing the masks of obsolete, or purged, contradictory ideologies. 'Ecstasy is the quality proper to any body that spins until all sense is lost, and then shines forth in its pure and empty form' (FS: 9). The figure of 'transeconomics' further delineates key features of 'trans'.

Mark Poster, in his introduction to *The Mirror of Production*, wrote that at the heart of contemporary political economy we see 'the increasing autono-misation of the signifier not only in the realm of language but in all aspects of social exchange' (MOP: 7). As we have seen throughout this volume, Baudrillard's analysis pertains to the interconnectedness of the structuring of economic value and the mode of representation, of the construction of objects and subjects, where such a distinction has cultural and historical salience. Poster's comment attests to this contemporary interconnection, theorised by Baudrillard in the 1960s. In the 1990s, the momentum of sign value has accelerated to the point where Baudrillard describes the logic of value as 'fractal', which, as mentioned above, refers to the complete absence of any form of reference for economic value. This shift is evident in the comparison between the impact of the 1929 crisis on economic value, and contemporary economic 'crises'. For example, the late 1990s 'Asian crisis' has been claimed to have effected a global recession, and yet the median value of a sample of stocks in information technology (especially net-work technologies) increased four-fold in the six-month period during which the global crisis gained full momentum and was finally acknowledged by finance pundits (Arnoux 1998a). As Baudrillard writes, 'the realm of mobile and speculative capital has achieved so great an autonomy that even its cata-clysms leave no traces' (TE: 27), reminding us too that the total volume of trade when he wrote in 1990 represented a fraction (one forty-fifth) of the total movement of capital. About the same period, Peter Drucker (1989) was stressing the profound uncoupling of capital transactions from trade in tangible goods and services. More recently, authors like Greider (1997) and Sussman (1997) have highlighted the massive increases in global financial transactions that are now completely unrelated to what some call the 'real economy'. Sussman, for example, notes that global currency exchanges now amount to well over US$1 trillion each day (1997: 38).

In addition to the notion of fractal replication, Baudrillard observes the 'orbital' quality of movement and flows pertaining to capital, information, signs. This is the orbital era, increasingly virtual, non-local. In effect, in the current hyperrealised world, most transactions between people are no longer geographically located in a specific place. Even when they are appar-ently geographically located, they are in their very logic taking place in an abstract space that has no geographical basis and which finds its roots in the political economy of the sign. The exponential growth of the Internet is nothing but a consequence of the western world having entered into a hyperreal mode of operation some decades ago. The mediation between local and non-local forms of social life has become a major challenge, which is not effectively addressed by current technology (Arnoux 1998b). In other words, the logic of the era of the 'orbital' is fast outpacing the technological capacity of the social dynamics that created it. Tourists, astronauts, satellites, debt, unemployment, DNA, nuclear waste, human beings (by virtue of the constructed functionality of our bodies – body parts) are all configured in terms that reflect the floating character of perpetual orbital circulation in the absence of a gravitational field. The central or core facet of this transversal *beyond* of transcendence and finalities is its inexorable growth, or 'growths'; its unrelenting positivity that renders everything productive simply of *more*, on and on. It is as if a system configured in terms of a purposeful linear progression from one point to another flips over into one of perpetual circular motion, recycling in simulated form all the old imperatives and ideologies, with no logic of possible transformation, reversion, or end. '[T]he causes themselves . . . are tending to disappear, tending to become indecipherable, and giving way to an intensification of processes operating in a void' (TE: 31). The logic of crisis shifts to that of catastrophe. 'Crisis' implies some critical point of decision and intervention in some kind of causal chain. 'Catastrophe' refers to the fatality of a system that supersedes its own ends.

> Something escapes us, and we are escaping from ourselves, or losing ourselves, as part of an irreversible process; we have now passed some point of no return, the point where the contradictoriness of things ended, and we find ourselves, still alive, in a universe of non-contradiction, of enthusiasm, of ecstasy – of stupor in the face of a process which, for all its irreversibility, is bereft of meaning.
>
> (TE: 33)

Baudrillard writes, in *The Transparency of Evil*, of the 'evidence' of this hyperreal state 'after the orgy', in terms that convey a sense of a social process that is compulsively increasing everything, in every way, across all spheres. He writes of the 'bloatedness' of information systems producing and disseminating more and more information, more and more data. We see a proliferation of reports, documents, plans, programmes, decisions, policies, procedures, all of which assume a linear process of planning. They are circulated with the *appearance* of a logical sequence of action and events, but as these reports proliferate it becomes less and less possible to have a conviction that anything actually happens in the sense of one thing leading to another. On the contrary, it is arguable that these 'projects' are figured on a circular plane with no linear trajectory. All anchor points in notions of causality or intervention having vaporised, they stage their reappearance in pure simulation; reports and plans that circulate regardless of an overall, overarching social or political project. The game seems to be simply to keep moving, keep thinking up new ideas, new ways of doing things, review, reassess, develop new initiatives, be proactive, create new markets: this is what matters more than what is actually done. If you stop moving, you're out of the game. 'Movement is all' (to echo Judith Halberstam, cited earlier). In *Fatal Strategies*, Baudrillard writes that the era of the transpolitical is that of anomaly: 'an aberration of no consequence, contemporaneous with the event of no consequence' (FS: 26). More recently, Baudrillard has commented on an aspect of the transpolitical as one instigating a persistent compulsion to document every detail, a sort of mania to be able to clarify and verify to the final degree, in a field ultimately defined by a triumphant undecidability (in Petit 1997: 75).

Fractal replication, orbital circulation, ineluctable positivity are all logics of non-reversibility, reminding Baudrillard of people who have lost their shadows: these people are either transparent and light passes through them, or they are lit from all angles, overexposed with no defence against the ubiquitous source of light. He refers to this state as one of 'whitewash', in which all activity is doomed to an aseptic whitewashing, or exposure to 'surround' light (positivity with no shadow side). Even violence and history are whitewashed. This eradication of negativity extends to the so-called 'cosmetic' surgical adjustments and changes to remodel facial and bodily morphology; the removal of unwanted forms, correction of negative traits to produce the simulated 'surgical face', modelled on the ideal. Having a mole on one's face, or wrinkles, a masculine jaw – none of these needs to be accepted as 'fate', but rather they are remodelled in accordance with the desired image. The fatality of sex need no longer be a part of our individual destinies: we can change our sex. Witness an Australian male in his early twenties who wanted to have the appearance of Barbie Doll. Now, after extensive surgical operations (including breaking and reshaping his jaw, nose, removing lower ribs, implants in breasts, buttocks, and upper thighs, and of course the removal of external male genitalia), he is indeed she, the Barbie-Doll lookalike who is going into modelling, darling. Baudrillard's notion of 'trans', with all its permutations, invokes a radical expulsion of the fatality of sex, which is replaced by the ubiquitous imperative of rights. We might have a *right* to be whatever sex we want (or both, or neither, or one today and another tomorrow, or one on top and another below, one inside and one outside, or all of these all at once).

Irigaray (1987) asks what in this context appears to be an absurd question: what man would want to give away his power in society and become a woman (p. 123)? Quite a few, it would seem. In a way commensurate with Baudrillard's analysis, 'power' in the sense she invokes seems to be something that is getting more and more difficult even to *give* away. The stakes have moved elsewhere. Irigaray's question is motivated through a valuing of sexual alterity, otherness, and thus her rejection of the 'pseudo-neutrality' that appears to result from any form of 'androgyny' or transgenderism. She rejects the possibility that a member of one sex might be able to 'identify' with the other gender. Baudrillard's analysis, however, insists that this kind of assertion cannot be made in an historical, cultural vacuum. Currently, in the west, his critique leads him to claim that the body is no longer a site of otherness but indeed one of identification (PC: 124), and it is precisely this logic that means we have urgently to repair it, perfect it, and turn it into an ideal object. As mentioned above, it is the body's resemblance to its model that becomes the source of eroticism, and not the encounter with otherness, which indeed would preclude 'identity' with the other, as Irigaray suggests.

The radical removal of 'otherness' is evident, possibly most significantly, within the embodied individual. Baudrillard refers to the fantasy of the double as the most ancient imaginary figure in the history of the body. The double 'haunts the subject as his [*sic*] "other", causing him to be himself while at the same time never seeming like himself' (TE: 113). Divided within herself, the individual subject faces the inevitability of her birth resulting from the union of two sexed beings, of her own individuation as a sexed being (who cannot be it all, who is divided, which is not to deny the existence of intersexed individuals who may or may not reproduce), and of her death. What Baudrillard refers to as 'the hell of the same' (the title of a chapter in *The Transparency of Evil*) is the current trend exemplified by the trope of cloning. He writes that our own culture and era must be the only ones to have attempted to turn the fantasy of the double into a flesh-and-blood reality. From the subject divided by sex, founded on the interplay involving Death and the Other, to the non-divided, singular 'subject' with no shadow, no fantasy of her double, her 'other', replicated through cloning the code, the matrix, to be 'born' into the light fully exposed on all sides: the 'bland eternity of the Same' (TE: 114). Like the sign, the 'subject' is fully positivised, and as such is not really a 'subject' any longer as the identical duplication ends the division constituting the subject – neither the one nor the other, merely the same. This in itself produces its own fascination; a kind of stupefied staring at the Barbie-Doll transsexual person vainly trying to find the point of negation, reversion, seduction.

Baudrillard, we know, argues that otherness, the symbolic, reversion, seduction, cannot ever be fully eradicated. The radical structural exclusion, or barring, of the symbolic might be understood to precipitate its return in self-destructive processes (TE: 122). Consider the endless chain of 'social diseases' and environmental issues increasingly plaguing the sanitised, desymbolised, postmodern 'social': increases in suicide, alcohol and drug abuse, drink-driving, domestic violence, BSE, depression, obesity, anorexia, allergies, chronic fatigue, chronic pain, global warming, economic recessions, market crashes, and so on. This return is what Baudrillard refers to as 'the transparency of evil'. Without the 'other', the 'self' is 'threatened with irradiation into the void' (TE: 122). Through this so-called liberation, which is more about a process of radical detachment and release into an orbital network, the concept of alienation disappears. The fully interactive individual, cloned, metastatic, is not alienated from him or herself, but is self-identical. '*He* [sic] *no longer differs from himself* and is, therefore, indifferent to himself' (IE: 108). Baudrillard argues that this indifference to oneself results from the absence of division within the subject, the suppression of the pole of otherness as the subject is inscribed in the order of identity, which 'is a product, paradoxically, of the demand that he [*sic*] be different from himself and others' (IE: 108).

> We have conquered otherness with difference and, in its turn, difference has succumbed to the logic of the same and of indifference. We have conquered otherness with alienation (the subject becomes its own other), but alienation has, in its turn, succumbed to identity logic (the subject becomes the same as itself). And we have entered the interactive, sidereal era of boredom.
>
> (IE: 109)

Shortly prior to writing *The Transparency of Evil*, Baudrillard published *The Ecstasy of Communication* (EC), in which he develops his insights related to the fate of 'the subject' as the Self-Same. The 'ecstasy of communication' subsumes the 'drama of alienation'. With oblique reference to psychoanalytic theory, the significance of the mirror in the construction of the subject divided by sex is replaced by the screen. Unlike the mirror, with its depth, transcendence, reflection, self, and other (and other side), the screen is a smooth, functional surface of operations, an immanent surface registering digital information flows. The subject and the screen form a continuous circuit, fully interactive, mutually networked. 'Ecstasy', then, refers to a sort of dazzled state of suspension in a fully positivised, virtual 'world' where communication is about the encounter with the sign, as sign; in fact, hardly an encounter, more a dissolution into a mutual state of positivity, connectivity, seamless interaction. This ecstasy is of the order of obscenity in so far as the obscene is the fully exposed, fully lit, no shadows, no secret, no seduction, nothing hidden. It is what it is. What it is has no reliance on any 'other' which it negates: in other words the logic of the ecstatic is that of the sign in the era of sign value, in Baudrillard's analysis. 'Information' has a kind of 'pornographic' quality to it where the 'more visible than visible' fascinates. Communication is not about a message, but about a fascination with the medium, now uncompromisingly dominant; the performative, the process of production rather than what is produced. Baudrillard describes ecstasy as the opposite of passion; along with fascination and obscenity, ecstasy is cool, while passion, desire, and seduction 'are games of a hot universe' (EC: 26).

Walters (1996), in her critical reading of Butler's work, is concerned about what she perceives to be a narcissism redolent in the writings of queer theorists. She refers more generally to 'these tales of modern queer life' as revealing what she describes as an 'obsessive focus on the self', a 'relentless narcissism and individualism' permeating these texts (pp. 856–7). A reading of Baudrillard's analysis suggests that this might be best understood not as narcissism but rather as illustrative of the preoccupations of the 'fractal subject'. Characterised within the general rubric of 'trans', Baudrillard writes that the fractal subject is no longer dreaming of his or her ideal image (narcissistic), but of the formula to reproduce him or herself into infinity. What matters is to resemble oneself – to be what one is – and to find oneself everywhere. As 'others' become less and less the horizon of the subject, difference becomes less and less a question of self and others and more a matter of crafting an endless differentiation of the self-same. This is an internal differentiation, fractally prolific. The subject's horizon becomes reduced to the manipulation of his/her images.

Butler (1997) claims that the subject is an effect of citationality, a subject-effect (p. 50), that the subject emerges from the bar itself (does not wilfully perform the barring but is performatively produced as a result of this primary cut) (p. 138), and that the agency of the subject is an effect of power (p. 139). Once again, Butler posits 'the subject' in an historical and cultural vacuum. This rendition of 'the subject' (certainly just a fragment of what she writes on the topic) is commensurate with her thesis of performativity and, following Foucault, the productive nature of power. Baudrillard's claim, by contrast, is that, in the contemporary configuration of what might be shorthanded as 'trans', 'the subject' is a bit of an anachronism, not much needed; in fact the circuitry works better without such a figure (Gane 1993: 174). Certainly we are all 'produced' as 'subjects' – a fate worse than being produced as 'objects', according to Baudrillard (IE: 80) – but this 'production' should not be taken at face value. Produced in a democracy of subjects with no objects we are, paradoxically, more compromised, and this is what needs to be analysed critically.

Earlier in this chapter I contrasted Butler's insistence on the inevitability of the 'law of the father' to Baudrillard's characterisation of simulation as less governed by a paternal than by a 'maternal law'. Now that the elements of this thesis have been introduced in more depth, it is useful to draw out this proposition and its implications more fully. In *The Ecstasy of Communication*, Baudrillard refers to the way immanence has replaced transcendence as the logic of transparency gains prominence (pp. 54–5), and immanence can be considered 'maternal' in character in so far as these concepts are mapped onto gender. Much earlier, in *Symbolic Exchange and Death*, Baudrillard notes the significance of a shift from transcendence to immanence, which, he argues, corresponds to a more advanced phase of 'vertiginous' manipulation of social relations (p. 60). He analyses the flotation of the categories of consciousness in parallel to the flotation of the categories of value and semiological reference, in turn ensuring the loss of the 'subject' as the psychoanalytic equivalent of the loss of the gold standard in terms of value, and the loss of the linguistic referent. He writes '[t]oday, individuals, divested as subjects and robbed of their fixed relations, are drifting in relation to one another, into an incessant mode of transferential fluctuations' (SE&D: 23).

'Manipulation' is a key word in this connection, characterising the 'politics' (if this is the appropriate word) of this 'current phase'. In this early text, Baudrillard discusses the phenomenon of the 'subject' being no longer divided, in psychoanalytic terms by building on his argument that the eroticisation of the phallic manipulation of the body is characterised as fetishisation, the fetish being the replacement for the desire for the mother, a desire for fulfilment never relinquished by the fetishist. This strictly incestuous situation renders the subjects undivided (not abandoning their phallic identity) and it no longer divides (the subjects no longer relinquish any part of themselves in a relation of symbolic exchange). These subjects are fully defined by identification with the mother's phallus (SE&D: 113) and exemplify the characteristics of the fractal subject, preoccupied, phobically, with 'manipulation'. Women are included in this depiction, annexed as they are to the phallic order (SE&D: 104). Manipulation in this sense of inducing a fusional and unbounded plenitude, Baudrillard claims, is even harder to stand against and refuse than the transcendental law of the father.

Baudrillard describes exchange that might be called 'sexual' between such 'subjects' as an exchange of pleasures rendered solely in the positive, or productive – I give to you and I give to myself, you give to me and to yourself – nothing is *taken*, but rather pleasures are exchanged as part of a 'performative interactivity' (TE: 47). In the contemporary west, an ambiguity of the sexes supersedes the ambivalence of sex. On the contrary, in accordance with symbolic exchange, the ambivalence of sex rests on there being no bar annihilating the ambivalence of the subject and the object, in Baudrillard's words, 'only an immediate, non-phantasmatic actualisation of symbolic reciprocity' (SE&D: 144). This is not fusional. 'Everything is already there, reversible and sacrificed' (see Chapter 5 for a discussion of seduction, reversion, sacrifice).

Transgender authors such as Whittle (guest editor of the 'Transgendering' issue of the *Journal of Gender Studies* 1998) assert or observe that in their assessment, transgenderism is at the cutting edge of radical politics. 'Trans' is 'high on the new agenda of identity politics' (Whittle 1998: 269). Nataf (1996) cites Baudrillard at the opening of a chapter on 'the postmodern lesbian body and transgender trouble', clearly assuming that his words provide support for Nataf's contribution, missing the critique they so obviously represent. In accordance with Baudrillard's view, movements such as transgender and queer cannot be considered to have the radical potential they purport. Said (1989) refers to Lyotard's thesis that the two great narratives of emancipation and enlightenment have lost their legitimising power. According to Lyotard, they have been replaced by smaller, local narratives 'based for their legitimacy on performativity', which Said describes as 'the user's ability to manipulate the codes in order to get things done' (p. 222). Said goes on to take issue with Lyotard's understanding of why this might be the case, but my point here is to draw attention to the link made between the shift to the performative and the 'smaller, local narratives'. Baudrillard refers a number of times, particularly in *Shadow of the Silent Majorities*, to what he views as the misguided understandings of those who consider the political stakes as revolving around exalting 'microdesires' (p. 40), or 'free[ing] libidinal energies, plural energies, fragmentary intensities' (p. 60);

the stakes today, in his view, are certainly not in any 'molecular hodge-podge of desire-breaching minorities' (p. 47).

The critical viewpoint presented in this chapter, based on an analysis of the work of Baudrillard, could not be further apart from the stance taken by the transgendered authors considered here, a stance they themselves also consider to be 'critical'. Those advocating transgenderism as a radical transgression of oppressive social processes of normative gendering do not ask how it is that, contemporarily, their discourses of fluidity and multiplicity intersect with the generalised proliferation of 'trans' traversing all spheres, and how their 'politics' might be complicit with hegemonic trends. Butler's concept of 'performativity' has contributed to motivating critiques of gender that are assumed to be deconstructive and denaturalising of gender. Baudrillard's analysis, however, suggests that the question of the structural logic of gender cannot be addressed by focusing solely on the sphere of semiotics. His critical theoretical engagement with the principle of the 'performative' reveals that this principle is indeed integral to simulation and sign value. 'Gender trouble' is exactly what one would expect at this point in time according to the very logic of western hyperreality, and at best little more than a smokescreen. Gabb (1998) hopes that we are moving towards a 'Utopian space where transformation and "difference" is celebrated, without the penalising loss of identity' (p. 304). To Baudrillard, this is precisely symptomatic of this era of simulation and relentless positivity, predicated on the radical exclusion of the symbolic. The fate of such an era is encapsulated in the theorem of the accursed share: 'anything that purges the accursed share in itself signs its own death warrant' (TE: 106). Chapter 5 will continue this discussion, focusing on seduction, reversion, and the significance of the 'accursed share'.

5 The Inevitable Seduction

The word 'seduction' has appeared a number of times in this volume, usually in conjunction with other terms such as 'symbolic exchange', 'reversion', 'otherness'; always in association with that which, in Baudrillard's terms, is structurally eradicated or barred by the ideological institutions of semiology and axiology. In Chapter 1, I referred, in note 18, to 'seduction' as that which is counter to production. Where production is literally making something appear, bringing into the realm of the visible or perceivable (or even performing, as in a theatre on a stage), seduction is that movement that removes from the realm of the visible, that vaporises 'identity', and is marked by ambivalence. Seduction is about reversion and disappearance, neither of which is recognisable within a productivist logic. In Chapter 2, I discussed the concern of feminists to articulate an 'otherness which is not the otherness of sameness', an 'otherness' which is not always and inevitably caught up in the oppositional logic of the binary form where the feminine is always opposed to, or different from, the masculine. Given this concern, Baudrillard's writing on 'seduction' is pertinent for consideration by feminists, and engagement by feminist theory.

The word 'seduction', in the Anglo-American context, is resolutely associated with a kind of predatory male behaviour bent on conquest (typically sexual), usually followed by abandonment of the seduced, or alternatively a female behaviour designed to turn the male on a path towards evil and his downfall. 'Seduction' is taken overwhelmingly to be an abuse and manipulation for selfish ends that aim purely to satisfy the seducer (subject), with no concern for the seduced (object or victim). When a male 'seduces' a female (especially a 'young and beautiful' one) for his 'pleasure', we have the ingredients for the objectification, domination, oppression, and manipulation of women by men, or of the feminine by a masculine order, ingredients which, of course, feminists revile. Alternatively, 'seduction', in its association with the feminine, is cast as the feminine resolution of the oedipal complex (see Grosz 1989: 137), and hence inevitably situated within the parameters of the Law. Given the intransigence of these meanings of 'seduction', it is exceedingly hard to release the notion of seduction from these associations in the process of considering Baudrillard's use of the term. It is crucial to acknowledge, however, that Baudrillard's use of the word 'seduction' is precisely in opposition to, and a process of critique of, these accepted readings; in fact, as will become apparent, his usage of the word problematises the very terms of these interpretations. In this chapter I will introduce Baudrillard's analysis of 'seduction', and consider its challenge to feminist theory. It is 'seduction's' quality of reversion, or reversibility, that points towards an important insight for feminist critique and understanding.

Seduction

> Seduction lies in the transformation of things into pure appearances.
>
> (SEDN: 117)

Baudrillard's theoretical works critique the productivist logic common to the major discourses of modernity: production itself, power, economic value, meaning, representation, the subject, identity, nature, desire, sex, sexuality, knowledge, the real. In other words, these constructs are, in different ways, relentlessly predicated on the ineluctability of presence, of increase, on the inalienability of existence in the positive, *against* the negative, the destructive, the absent. Foucault, whose work has been so eagerly embraced by feminist theorists, has even formalised the transformation of the seemingly negative into the positive, reflecting the fact that the binary scansion of 1/0 registers absence as another positivity, so that all discourses are now understood as 'productive'. Accordingly, the exercise of power, rather than being understood as a prohibition, is a force that *produces* the social; it has effects.

Contrary to those feminist writers who claim or assume that there is, or can be, no position outside the Law, Baudrillard's notion of seduction is precisely about that which challenges the Law. Seduction does not oppose production, but rather transforms it, annuls its singular and transcendent positivity, and reverses its assumption of unilinear accumulation. 'Seduction' is not about negation, it is about neither presence nor absence, but about a process whereby absence 'eclipses presence', or where absence 'seduces' presence rather than opposing it. Its strategy is both to be there and not be there, hence its ambivalence. Seduction is an inverse power; in itself it has no power; its power is to annul the power of production (the positive, non-reversible assumption of identity) through reversion. The logic of production is one of accrual; seduction is not that which negates or opposes that accrual, but that which transforms it. Baudrillard insists that 'everything demands to be exchanged, reversed, and abolished within a cycle' (SEDN: 45), hence the illusory nature of production, or of any non-reversible ontology.

Seduction is precisely not of the order of representation; the distance between sign and referent, discourse and world, which marks an order of representation is abolished. In Baudrillard's writing, the whole edifice of representation, of a semiological structure that codifies 'reality', is deemed to be an ideological process that reduces the symbolic, in other words, that obscures or bars the inevitable cyclical process of presence, seducing absence, seducing presence: of creation and destruction, life and death, appearance and disappearance, truth and illusion. A poststructuralist ontology, postulating the social construction of reality through a critical rendition of the idea that meaning obtains through language and not through its relation to an extradiscursive world, only goes part of the way. It still posits the inevitability of this linguistic structuration, of the Law, of the binary structuring of meaning where deconstruction remains in the realm of the semiotic, and is of uncertain import. Baudrillard's notion of seduction is not only critical of the assumptions of reference, but, through a critique of the conditions under which reference becomes possible, develops a critique of the entire process of codification. Materialising the world through a representational linguistics (reference or no reference) works against the seductive interplay of signs.

Seduction is therefore also about the annulment of signs, their reversion, and the transformation of their meaning into 'pure appearance'. Baudrillard places considerable emphasis on 'appearances', the 'play of appearances', and this needs discussing. In contrast to notions of resignification employed by Butler and others, whereby another meaning is deemed to replace an existing one, the reversion of signs annuls meaning through returning the sign to the immediacy of its site of action. The best way to convey a sense of the significance of 'appearances' to seduction, and how consideration of the play of appearances shifts the site of analysis from one solely focused on semiotics, is to use an example.

Camilla Power and Leslie Aiello (1997), both paleoanthropologists, develop an interpretation of prehistorical data to address the question, how did humans become a symbolic, culture-bearing species? Using an evolutionary framework they establish a hypothesis, develop an argument for the 'evidence' that would support it, and consider that the existing evidence lends cautious support for their hypothesis (certainly no less plausible than competing explanations, in their assessment). They preface their discussion with reference to the work of symbolic anthropologists who have stressed the interdependence of speech and ritual. Humans, as they speak, 'trigger' acts of identification of constructs that have a mutual authority amongst a group. But speech itself cannot establish these constructs in the first place. A mutual construct can only exist through being emotively experienced, they claim, and this is only possible through ritual. 'Collective ritual action is the source of those shared, morally authoritative symbolic constructs without which speech would have no force' (Power and Aiello 1997: 154). A theory of speech origins, therefore, has to incorporate an understanding of the earliest instances of ritual.

Asking what selection pressures might have led individuals to 'engage with displaced and imaginary constructs' and to share those constructs with others, Power and Aiello advance a thesis linking female reproductive strategies, the emergence of symbolism, and the sexual division of labour. In a context characterised by the evolutionary loss of oestrus as a sign of fertility, they propose that 'symbolism emerged as a set of deceptive sexual signals aimed by female kin coalitions at their mates to secure increased male reproductive investment' (p. 154). For a variety of reasons developed by Power and Aiello, which I will not go into here, reproductive success was enhanced if females reduced the amount of time males spent engaged in sexual activity with other females, and increased the amount of time they spent with the one female. This set of conditions, they argue, led human females to develop a ritual process of signalling to males deceptive signs of menstruation. Thus, within kin coalitions, they suggest that non-menstruating females might have 'borrowed' the blood of a menstrual relative. 'Confusing information available to males by showing the same reproductive signal at the same time, coalition members could then retain both the attractions of menstruation as an indicator of impending fertility, and the advantages of synchrony for maximising male parental investment' (p. 157). Power and Aiello give this process the term 'sham menstruation', which, they claim, may well have developed into the females' use of blood-coloured pigments to paint their bodies.[1]

Power and Aiello claim that this rendition of 'sham menstruation' provides a basis for the emergence of ritual and symbolic activity. A 'signal' that was specific to the individual and that could gain the attention of males on a one-to-one basis was also one that could become collectivised, so to speak, among females in the group, making the deception one that is shared and maintained by the group. Power and Aiello argue that this process represents a vital step towards 'sustaining an imaginary construct and sharing that construct with others – that is, dealing with symbols'[2] (p. 158). Ritual body-painting within groups of human females would recreate the authoritative construct of 'fertility' or 'blood'. Power and Aiello go on to discuss how this kind of ritual could have led to the emergence of taboo. They also pursue their analysis of the associated structuration of ritualised work division and gender roles.

I have chosen to detail this example not to endorse it or debate its validity, but rather to illustrate some of the key facets of 'seduction' as Baudrillard uses this term. It is clear in this example that the ritual process is an enactment that literally involves the play of appearances. It is not a question of 'meaning', with the borrowed blood or red pigment 'representing' menstrual blood to 'mean' specifically impending fertility (as this would assume prior shared constructs of fertility and trade-offs between investing time and energy in relating to one female or several), but rather their use has to be understood as a symbolic action – 'collective ritual action' with no depth of meaning, involving a superficial play of signs; the unmediated resonance of signs that removes them from the domain of the code (that is, amenable to monosemic interpretation), and creates a symbolic world. In this emerging world, the males are seduced into ritualised patterns of tribal behaviour and in doing so move towards the symbolic, the human cultural sphere.

Baudrillard is explicit that seduction supposes a ritual order (SEDN: 21), not a 'natural' order (p. 2). '*Only rituals abolish meaning*' (SEDN: 138); in other words, in the act of ritual, it is the immediacy of the performing that counts; it is not a question of reference, generalisation or abstraction. The circulation of signs, their appearance and disappearance, is a superficial affair played out on the surface of things.

Seduction is not of the order of the real (SEDN: 46) but of that of artifice (p. 2), of the order of rituals and signs (symbolically reversible), of the *seduction* of the real. Where the grand systems of meaning and value, semiology and production, assume hegemony, seduction as artifice, as detouring from a truth, as the play of appearances, is constructed as evil, as untruth, a truly wayward path of black magic. Indeed, to seduce is to turn the other from his or her 'truth', and to be seduced is to be turned from one's 'truth' (SEDN: 81), a capacity to deny things their assumed 'truth' (SEDN: 8), a return to illusion through artifice. Baudrillard writes that the strategy of seduction is inevitably one of deception, '[i]t lies in wait for all that tends to confuse itself with its reality' (SEDN: 69–70). It sabotages assumptions of the real and the truth of the real. Against production, seduction is ultimately the more powerful:

> For if production can only produce objects or real signs, and thereby obtain some power; seduction, by producing only illusions, obtains all powers, including the power to return production and reality to their fundamental illusion.
>
> (SEDN: 70)

'Deception', of course, is only deception from the perspective of a truth of the real, if one assumes there can be such a 'thing'. If deception is the strategy of seduction, it speaks to the reversible quality of seduction: seduction is reversion and as such is immediately reversible.

As seduction is not of the order of representation, so it is fundamentally of the order of the 'secret'. In other words, it cannot be revealed; as Baudrillard writes, '[e]verything that can be revealed lies outside the secret' (SEDN: 79). As with the ritual of 'sham menstruation', the secret is indeed shared, of the order of 'an indestructible pact' (SEDN: 89), and it maintains its power through remaining unspoken; in fact it cannot be spoken (in the sense of represented, hence the notion of symbol). Implosive, initiatory: 'one enters into a secret but cannot exit'; its strength lies in 'the power of an allusive, ritual exchange' (SEDN: 79), a ceaseless, symbolic exchange.

Seduction is implicitly a challenge in which each engages the other in a reciprocal obligation to respond: the relation, if this is the right word, is thus dual/duel. In the English translation of *Seduction*, the translator, Brian Singer, notes that the French word *duel* has the double meaning of both dual and duel in English, conveying simultaneously agonistic relations and reciprocal challenges (SEDN: 42). Baudrillard asks, what could be more seductive than a challenge (SEDN: 82)? He evokes a sense of the parties to the seductive encounter being constructed through this dual/duel relation, which has the vertiginous intensity of a continuing escalation of stakes in a 'game' that has no end. To be seduced is to challenge the other to be seduced; the seduction has no end because the 'dividing line that defines the victory of the one and the defeat of the other, is illegible . . . there is no limit to the challenge to always be more seduced' (SEDN: 22). This dual/duel relation of the symbolic order is radically different from a theory of relations between those who are 'different'.

In *The Transparency of Evil*, Baudrillard observes how, within the symbolic realm, forms of relation are not dependent on the distinction between ego and other. He gives the example of the Pariah and Brahmin: the Pariah is not 'other' to the Brahmin, but rather *'their destinies are different'* (TE: 127). The two are not 'differentiated along a single scale of values', but rather they are 'mutually reinforcing . . . parts of a reversible cycle like the cycle of day and night' (TE: 127). Reversible moments: one changes place with the other 'in an endless process of seduction'. Baudrillard is careful to distinguish this process of reversion from a mystical one of fusion. Although the reversion of seduction tracks diagonals and transversals across oppositions between terms, breaking or dissolving this structure, it does not lead to fused or con-fused terms. Rather, it leads to dual/duel relations. 'It is not a matter of mystical fusion of subject or object, or signifier and signified, masculine and feminine, etc., but of a seduction, that is, a *duel and agonistic* relation' (SEDN: 105). Again, in *Fatal Strategies*, Baudrillard underscores the importance of seduction as dual/duel. There he writes 'I cannot seduce if I am not already seduced, no one can seduce me if he [*sic*] is not already seduced' (FS: 105).

Baudrillard's notion of seduction has some apparent points of overlap with Butler's notion of 'performativity', where the latter is 'that mode of discourse that produces what it names'. The appearance is deceptive, however, in that 'seduction' seduces production, whereas 'performativity' is of the order of production through and through. As analysed in Chapter 4, performativity and resignification, with the assumption of the productive nature of power, run counter to reversion and the critical epistemology and ontology underpinning seduction and Baudrillard's notion of the symbolic. In Chapter 4 I argued that the political agendas for transgenderism and their claims regarding the deconstruction of the binary of sex can arguably be understood as complicit with hyperreal trends. Interestingly, the 'trans'-person, whose 'play' is one of seducing the signs of sex through the power of his or her appearance and disappearance, has more chance, if we follow Baudrillard's analysis, of 'subverting' identity (really seducing identity), than a transgenderist concern to reinscribe another trans-identity. Where the game of trans is one of a superficial play of appearances, perhaps its seductive power is greater than when it invests the game of seduction with the weighty 'political' agendas associated with 'feminism' and/or queer, when these are grounded in the finalities of 'identity' and 'liberation'. In fact, it could be argued in accordance with Baudrillard that the latter actually serves to reinstate the Law against the Rule, precisely undermining the ambivalence of seduction of transvestitism or transsexualism in its dual/duel encounter.

The Rule and the Law

> [S]eduction is what tears you from your own desire to return you to the sovereignty of the world.
>
> (FS: 142)

The significance of the Rule by contrast to the Law will be discussed in this section, in conjunction with the notion of the 'accursed share', before going on to examine Baudrillard's view on the implications of seduction for sex and sexuality, and giving consideration to the feminist response.

Baudrillard uses the concept of the Rule, as in rules of a game, to convey the dynamic of seduction in contradistinction to that of the Law. Baudrillard observes that the Law describes a potentially universal system of meaning and value, based as it is on the assumption of a fundamental transcendence. The crucial point is that 'the Law constitutes itself into an instance for the totalization of the real' (SEDN: 134). Remembering Baudrillard's concept of 'ideology' as the semiological reduction of the symbolic, this assumed totalisation of the real is the supreme ideological form. In its universalisation, the Law transcends the individual, the group, the social dynamic of action. The Rule, by comparison, is immanent to a specific and limited 'system'; it is not transcendent, nor does it aspire to universality (SEDN: 134). It is the transcendence of the Law, the assumed transcendence and totalisation of the real, that establishes the universality and irreversibility of meaning and value. By contrast, it is the immanence of the Rule, and its arbitrariness, that lead 'in its own sphere' to reversibility, both of meaning and, indeed, of the Law.

> For us the finite is always set against the infinite; but the sphere of games is neither finite nor infinite – transfinite perhaps. It has its own finite contours, with which it resists the infinity of analytic space. To reinvent a rule is to resist the linear infinitude of analytic space in order to recover a reversible space.
>
> (SEDN: 134)

The Law pertains to that order of a linear scale, or crystalline structure, on which discrete items, or individual 'identities', can be differentiated in accordance with a transcendent value of equivalence or difference. This order is cumulative; more can be added, they can be removed and replaced, or they can change places. It excludes, however, what Baudrillard terms 'seduction': the cyclical reversion of terms that is not of this order, and furthermore dissolves it. Baudrillard comments that the Law 'establishes equality as a principle' (SEDN: 136): in the sense that everyone is equal but different before the Law, there is no 'equality' in terms of the Rule. Equality is conceptually dependent on this transcendent scale whose axiom is the ontological priority of discrete 'identities': everyone/thing is inexorably separate and individualised (essentialised, furthermore) according to the terms of the Law. The order of the Rule, by contrast, establishes dual/duel relations where 'individuals' are constituted through reciprocal encounters, 'being' nothing more than the histories of those encounters, continually challenged and seduced, reversed, transformed. This 'order' is not mediated through representational structures, which presume a transcendent 'reality' or 'realities'. The Rule only exists when shared; the Law 'floats above scattered individuals' (SEDN: 136). Baudrillard makes the astute comment that, in a sense, 'we are more equal within ceremonials than before the Law' (SEDN: 137), where, in the ceremonial, there is no unilinear scale of differentiation.

The order of the Rule, as arbitrary, ungrounded, without reference, counters the idealism of a transcendent Law that assumes a codifiable Real. The Rule is resolutely 'material' in the sense of the quotation from *Fatal Strategies* cited at the opening of this section: seduction 'tears' one away from being caught up in the phantasmatic 'socially constructed' Real of one's 'desires' and 'beliefs', and 'returns' one to the 'sovereignty of the world', in other words to being challenged and seduced by that which cannot be represented or codified, cannot be ideologically reduced but is continually symbolically exchanged. Baudrillard refers to the logic of the symbolic sphere of cultures of symbolic exchange as one where there is no remains, no residue; all stakes are constantly consumed and reversed (SEDN: 135).

> Ko maru kai atu
> Ko maru kai mai
> Ka ngohe ngohe.[3]

The logic of symbolic exchange that eschews internal accumulation is at the heart of Bataille's notion of the 'accursed share' (1967, trans. 1988). In Chapter 1 reference was made to societies based on symbolic exchange, whereby they actively avoid the accumulation of any surplus and actually institute its destruction through, for example, ritual encounters such as the potlatch where wealth or surplus is expended, lost, for no return. Mauss (1966) observes how in some potlatch systems one expends everything possessed and keeps nothing (p. 35). 'The accursed share' is that portion, item, object, being that threatens the cyclical reversion at the heart of culture by its status as accumulative. It is destined to be ritually 'sacrificed' and reversed. I will come back to the question of the notion of sacrifice below, in conjunction with a discussion of the 'exchange of women' in societies of symbolic exchange. The point of importance here is the connection between seduction, the Rule, the reversion of stakes, and the notion of the accursed share which symbolically embodies that which has not been reversed.

Baudrillard discusses how the Law can be obeyed or transgressed, but it is not possible to go beyond its terms. The Rule is observed, not obeyed; it is not possible to 'transgress' a rule. On the contrary, if one does not observe it, one is no longer 'playing the game'. To cheat is to transform the ceremonial conventions of the Rule, or game, into the economic logic of the Law. The cheater, according to Baudrillard's discussion, fears the vertigo of seduction (in other words, being abandoned to, and taken up by, the challenge and reversion of the game) and, by attempting to 'win' through turning the stakes into a purpose, into surplus value, destroys the game. Baudrillard writes that 'the cheater is *autonomous*: he [*sic*] establishes a law, his own law, against the arbitrary rituals of the rule – this is what disqualifies him' (SEDN: 140). The transfinite space of the Rule 'delivers' one from the universality of the Law. The ritual sign is not a representative sign (think of cards in a poker game), it is not worth *understanding* in the sense of ascertaining its 'meaning', and hence, again in Baudrillard's words, 'delivers us from meaning' (SEDN: 137).

Moving more specifically to those games that are understood to be predicated on 'chance', Baudrillard is clear that it is not a matter of *believing* in chance, but challenging 'chance'.

> Belief is an absurd concept, of the same type as motivation, need, instinct, i.e. [better translation: 'or even'], drive, desire, and God knows what else – facile tautologies that hide from us the fact that our actions are never grounded psychologically in belief, but in stakes and challenges.
>
> (SEDN: 142)

According to Baudrillard, the gaming table has an enduring attraction not because of the money, but through the unmediated seduction of the order of things. To throw a fragment of value in the face of chance, where 'chance' is understood as an instance of some universal, transcendent law, is not to win the favour of a 'chance' hit, but precisely to challenge chance by dismissing its transcendence and turning it into an agonistic partner. The game is then predicated on chance declaring itself favourable or hostile. In other words, in this formulation 'chance' does not exist. 'Chance' as an adversary no longer bears any resemblance to the modernist notion of chance in its random, aleatory sense, where it is subject to the laws of probability (in contrast to the rules of the game). The gaming table would not hold its fascination and enchantment if the statistical abstraction of the random 'win' was all that was at stake. Rather, gaming opposes the logic of the Law, and in fact radically interrogates chance. The notion of a law of randomness and probability literally encounters a duel and agonistic challenger who seduces the law and transforms the universe into a contingent world challenged into existence.

Having established some of the key aspects of Baudrillard's notion of 'seduction' and the significance of reversion, I will turn now to consider his writing on seduction in relation to sex, sexuality, and desire. Subsequently, I will return briefly to the question of the paradigm of 'chance' to consider Baudrillard's critical comments on Deleuze's 'ideal game'.

Seduction, Sex, and Sexuality

> To seduce is to die as reality and reconstitute oneself as illusion.
>
> (SEDN: 69)

There are a number of points that need to be clarified at the beginning of this discussion, as it seems, from a reading of the English-language literature on Baudrillard's writings on seduction, that the possibilities for applying inappropriate assumptions and taking huge and unwarranted liberties with isolated, decontextualised statements made by Baudrillard are limitless.

Baudrillard is explicit in his view that the oppositional structure of male/female, masculine/feminine, apart from being historically and culturally specific, is fundamentally a 'masculine' opposition. This inevitably essentialist oppositional structure establishes the masculine 'sex' in the positive, and the feminine as 'other', as opposite to the masculine. Baudrillard is resolutely critical of this structure and its attendant assumptions. The institution of the poles of two inalienable sexes is but one more instance of the hegemony of production against seduction. All masculine power is the power to produce; the masculine is synonymous with power and production, understood within Baudrillard's critique of these constructs; 'all that is produced . . . falls within the register of masculine power' (SEDN: 15).

Baudrillard's critique of the structural imperative of masculinity is grounded in his analysis of seduction. The feminine, when he uses this term, does not equate with 'women' (nor the masculine with 'men') (Baudrillard in Gane 1993: 86). It is vital to appreciate the significance of this insistence on his part. Furthermore, the feminine does not oppose the masculine; rather it seduces the masculine (SEDN: 7). The 'feminine' *is this power of seduction*, that is, this power to annul the masculine, and to annul the power of production. It seems, then, that Baudrillard's construct of the feminine and masculine views them as co-dependent, the one emergent and the other seductive. The feminine is not a 'sex' in the sense of a sex opposed to the other sex, but is rather what counters the sex that has erected itself as sex (SEDN: 21): as the sexual subject. Femininity 'causes the sexual poles to waver', it is 'what abolishes the differential opposition' (SEDN: 12). In Baudrillard's terms, the feminine cannot be considered as a 'sex' but 'as the form transversal to every sex, as well as to every power' (SEDN: 15). The feminine as seduction could not possibly inhere in a sex, as 'woman', which is a construct instituted (in accordance with the masculine) as the other of 'man' within a polar opposition; it rather traverses sex as it traverses power and production, seducing and abolishing the oppositional terms. As such, masculinity, Baudrillard argues, has always been somewhat residual: a secondary formation whose weakness and fragility are evident in the extraordinary efforts it has to go to in the endeavour to defend itself against the seduction that continually haunts it. He even hypothesises, ironically, that the feminine is in this sense the only 'sex', as the masculine has to sustain such an effort to exist against, in opposition to, the feminine (SEDN: 16).

The power of annulment immanent to seduction is the capacity to deny things their truth. It is the capacity to return the semiological and axiological instantiations of the Law to the pure play of appearances, to the sphere of the Rule, and by doing so, in fact, foiling all systems of power and meaning with quite simple gestures. It is this power of annulment and reversion associated with the feminine that leads Baudrillard to state that the feminine indeed prevails, as the seductive form prevails over the productive. This power of seduction, of a ruthlessly non-essentialist ontology, is best evoked by Baudrillard's ironic statement that '[n]othing can be greater than seduction itself, not even the order that destroys it' (SEDN: 2). As he observes, structures can adapt to their being subverted or overturned, because the transformation occurs within the terms of the structure, in accordance with the Law, but they cannot survive the reversion of these very terms. Seduction, therefore, also reverses and abolishes the oppositional terms of conventional semiology (SEDN: 104).

Why has femininity – as seductive – become associated with 'women', and masculinity – as productive – with 'men'? Or rather, why has the seductive become associated with the feminine and the productive with the masculine? There can be no absolute or definitive answer to this question, beyond historical and cultural circumstance. In asking this question, it is important also to remember that it is entirely derivative, and reliant on a polar oppositional structure of different 'sexes' within which some essential core defines them. Again, this is a masculine construct in that the masculine as productive is the impulse towards creating distinctions, towards the definition of things, in contrast to the feminine as seductive, as the impulse that puts this very definition into question, dissolving the terms of the opposition. The feminine and masculine are:

> undoubtedly merely reversible moments . . . following upon one another and changing places with one another in an endless process of seduction. One sex is thus never the other for the other sex, except within the context of a differentialistic theory of sexuality – which is basically nothing but a utopia. For difference itself is a utopia: the idea that such pairs of terms can be split up is a dream – and the idea of subsequently reuniting them is another.
>
> (TE: 127–8)

At heart, there is absolutely no reason whatsoever why the seductive has to be associated with the 'feminine', and the productive with the 'masculine'. This is purely an historical and cultural, mythical phenomenon that has been unfolding over many millennia. In the same way it is an historically and culturally specific condition of western modernity that, according to Baudrillard's work, the structures that exclude the symbolic and the seductive, that posit production, power, growth, knowledge, truth, value, and meaning relentlessly in the positive, that are hegemonic and trending to catastrophe, are masculinist.

> If we continue to speak this sameness, if we speak to each other as men
> have spoken for centuries, as they have taught us to speak, we will fail
> each other. Again . . . words will pass through our bodies, above our
> heads, disappear, make us disappear.
>
> (Irigaray 1980a: 69)[4]

> Everything returns to the void, including our words and gestures. But
> before disappearing, certain words and gestures, by anticipating their
> demise, are able to exercise a seduction that others will never know.
>
> (SEDN: 84)

As noted in Chapter 2, when feminism critiques the bar that splits male and female into two different sexes, formulated in accordance with the logic of identity/difference, Baudrillard supports its impetus and would presumably agree with its analysis. Indeed, in 1973 Baudrillard wrote how the 'position of revolt' for those social groups 'that fall under the structural bar of repression' cannot be understood in terms of economic exploitation, but rather in terms of revolt against 'the imposition of the code, which inscribes the present strategy of social domination' (MOP: 134–5). When, however, feminists are preoccupied with 'female subjectivity', with being a 'woman' as a sex, 'a sex in its own right', with being 'subjects of desire', with 'feminine desire', this is an entirely different matter. Baudrillard's writing on seduction provides the basis for understanding the viewpoint that leads him to reject this kind of discourse outright.

In a 'culture' (if one can call it that) that relentlessly seeks to exclude the principle of seduction/reversion as outlined here, and where the values of the productive dominate absolutely, to be rendered a 'non-subject', with no 'agency', no 'desire', to be 'feminised' if this is what this means, is *intolerable*. In such a context, to have a consciousness of the implications of such a status and to read, for example, a text that positions women (she, her) as the object of exchange, along with animals, food, and other gifts, by the unmarked term, the other sex – men, is *intolerable*. The rage and pain of this intolerable erasure and subjection of the feminine have produced an outpouring of theory and critique by western feminists, which rival the best theory and philosophy produced by non-feminists. Baudrillard's writing on seduction shifts the inquiry from what has tended to be the dominant feminist focus – how to achieve subjecthood, agency, autonomy, desire, in alternative and non-oppressive formulations and social structures – to fix the critique more firmly on the problems inherent in this cluster of notions, and hence the underlying subjectifying impulse. Baudrillard takes this latter focus of critique further than I have seen feminist theory achieve hitherto.

It is impossible to know which texts, or authors, Baudrillard is referring to when he questions 'the women's movement' or 'feminism'. It appears that he refers predominantly to the works of authors like Luce Irigaray and Hélène Cixous, but possibly equally to those feminists agitating visibly in the arena of state politics. Whatever, in *Seduction*, published in 1979, he questions then what it is that he observes 'the women's movement' opposes to the phallocratic structure: autonomy, difference, a specificity of desire and pleasure, a different relation to the female body, a speech, a writing, but not seduction (SEDN: 8). He surmises that feminists reject seduction through a suspicion of artifice and the assumption that seduction represents a 'misappropriation of women's true being'; the 'truth' of this being is to be found 'inscribed in their bodies and desires' (SEDN: 8). Thus, in terms of this analysis, rather than claiming any desirability in the mastery of reversion through the artifice of appearances, feminists prefer to accede to truth and meaning, and claim women's (right to the) autonomy of their desires, their sex, their pleasure, and to sovereignty over the Real, alongside men. This claim to mastery over the Real indeed gives women access to power on the same terms as men. Sex is indifferent, and becomes a matter of indifference. Irigaray's quest to renew a different sexual difference and have both women and men aspire to their autonomous subjectivities, with their unique desires, seems increasingly problematic. If we are all desiring subjects, who will be the other we will desire?

Baudrillard observes how 'sexual liberation' appears to lie in the rights, status, and pleasure of women. The absence of sexual desire and pleasure is deemed by feminists to be symptomatic of oppression, and it is the conviction of the advocates of 'sexual liberation' that this achievement of an autonomous feminine desire and sexual pleasure (jouissance) is one significant route to subjecthood. His claim, however, is that this 'promotion' to the status of subject means losing the ironic power of that which is of the order of seduction, and becoming trapped within the hegemonic order of sign value, the most abstract form of 'masculine' productive power.[5] Subjectivity, agency, desire, and pleasure, all these characteristics of a 'sex in its own right' mean a radical loss of irony and seduction (and a naïve belief in the 'truth' of the 'real'). Baudrillard argues that it is the enduring illusion of enlightenment humanism to assume the liberation of a servile sex, race, or class in the very terms of its own servitude (SEDN: 17). In other words, subjectivity, agency, desire, and pleasure are the very terms used to inscribe, signify, and ascribe feminine servitude into the so-called Real.

It was commonplace among the feminist community in the 1970s to hear the lament that 'men will never give up their power'. If women attained the 'power' of the subject, the power of desire and agency, they would not 'give up their power' either. It is not, however, that they would not 'give it up' because they would not see a reason to, or because they would be perversely attached to power. Rather, one actually cannot 'give up' the status of subject, the condition of autonomy. How does one stop being a subject? How does one 'give up' being autonomous? The absurdity of this notion reveals the power of seduction as, apart possibly from some forms of meditation, the only means of annulment of the irreversible phantasm of the subject and its interminable desire.

Baudrillard develops a critique of 'sexuality' and 'desire' in *Seduction*, expanding on his critique of Deleuze on desire in *Forget Foucault*, which I discussed in Chapter 2. In developing this critique he posits the entire emphasis on 'sexuality', 'desire', and 'sexual pleasure' as fundamentally 'masculine' in the productive sense discussed above, and questions what women gain, and what they lose, by embracing this emphasis, albeit in a supposedly subversive 'difference'. Citing the work of Irigaray, Baudrillard comments on the almost religious nature of the obsessive profundity associated with the 'ethical truth of desire' incarnated in the body. If there is a feminist concern to contest the assumption that 'anatomy is destiny', it is certainly not evident to Baudrillard in this kind of feminist writing.

In accordance with the primary dictates of production, 'sex has become . . . *the actualization of desire in pleasure*' (SEDN: 38). This imperative to produce desire and to actualise this desire in 'pleasure', this insistence that investments must be ceaselessly renewed, and that value must 'radiate without respite', Baudrillard argues replicates the model of regulation of exchange value (SEDN: 38), where capital must circulate and flux and liquidity are paramount. 'Sexuality' is simply the mode of appearance of this model at the level of the body, according to Baudrillard's analysis. The primary importance placed on the use of the energising drives is common to productive forces and sexual libidinal forces (the psychic metaphor of capital). In fact, the assignation of sexual drive or desire to individuals, Baudrillard argues, is an extension of the ideal of private property in that each person is assigned an amount of capital to manage: 'a psychic capital, a libidinal, sexual or unconscious capital, for which each person will have to answer individually, under the sign of his or her own liberation' (SEDN: 39).

This form of 'sexuality' replaces seduction, 'liquidates' seduction, in Baudrillard's words, emptying it of its symbolic substance. '*It is then the absent form of seduction that is hallucinated sexuality* – in the form of desire. The modern theory of desire draws its force from seduction's liquidation' (SEDN: 40). In place of seduction, an 'economy of sex', productive, autonomous, natural; sex as a simulation model. In the same way as value and energy imply irreversible processes, so too does desire. In this sense, Baudrillard claims that 'Freud was right'; there is one 'sexuality', one libido, and it is 'masculine'; masculine in that it is productive, phallic, repressive, marked by the Name of the Father. Baudrillard writes that there is none other, and it is, in his view, pointless to 'dream' of the possibility of some 'non-phallic, unlocked, unmarked sexuality' of the feminine somehow having passed through to some other side of sexuality. The structural paradigm of 'sexuality', heterosexual of course, is such that the female (as the feminine) is absorbed by the male (as the masculine); either this structure remains in place or it collapses. If it collapses, there is no longer either male or female, in these terms, as these forms are structural prerequisites to 'sexuality' in the contemporary asymbolic sense (SEDN: 6). In a way, he argues, this is what is happening today. In the western hyperreal rendition of 'sex' and 'sexuality', devoid of challenge and seduction, it might as well be considered as a kind of 'sport' or form of 'exercise', as some fitness psychologists in North America have seriously suggested, in the interests of physical and mental health, and longevity. Sexes become interchangeable in a combinatorial matrix. Baudrillard observes how, today, 'everything is converging towards the non-differentiation of the structure [of sex] and its potential neutralisation' (SEDN: 6). Where seduction intensifies through pushing the poles of the two terms towards each other (SEDN: 104), the fractal logic of hyper-real simulation disperses the terms into a neutral orbit. Psychoanalysis is as incapable of engaging with this imploded form of sexual neutralisation as it is with seduction. As Baudrillard writes, the axiomatics of psychoanalysis are sexual, and the fact that we see the decline of psychoanalysis and 'sexuality' simultaneously enables us, he suggests, to 'glimpse a parallel universe' (SEDN: 7).

The inevitability of 'sexuality' and 'desire' as 'masculine' is brought into sharper focus in Baudrillard's brief discussion in *Seduction* on pornography.[6] One way of interrogating the dynamics of the production of contemporary pornography is to understand its intensification as a form of 'generalised pornography', less sexually specific as such: the 'violence of sex neutralised' (SEDN: 27). Pornography is more about the obscenity of visual representation – the more real than real, simulated, hyperreal – than it is about anything else. And why are women overwhelmingly the 'sex objects' of pornography? Today, in Baudrillard's analysis, because they more easily represent that imaginary characteristic of sex that animates 'sexuality', that is, the irreversible, seamless production of desire and sexual pleasure. Linking this observation again to the economic logics of a hyperreal society, sexual 'liberation' requires a 'sexually affluent' society. No scarcity of sexual 'goods' will be tolerable. The erection of the male is constructed as intermittent and fragile; the female sex is, by contrast, better representable (an irreducibly violent representation) in terms of that which is continuously available, and it is this character of 'sexuality' that, Baudrillard argues, has come to dominate our phantasies (SEDN: 26).[7] He postulates that the contemporary practice of using female sexual imagery to sell everything from washing machines to computers, and on and on *ad nauseam*, is precisely about 'conferring on objects the imaginary, female quality of being available at will, of never being retractile or aleatory' (SEDN: 26).[8]

Baudrillard contrasts the logic of pornography to that of the *trompe l'oeil*. Where the latter removes a dimension from 'real' perspectival space, pornography adds a dimension to the space of sex, making sex more real than real, hyperreal, which accounts for its absence of seduction (SEDN: 28). It is this phenomenon of the hyperreal excess of reality that fascinates in pornography; a pornography of the real and its vaporisation into the hyperreal. 'Pornographic voyeurism is not a sexual voyeurism but a voyeurism of representation and its perdition, a dizziness born of the loss of the scene and the irruption of the obscene' (SEDN: 29). In such an instance of the obscene (literally outside the 'scene', the anatomical zoom), perspectival space vanishes, as sex is so close it merges with its own representation: this signals the end of the 'scene' as such, the end of illusion, of the imaginary, of phantasy. This is a pornography that 'decomposes bodies into their slightest detail' (EC: 43). In this new form, the pornographic obscenity of the real is not, according to Baudrillard, a representation of a violence of 'real sex', but the production of a neutralised sex whereby sex is 'outrageously "rendered"', where that 'rendering' is one of 'something that has been removed' (SEDN: 29). In parallel, is not the simulated 'scene' of sado-masochistic performance and sexual pleasure one of 'rendering' in an 'obscene' form a phantasm of precisely that which has been removed: seduction, sexual stakes, and an agonistic challenge?

To convey the significance of the 'loss of distance', and consequently the 'scene', implicit in the pornographic representation, Baudrillard draws an analogy with quadraphonics. This is a sophisticated sound system by which the notion of listening to music is transformed into an experience of a kind of technical delirium, where, in an environmentally monitored and conditioned room, one 'experiences' music through four dimensions, one of which is a 'visceral dimension of internal space' (SEDN: 30). This implosion of distance is the key point here. Baudrillard describes pornography today as a kind of 'quadraphonics of pornography', where the 'hallucination of detail rules', like the technical perfection of the more-real-than-real sound (SEDN: 31). Baudrillard makes the connections with the broader cultural paradigm:

> Everything is to be produced, everything is to be legible, everything is to become real, visible, accountable; everything is to be transcribed in relations of force, systems of concepts or measurable energy; everything is to be said, accumulated, indexed and recorded. This is sex as it appears in pornography, but more generally, this is the enterprise of our entire culture, whose natural condition is obscene: a culture of monstration, of demonstration, of productive monstrosity. No seduction here.
>
> (SEDN: 34–5)

Baudrillard is clear that 'liberated desire', positioned entirely on the side of demand, within a productivist logic with no restrictions, loses its imaginary. With nothing to counter want, no prohibitions, no limits, desire appears everywhere, but this apparition through the proliferation of its images is a generalised simulation (SEDN: 5). Seduction is not of the order of desire, or of the contemporary order of simulation. Seduction is about the ability to turn appearances on themselves, 'to play on the body's appearances, rather than with the depths of desire' (SEDN: 8). Contrary to Irigaray's argument, which Baudrillard cites in this context, it is seduction that is opposed to 'anatomy as destiny'. In Irigaray's writing he confronts the profundity of claims regarding the depths of desire. Nowhere does he find the body worked by artifice and appearances, the body seduced or to be seduced. At no point is the body to be turned from one's 'truth' and seduced, but rather he finds precisely a quest for the truth of one's (feminine) desire. Where Irigaray is concerned to augment 'sexual difference' as a part of a strategy to undermine the phallocratic order, Baudrillard claims that 'seduction alone breaks the distinctive sexualisation of bodies and the inevitable phallic economy that results' (SEDN: 10).

Where psychoanalysis turns the manifest discourse (superficial, apparent), towards its truth (a deeper, latent discourse), seduction employs discourse at its most superficial and turns it away from any deeper truth. Seduction is not about interpreting hidden meanings. Rather, it debunks any pretence to say and establish the truth or meaning of 'what is' in any finite, fixed, and absolute way, as pure illusion.[9] In fact, in *Seduction*, Baudrillard claims that the 'shroud of psychoanalysis has fallen over seduction' (p. 57), through its insistence on the depth of hidden meanings. According to Baudrillard, Freud was initially persuaded by the significance of that which might be called the seductive in Baudrillard's terms, but he abolished this in favour of instituting a 'machinery of interpretation' (SEDN: 57; SE&D: 1–3). Subsequently, Lacan, he argues, presents a kind of imposture of seduction with his dazzling mastery of the Word, the bewildering play of signifiers, but an imposture all the same, as the apparent Lacanian seduction occurs within the terms of the Law. Baudrillard wonders if Lacanian discourse does not reveal a vengeance on Freud's foreclosure of seduction (SEDN: 58).

Seduction is an escalation of stakes, seducing through being seduced; Baudrillard describes seduction as an 'endless refrain' where '[t]here is no active or passive mode . . . , no subject or object, no interior or exterior: seduction plays on both sides and there is no frontier separating them' (SEDN: 81). There is a passion in this process that cannot be understood in terms of desire, libidinal investment, or an origin (such as a drive). Its intensity draws from this immediate reversion, from the gaming, from the challenge, from the appearance and disappearance of signs. Cosmetics can be seen in this way: they have no 'meaning' as such. As Baudrillard points out, if desire exists in the terms that modernity postulates, then it follows that the imperative will be to ensure that nothing interferes with its natural expression and harmony; cosmetics will be deemed hypocritical in their effacing of the real and the natural. If, on the other hand, desire (understood in the modern, psychoanalytic sense)[10] is a myth, which is the postulate of seduction, then nothing can prevent this mythical construct being put to use by signs, which, as they have no 'natural' limits to contend, efface the world through their appearance and disappearance. Such is their power (SEDN: 93).

I indicated at the concluding paragraph of the previous section that it would be useful to return to the question of the paradigm of 'chance' to discuss briefly Baudrillard's critical commentary on Deleuze's 'ideal game' in *Logique du Sens*. It is now possible to see how Baudrillard's notion of seduction is the point of departure for a critique of the assumptions of both 'chance' and 'desire'. In Deleuze's 'ideal game', these two concepts converge to produce a basis for his 'nomadic economy of desire'. In Baudrillard's view, the attempt to liberate and multiply 'chance' as a revolutionary variable achieves nothing more than reasserting the mirror image of causality: it assumes that the world is either caused or aleatory. The hegemonic rule of causality or determinacy (non-contingency) is, of course, not subverted by the assertion of its opposite. Baudrillard condemns the idea that an increased indeterminacy would 'give rise to the simultaneous play of every series, and, therefore, to the radical expression of becoming and desire' (SEDN: 144–5). He contests the notion that 'more' chance leads to a more intense game, or that greater contingency necessarily provides the basis for a more enlightened view of the world. He notes that many cultures do not have a word or concept that corresponds to 'chance', as nothing for them is computed, not even in terms of probabilities. In fact, the more Baudrillard writes about this, the more the idea of an aleatory universe seems repugnant to him: 'insane', 'demented' (SEDN: 146). The unconditional 'liberation' of chance in Deleuze's framing of a nomadic economy of desire is, in Baudrillard's analysis, 'part of the political and mystical economy of residues at work everywhere today, with its structural inversion of weak into strong terms' (SEDN: 146).

Critics of 'Seduction'

> Before this old monk studied Zen twenty years ago, seeing a mountain, the mountain was a mountain; seeing water, the water was water. Later, I met my teacher and attained some realisation. Then a mountain was no longer a mountain, water no longer water. Now, after further accomplishment, seeing a mountain, mountain is mountain; seeing water, water is water. I ask you, are these three views the same or different? If you can answer, you'll meet me intimately.
>
> (Ch'in-yuan Wei-hsin, in Maezumi 1978: Commentary One)

You know the Zen saying that when you begin there are mountains and rivers, then no mountains and no rivers, but you have to come back to mountains and rivers. So here we are. And there are lots of women, and they're just not given equal respect as females. That whole shadow has not been gotten rid of . . . because it fits right into the shadow of the people.

(Jaqueline Mandell, in Friedman 1987: 257)

Feminist responses to Baudrillard's writing on 'seduction' are, I think, missing something important. In those few instances where there is a response, generally the outrage is palpable. Overwhelmingly feminists see women, the feminine, as having been constructed by men, the masculine, to suit their ends, their identities, their existential dreams and nightmares for too long. Baudrillard's writing appears to be read as an arrogant extreme, as one of the more blatant examples of a male philosopher/theorist yet again telling women what is good for them, and even though it might not seem to be what they want, listen to him because it really is, and he knows (for example, Gallop 1987). I do not wish to belittle this concern, and it may well be justified on occasion. Nor am I interested in analysing 'why' some feminists respond to his work in the way they do (a favourite approach taken by feminists to Baudrillard is to explain his writings as a symptom of his own misogynist fears, etc.). My concern is to ask whether there is something important in his theorisation and 'challenge'. He directly challenges feminists to put their *ressentiment* aside, and respond to the significance of 'seduction' as a principle of reversion.[11] Never mind the (undoubtedly pressing and important) preoccupations with 'women' and 'men': put this aside for the moment, one can always 'come back' to the mountains and rivers. But nothing of this has happened. His work has been interpreted from particular sets of feminist assumptions, which, for all their diversity, are surprisingly convergent when confronted with Baudrillard's ideas.

Baudrillard's challenge only makes sense, or makes better sense, if one approaches the task of responding to the notion of 'seduction' in the context of his entire critique of the political economy of the sign. Sadie Plant's discussion (1993), for example, appears to focus mainly on Baudrillard's book *Seduction*, certainly not citing any works written prior to this, and she draws conclusions that are not convincing when in fact considered in the light of Baudrillard's prior works, including *Mirror of Production* and *Symbolic Exchange and Death*. As Plant criticises Baudrillard for apparent claims to knowledge of something women do not know, she claims to know something about Baudrillard that he himself does not: that is, that he deploys 'seduction' as some sort of protective device against the demise of his own identity (and by extension that of all males). Throughout her chapter, Plant returns to this theme of identity, subjectivity, against the void, claiming that 'seduction' is for Baudrillard a convenient buffer between the security of identity and the attraction of the void. According to Plant, it is what he calls seduction that enables him to experience the vertigo of approaching the void (or what she assumes she reinvents as the appearance of the void), but secure in the knowledge that his identity is not really threatened; it is really all a game.

Throughout his work, Baudrillard is careful to situate seduction as that which annuls the terms of a binary dichotomy of identity/void, or individuation/death impulse. This annulment of terms cannot be understood to 'protect identity'; as we have seen in this volume, Baudrillard's work is precisely, integrally about a critique of 'identity', or equally about the importance of undermining the grounds on which the very notion of 'identity' is possible. His critical, historically situated deconstruction of production, value, and semiology theorises the conditions under which 'identity' attains any kind of meaning and political purchase. A reading of *Symbolic Exchange and Death* acquaints the reader with Baudrillard's analysis of the construct of 'death' and the 'void'. Certainly, in *Seduction* he states that 'the attraction of the void lies at the basis of seduction' (p. 77). My reading of this is not that Baudrillard is seriously reifying 'the void', but rather that the process of seduction works through the attraction of poles: distinctions are continually made and seduced, reversed. In a fractal logic of dispersal with the loss of all forms of referentiality and the implosion of poles to the benefit of a logic of the pure positivity of the sign, seduction 'works' at one level removed. Interestingly, Plant in writing against Baudrillard comes perilously close to agreeing with him: 'Seduction has found its own ways of becoming real, none of them dreamt up by the masculine subject. The feminine is not absorbed by the masculine, but begins to dissolve it' (Plant 1993: 101).

Plant is frequently what can only be described as scathing about Baudrillard's use of the terms 'game', 'secret', 'ritual', 'ceremony', as if it is supposedly obvious to the reader why these words and concepts are so problematic and hardly worth serious contemplation. Like those few others who have responded to Baudrillard's work on 'seduction', Plant reiterates Baudrillard's claims in a way which, again, assumes that it is obvious to the reader how both (Plant and reader) share a common view on not only the absurdity, but also the anti-feminist nature, of these claims. Plant asserts that 'seduction' is no threat at all (1993: 90), with no justification for this counter-assertion. When Baudrillard has developed an entire theorisation over several books to arrive at his analyses of 'seduction' and the significance of reversion against the assumptions underlying other theoretical paradigms of power, social change, and 'liberation', it is inadequate simply to say no, it is not the case. The apparent security of the knowledge that one can make such an unsubstantiated assertion with ease possibly testifies to the presuppositions the author makes about the shared knowledges of feminism(s), which are assumed to be beyond criticism, challenge (or seduction). Goshorn (1994) is of the view that Baudrillard 'accuses a universalised feminism of being anti-seductive' (p. 266). He refers to Gallop's concern that Baudrillard remains unseduced by feminism, claiming evidence of Baudrillard's 'rigidly irreversible' opinion (p. 266). On the contrary, Baudrillard is not concerned to comment on feminism as such, but to point at the unavoidability of reversion and seduction, and in so far as 'feminism' ignores, excludes, or rejects seduction, it is this exclusion that is of importance. If it is the desire of feminists to ensure the finalities of 'identity', the 'female subject', or to take up any irreversible position, then neither Baudrillard nor anyone else can be 'seduced' by this discourse; he/they might rather present a challenge (or join the cause).

Reading Plant, it seems that any discourse that would question the feminist assumption that women's interests are best served through the attainment of an autonomous, desiring subjectivity must be deluded, politically motivated against women, and opposed. There is no room for even considering the paradoxes and tensions generated through an acknowledgement of the points Baudrillard is making about the fiction of power and the power of 'seduction' or reversion on the one hand, and, on the other, the inevitability of a need to ensure women's rights, freedoms, and autonomous decision-making in a male-dominated world where subjectivity, identity, value, and production rule. His writing is deemed to oppose women's 'liberation', and is singularly ridiculed and condemned outright. I argue that Baudrillard's point is more complicated than this, and it is this more complicated picture that is of interest here.

Soon after *Seduction* was published in 1979, a review appeared by Luce Irigaray in a French journal (1980b). Her review is headed with a quotation taken from the book: 'woman is nothing and that is her power', her reaction to which appears to animate her response to the book as a whole. Like Plant (1993), Moore (1988), Gallop (1987), and Kellner (1989) on behalf of all feminists, Irigaray is incensed by Baudrillard's apparent arrogance to dare, as a male, to assume knowledge of anything of the feminine, or even worse to assume the possibility of appropriating the feminine for his masculine self. Kellner is convinced this is insulting to women, or at least feminists, indeed, claiming that *Seduction* is an 'attack on feminism' (p. 143). Kellner, unwaveringly consistent throughout his book, proclaims Baudrillard to be sly and essentialist, falsely designating masculine and feminine as 'ontological realities' when they are in fact 'social constructs' (p. 146), a curious interpretation of Baudrillard's work, to say the least.

Irigaray adopts an interrogatory, accusative, sarcastic approach, questioning Baudrillard on his claims, for example, that 'power is nothing', that 'the feminine is elsewhere', that seduction is subversive. Her questions are purely rhetorical, asked in a fashion that, again, assumes that the reader will automatically see what the problem is with these absurd statements, without her having to explain. The fact that she does not begin to engage with his ideas in their own terms suggests that she is of the view that they do not have any value or credibility, and that she considers them to be simply misogynist ravings (and we, reasonable and educated folk, will all see the point and agree with her). Once again, *it speaks for itself*; Irigaray knows her readership. Certainly, Baudrillard writes in a provocative manner, but he is never, or seldom, provocative just for the sake of attack. His provocations are generally deeply ironical and serve to reveal problems with the ardent attachments of those who take such umbrage. This issue of irony and offence will be discussed further below in the context of Baudrillard's (in)famous statement about sacrificing a woman in the desert.

Irigaray focuses her review, in the main, on Baudrillard's use of Kierkegaard's story in *Diary of a Seducer* (one chapter in *Seduction*, around twenty pages). It becomes clear that her reading of the story is very different from Baudrillard's. She criticises Baudrillard for leaving some bits out of his citation of Kierkegaard. It is equally the case that Irigaray is highly selective and leaves some bits out of her references to Baudrillard (and she, after all, is reviewing a book). Baudrillard's reading can be viewed as a kind of mythical use of the text to make a couple of key points about 'seduction' in what tends to be considered its 'sexual' context. He wishes to distinguish a crude form of 'seduction' from that consistent with symbolic exchange. The former is precisely the rather grotesque formula that feminists and others find repugnant or worse, cast by Baudrillard as 'an immoral and libertine exercise, a cynical deception for sexual ends' (SEDN: 99). This distinction enables him to articulate a process of seduction that is significantly different. The seduction Baudrillard alludes to is about the reversion of those qualities of 'self' that fix the 'identity' of the 'subject' within a kind of additive formulation which precludes being seduced; in other words, which precludes becoming 'nothing', dying to oneself and being reconstituted as an illusion. The art of this process of reversion is the feature of Kierkegaard's text that, in my interpretation, interests Baudrillard, and his claim is that the jouissance of 'desire' is only one rather insignificant part of the exquisite seduction where one is literally taken out of oneself. Baudrillard writes that a 'vulgar' form of seduction might proceed by persistence, but he distinguishes this from a form of seduction that proceeds by absence, 'or better, it invents a kind of curved space, where signs are deflected from their trajectory and returned to their source' (SEDN: 108), creating a state of suspense. This is not a process of conquest (one can only seduce if one is already seduced).

Seduction is of the order of symbolic exchange. In addition to a process of on-going reciprocal exchanges, seduction also involves importantly the cyclical reversion of any feature, element, construct, that posits itself in identifiable terms (identity/difference) as that which cannot be reversed, as the presence of an apparently enduring essence. The non-reversible is residual and must be destroyed to annihilate the possibility of the institution of power, of an accumulative logic understood as damaging or dangerous to the reversible logic of the symbolic. Baudrillard refers to the so-called 'seductive' antics of the likes of Don Juan and Casanova, describing them as 'impure seducers', precisely because they are dedicated to the accumulation of this residue (SEDN: 101). Similarly, the caricature of women as seducers through a kind of coyness and flattery is of the same order of crudity, in Baudrillard's terms. This is not what the seduction he is referring to is all about. This much is abundantly clear from his text. Seduction is about being seduced.

None of this is clear from Irigaray's review. Kierkegaard and Baudrillard are both, according to Irigaray, referring to a story of a rape and violation of a young and beautiful woman; the seducer attempts to possess her through his more sophisticated ploys and tactics. She is a victim, brutally prevented from finding herself. These victims are all, or mostly, women, captive in a world not of their making. A diabolical destiny indeed, and to valorise such a scenario would be problematic in the extreme. This, however, is precisely not what Baudrillard is talking about, and such a singular reading is surely surprising. Maybe not, read from a certainty of the importance of the sovereignty of the 'female subject', her 'desire', and her 'pleasure', protected from seduction by all the mechanisms it might be possible to muster. This is not to say that Baudrillard's depiction of seduction as a process of reversion is, in all its guises, a kind of painless and endlessly pleasurable delight. In the realm of symbolic exchange, seduction is also sacrificial. As Baudrillard writes, 'seduction always seeks to overturn and exorcize a power' (SEDN: 87). In Kierkegaard's story, it is Cordelia's power of grace or desire that is to be reduced to nothing.

Louise Burchill's discussion (1984) of *Seduction* also focuses on Baudrillard's writing on the *Diary of a Seducer*, and, like Irigaray, she is critical of his use of the text, but in quite a different way. Burchill's critique leads her to conclude that Baudrillard's discussion of 'seduction' really, and inevitably, secures his grounding in 'identity', or 'positionality'. She draws on Irigaray's notion of a 'sensible transcendental' as a parallel to what she claims is a 'third term' in Kierkegaard's work, a third element that, she argues, Baudrillard ignores. This third element, she claims, is vital for the 'aesthetic seduction' in Kierkegaard's story. A third element enables a mediation between the two terms:

> When described in such terms the movement extracted from Kierke-gaard's conceptualisation of a turning point, an articulation, between two worlds, evokes (however aleatorily) the attempt of Luce Irigaray in *Ethique de la Différence Sexuelle* to think a different dialectic, in which the movement is one not of subsumption but an articulated 'becoming' (devenir) of both two terms (each irreducibly other), and two orders (precisely those of the immanent and the transcendental); no longer then is there a bifurcation of the one from its other but rather there is established between the two a constant relay, an indeterminate relation, through the intermediary of a third (field): that which Irigaray calls a 'sensible transcendental'.
>
> (Burchill 1984: 37)

Here we see both Irigaray's and Burchill's concern that no term be annihilated, reduced to nothing. All must be retained in their positive presence. Rather than a process of two terms mutually seducing and being seduced, which, in its fullness, leads to there being no trace of either, they prefer to secure the two in their inalienable 'otherness' with an intermediary acting as a kind of go-between. This 'third field' is deemed necessary to enable an exchange between the two irreducible (and unseducable) terms (I acknowledge that I am not commenting on the Kierkegaard text here at all).

Burchill appears to interpret 'reversibility' in Baudrillard's work to mean literally, and only, two terms changing places; 'an atomistic, bi-polar universe', where the young girl is 'articulated in an *irreversible* relation with the Seducer' (1984: 34). Burchill then argues that these two terms are inevitably based on a positionality (and therefore too that Baudrillard's theorisation cannot escape this inevitability). In my reading of Baudrillard, first, 'positionality' is not such a problem and is not bound up with these ontological concerns evident in Burchill's rendition; Baudrillard is relentlessly critical of ontological positions. Secondly, it is not that the reversion is best understood as only a simple swapping of places, whereby both terms remain, but simply switched around. Reversion is rather an annulment of pretences to establish and fix the truth, real, desire, power. Casting reversion in this less singular way does not evoke a 'bi-polar universe'. Indeed, the process of emergence and reversion can be viewed as a dual and cyclical movement, but this does not reduce it to exclusively two terms. There is no reason why we are only talking about two terms; what is clear is that there is no intermediary.

Burchill's presumption of reversion as only a naïve changing of places is evident in the following: 'Baudrillard's two poles of seduction (feminine/animalistic: masculine/strategic) demonstrate a radical disparity which must be correlated with the staggering of the two different phases: as such, no simple reversibility can, in principle, be stated to operate between the two poles' (1984: 35). Is she claiming that because of the sequence of time separating the two phases, one cannot *become* the other? But whoever said that night *becomes* day? It is not a matter of *becoming* anything, but rather a cycle of being and not-being, through reversion and transformation. Ironically, Irigaray would agree: '[w]inter is not summer, night is not day, every part of the universe is not equivalent to every other. These rhythms should be enough for us to build societies. Why has man wanted more?' (1987: 88). Good question.

I agree with Goshorn's view that Baudrillard's theory of seduction is significant for feminist theory both philosophically and politically, that it is not 'an embarrassment'. Goshorn also contends that seduction needs to be 'brought out of its eighteenth century trappings and into the present' (1994: 280); my own view is that this pertains more to the preconceptions of readers than to the analysis Baudrillard presents. Enduring confusion surrounds Baudrillard's use of the concept of 'seduction' in conjunction with 'sacrifice' and 'symbolic exchange'.

Baudrillard's Sacrifice

In *America*, published in 1986, Baudrillard made the following outrageous statement, for which he has undoubtedly (and deservedly) become infamous, among those few feminists who have taken any interest in his work:

> Death Valley is as big and mysterious as ever. Fire, heat, light: all the elements of sacrifice are here. You always have to bring something into the desert to sacrifice, and offer it to the desert as a victim. A woman. If something has to disappear, something matching the desert for beauty, why not a woman?
>
> (AM: 66)

As this statement has fixed the attention of a number of commentators, my intention is to analyse the discussion it sparked, for the purpose of exploring possible miscomprehensions, and situating the notion of 'sacrifice' in the frame of Bataille's notion of the 'accursed share'.

Moore and Johnstone (1989) ask Baudrillard in an interview, 'what is the point of such a gratuitously provocative statement?' His response speaks to the question of how he views the notion of sacrifice, which I will go on to discuss, but we do not really get a response to the 'why so gratuitously provocative' part of the question; it can only be intended as a massively disguised challenge (remembering that Baudrillard does defend at least the attempt to be a 'theoretical terrorist' as a kind of 'position' of last resort),[12] or an indication that Baudrillard really has never had an intention of a dialogue with feminism (which is not entirely convincing). Possibly we do not get a response from Baudrillard to this aspect of the question partly because the interviewers do not pause there, but suggest a corollary: the sacrifice of a postmodern philosopher in the centre of the city, which Baudrillard thinks is a great idea (even assuming it would be him).

This 'sacrifice' statement of Baudrillard's is indefensible, and no amount of analysis of 'what he might have meant' excuses it. I say it is indefensible because, precisely in accordance with his analysis, it is arguable that 'women' are being destroyed in huge numbers through horrendous violation and dismemberment in our contemporary world exactly in conjunction with the eradication of the logic of sacrifice and the symbolic from the western hyperreal consumer society. Thus, to suggest this 'sacrifice' in what appears to be a flippant tone, in its context of comment on the American desert, is to show little respect for the tragedy of this violence. To clarify the point about contemporary 'sacrifice', we need to revisit Baudrillard's writing on the significance of the sacrifice in the context of symbolic exchange, and the feminist critique of the objectification of women implicit in the 'exchange of women' in societies of symbolic exchange.

I have referred above in this chapter to the notion of the sacrificial as that process where the 'accursed share', as that symbolically embodying that which has not been reversed, is 'sacrificed'. In Baudrillard's analysis of cultures of symbolic exchange, sacrifice is about nothing more than this reversal of power, or accumulation, reversal of the power that accrues from having given without having been given. 'This is the essence and function of sacrifice: to extinguish what threatens to fall out of the group's symbolic control and to bury it under all the weight of the dead' (SE&D: 138–9).

In response to Moore and Johnstone's question, Baudrillard replies that he does not view the question of sacrifice in a negative manner, but rather sees it as something to be valued for its reciprocity. Without reciprocity, something has to die, and, he says, in relation to this statement it is identity: 'in the desert one loses one's identity'. In saying 'something has to die' he reiterates that he means this in the sense of removed; ritually and symbolically reversed. I think this reference to 'removed' has to be understood in the context of Baudrillard's critical analysis of death as a western invention, where death is dichotomously split from life as its binary opposite, and not to be understood metaphorically, as Gane (1991b) suggests. Irigaray (1987), in 'Women, the sacred, money', assumes an entirely different meaning of 'sacrifice', calling 'our own' society 'sacrificial', and, without actually exploring the term itself, appears to use it to connote an action whereby one agency precisely removes or destroys a victim to ensure a benefit accrues to that agency (a process somewhat reminiscent of Baudrillard's 'crude' or 'vulgar' seduction). Irigaray does not elucidate any distinction between cultures of symbolic exchange and 'our own'.

In the interview of Baudrillard by Moore and Johnstone, Baudrillard, again provocatively, makes a final comment that making the woman into an object of the sacrifice 'is perhaps the greatest compliment I could pay her', and we are left to wonder what on earth is at stake here. Mike Gane (1991b), in a discussion of postmodernism, Marxism, and feminism in relation to Baudrillard's work, is also concerned with this apparently gratuitous 'compliment' statement. Gane's comments might help reveal something of the irony and challenge in Baudrillard's 'compliment'. Gane refers to Baudrillard's reflection in *Cool Memories* (CM) on a story about a Japanese man who invites a young Dutch girl to a meal and then to read poetry, during which he shoots her, then proceeds to eat her. Gane makes the point that these sacrificial images are purely artificial: the murder ('sentimental cannibalism') has something of an air of ritual and sacrifice. He comments in a parenthesis 'presumably Baudrillard would argue that the Dutch girl is paid a compliment'. Possibly the irony here is that the question of the compliment is judged as such not by Baudrillard, but in the very terms of the sacrificial object: if having beauty and its contingent identity are so dearly prized, to be designated the sacrificial bearer of these qualities, chosen above all others, is a 'compliment' indeed. There are undoubtedly a multiplicity of interpretations, probably the most important of which relates the sacrifice in the desert to the biblical account of Abraham being incited by God to sacrifice in the desert that which he most cherished in the world, his son Isaac. Abraham was stopped by the intervention of Yahweh's angel, as he had proved his faith (Genesis 22). This analogy would have the woman to be sacrificed in Baudrillard's comment parallel to that valued above all else. To understand his comment in terms of the notion of the accursed share, it is not a matter of woman-as-object, as inalienable, ontically positive, produced self, but of the reversion of her/him (as sex object of desire) to the world of the symbolic, of seduction.

Regardless, the question of the bifurcation of an agent of sacrifice on the one hand – he (subject who chooses) – and a sacrificial victim on the other – she (object as chosen one) – is at the heart of a key issue of contention that has traversed feminist theory for many decades: men are subjects who choose, decide, intervene, and women are objects of choice, decision, intervention, and indeed 'exchange'. In 1978 Gayle Rubin published a paper with the title 'The traffic in women', which was to become a pivotal contribution for developing (English-language) feminist theorising on this very kind of question. Rubin employs a combination of Marxist and Freudian theory to develop a critique of those social conventions, prevalent from the earliest historical times and across cultures, in which women are objects of exchange among men, arguing that this is crucial to understanding patriarchy and women's oppression. Rubin coined the term 'the sex/gender system' to characterise what she terms 'the specific social relations' of the oppression of women. She analyses the work of Claude Lévi-Strauss to identify those features of kinship systems that figured these social relations, and the work of Marx to position these sets of relations within a framework of 'political economy'.

From the standpoint of Baudrillard's work, and any anthropological, social theory building on the work of Mauss, Sahlins, and Bataille among others, Rubin's argument is flawed in its Eurocentric assumptions about the universality of the economic paradigm, and that of the unconscious. She discusses societies of symbolic exchange as if these social groups automatically functioned on the basis of the economic logic of utility and their objects of exchange took the universalised form of the commodity. Rubin therefore applies this same logic to her understanding of the exchange of women in these cultures, which presents fundamental problems. Marcel Mauss (1966) exposes the folly of the application of such assumptions to such social groupings. Interestingly, Rubin does refer to Mauss in her discussion, but persists in her use of these assumptions regardless. For example, with reference to 'gift exchange' she writes: '[i]n a typical gift transaction, neither party gains anything' (1978: 158); 'the other purposes served by gift giving only strengthen the point that it is a ubiquitous means of social commerce' (1978: 158); and '[t]he relations of such a system are such that women are in no position to realize the benefits of their own circulation . . . it is men who are the beneficiaries of the product of such exchanges – social organisation' (1978: 159). Rubin continues to talk in terms of 'rights', 'property', 'trade', 'merchandise'; she dichotomises 'social' and 'natural' 'worlds', asserting that a kinship system in the kind of societies Lévi-Strauss described was to be understood in terms of 'production'. Irigaray (1977), writing at the same time as Rubin, makes the same assumptions in her two essays 'Women on the market', and 'Commodities among themselves'. Irigaray does critique the problematic concept of equivalence in the economic paradigm, but assumes this concept operates universally and applies it to her understanding of 'exchange of women' in cultures of symbolic exchange.[13] Strathern (1988), on the other hand, argues on the basis of her anthropological study that there is only one example in fact (and it is obvious which cultural formation this refers to) where men's transactions are directed towards a discernible and discrete sphere of female activity.

In Chapter 1 of the present volume, the entire edifice of 'political economy', assumed to be predicated on all of these concepts, has been critiqued with reference to the early work of Baudrillard (published prior to the mid-1970s) for its universalist presumptions, and argued by Baudrillard to be entirely 'other' from societies of symbolic exchange, where none of these concepts is applicable. Mauss (1966) is explicit that it is not possible to reduce such exchange to a binary of a subject of exchange and an object exchanged. That which is exchanged takes on its being in the act of exchange, and in the same movement the exchanger is constituted through the act of exchange. It is not appropriate to construct such a process in terms of agency, subjecthood, possessions, gains and losses, and so on. Objects (for want of a different term) that are exchanged cannot be conceptualised as entirely separate from those exchanging them: Mauss is writing about a form of gift exchange in which 'persons and things become indistinguishable' (1966: 46). Building on this work, Baudrillard makes the point that in these forms of gift exchange, the status of 'goods' (again, for want of a better word) that circulate within the exchange has more in common with language than with the dictates of an economic relation. The goods are 'neither produced nor consumed as values'; their function, according to Baudrillard, 'is the continuous articulation of the exchange' (MOP: 98). Baudrillard writes how, in societies of symbolic exchange, all signs have the function of actualising exchanges in their non-mediated appearance and disappearance (SE&D: 107). The exchange is not a 'negotiation' of identity by a subject with another, nor is it about the active manipulation of signs by a subject: rather, the process of the exchange consumes the subject's identity, eliminates it. This makes it possible to understand processes of symbolic exchange with the dead; how ancestors are active partners in exchange (see SE&D: 131–2).

In contrast to Rubin, for whom the exchange of women in societies analysed by Lévi-Strauss is a mechanism designed by group 'men' for their own collective benefit at the expense of group 'women', Baudrillard indicates that the exchange of women is better understood as a strategy of the group: '[i]t is essential that everything (women in this case, but otherwise birth and death) becomes available for exchange, that is, comes under the jurisdiction of the group' (SE&D: 134). In this context, it is not possible to identify the 'group' as men only. Rubin's formulation makes assumptions about boundaries, groups, power relations, all of which are redolent of capitalist 'political economy'. As Baudrillard has argued so vehemently, to project our concept of power and power relations 'indiscriminately onto earlier forms of domination is to miscomprehend all that the earlier formations can teach us about the symbolic operations of social relations' (MOP: 96). This is equally the case for psychoanalytic theory, which Rubin claims is 'a theory about the reproduction of kinship' (1978: 163), clearly assuming a universalist, transcultural, transhistorical application. Baudrillard's analysis, on the other hand, claims that our knowledge of symbolic exchange indicates a social order opposed to a psychical principle of prohibition; 'a symbolic process opposed to an unconscious process' (SE&D: 136).

> The symbolic is precisely this cycle of exchanges, the cycle of giving and receiving, an order born of the very reversibility which escapes the double jurisdiction, the repressed psychical agency, and the transcendent social instance.
>
> (SE&D: 136)

Processes of symbolic exchange around kinship are based on initiation as well as incest prohibition. Fathers are exchanged; given and received, passed through generations of initiates in the form of already dead and always living ancestors (a point Baudrillard contrasts to the notion of the biological father who is indeed inexchangeable with his immutable Word) (SE&D: 137).

It is not the case that women do not enter into exchanges in these cultures, and Mauss discusses some instances. Although there appear to be no reasons to accept the analysis of women's oppression developed by Rubin, there is still something important in the fact that men are not exchanged in the same way as women. It does remain to address the question why women are much more frequently those exchanged, especially in kinship structures of marriage, even though it is not credible to discuss these exchanges in cultures of symbolic exchange in terms of western, mercantile, economic transactions with all their attendant concepts. Baudrillard writes, somewhat frustratedly, of his concern at the profound confusion he observes in these 'pious discourses' that want to rescue the so-called 'sex object' and restore her to her rightful place as a subject of production (SEDN: 92). Possibly this observation points to the heart of the issue, and underlies Baudrillard's 'compliment': it opens ironically onto a systematic critique of the superimposition of the productive on the 'masculine' and the seductive on the 'feminine', an ideological process that needs to be sacrificed.

Seduction is a principle of reversion in accordance with symbolic exchange as a social process constitutive of culture. Historically, seduction has been associated with the feminine, and by extension with 'women', and production with the masculine, with men. This association, couched in terms of a strict dichotomous bifurcation, is predicated on a dichotomous construct of sexual 'difference' Man/Woman, and a dichotomous construct of production/ seduction: a structure that in actuality renders Woman and seduction untenable and contradictory, as seduction is precisely outlawed in a binary logic, as is 'Woman'. Such a dichotomous structure is historically recent, and an invention of the west. It is alien to cultures of symbolic exchange. It appears to be the case, however, that the association of seduction with the feminine has a very long history and is indeed evident in early cultures of symbolic exchange.

Rubin writes:

> [m]en and women are, of course, different. But they are not as different as day and night, earth and sky, yin and yang, life and death. In fact from the standpoint of nature, men and women are closer to each other than either is to anything else – for instance, mountains, kangaroos, or coconut palms.
>
> (Rubin 1978: 162)

Here Rubin places her analysis firmly within the rubric of the logic of 'identity/difference'. 'From the standpoint of nature'? Even within the terms of its own logic this statement is not correct: from the criteria of presence of ovaries, female *Homo sapiens* are more like female kangaroos than they are like male *Homo sapiens* (female *Homo sapiens* ≡ female *kangaroos*, modulo $\mathfrak{R}$ (ovaries)). The entire problematics surrounding the couching of notions like day and night, life and death, within a logic of 'difference' has already been rehearsed in this and previous chapters. The point I am stressing here is that within the symbolic realm of culture, the distinction between bodies of gestation and birth and those not so will arguably be of more than a little significance, considering the drama of the cycle of death, pro-creation, and birth. Furthermore, Rubin's comment is fundamentally under-mined by those tribal groups that define themselves precisely through their symbolic 'being' with a particular mountain, animal, or plant species. This is a ritual, symbolic process of exchange that does not let itself be inscribed as 'identity' or as pertaining to the 'economic'.

The reasons why the seductive, the reversible process, should become associated with the feminine are cultural, historical, and indeed intensely problematic. This association is problematic because it abstracts the process from its site of gestures and flux to invest it in a fixed form. Production and seduction become separated and ontologised into 'different sexes' (amongst other things). My reading of Baudrillard's work is that this separa-tion is a crucial problematic for feminism. For feminists, in the endeavour to reject, subvert, and go beyond the association of women, or the feminine, with seduction, with lack, with absence and powerlessness, the mistake is to reject seduction itself, to reject the principle of reversion. This rejection or eradica-tion is central to the hegemonic political economy that is a masculinist order of meaning and value. What needs to be rejected is the erasure of seduction and reversibility, and its exclusive association with the feminine. Reversion traverses all 'sexes' in their non-essentialist appearance and disappearance.

Such a conclusion does not lead to a nostalgic romanticising of cultures of symbolic exchange. On the contrary, Baudrillard is clear that a strong 'symbolic order' was that of a ferocious hierarchy (SIM: 84), and this is abundantly evident from a reading of the literature. Taking symbolic exchange as a critical point of departure for an analysis of semiology and axiology, however, has led Baudrillard to a critical understanding of the significance of seduction. My argument is that this is important for feminism. At the beginning of this discussion on Baudrillard's 'sacrifice' statement, I suggested that contemporarily, the destruction and violation of women could arguably be understood in conjunction with the eradication of 'sacrifice' and the symbolic from western, hyperreal society. If women are associated with seduction, and seduction is annihilated (along with the possibility of sacrifice to ensure reversion), then men are relentlessly consigned to 'identity' with no relief, exposed on all sides, fully positivised, a kind of pornography of masculinity that has erased its only possibility of transformation and death. This must engender its own form of madness.

6 Feminism and the Power of Dissolution

The final chapter of Baudrillard's early text, *Symbolic Exchange and Death*, has the title 'The extermination of the name of God'. In this chapter he develops a discussion of language instanced, through the poetic, not as a structural operation of representation by signs, but as a symbolic operation that effects the deconstruction of the sign and representation. This discussion extends the insights derived from consideration of Baudrillard's notion of 'seduction', and brings the examination of Baudrillard's work back to the point where I began, with the significance of the interpenetration of the logics of value (economics), representation (linguistics), and subjectivity (psychoanalysis). The final chapter of this present book will revisit this fundamental interweaving so vital to Baudrillard's work, through a brief outline of the central arguments he develops in relation to poetic language.

According to Baudrillard, today we are confronted with a form of 'cool seduction', and, possibly, with the 'revenge' of the object. The digitality of the 'norm' is replacing the Law, he claims in *Seduction*. If seduction and simulation are both implosive, what is at stake in their mutual implication? This chapter will explore the questions raised by Baudrillard's writing on 'the object', and the kind of anti-politics it anticipates.

The Enjoyment of Poetics and the Poetics of Enjoyment

> For used words are not volatilised, they accumulate like waste – a sign pollution as fantastic as, and contemporary with, industrial pollution.
>
> (SE&D: 203)

In the final chapter of *Symbolic Exchange and Death*, Baudrillard returns to an intensely focused discussion of what he deems an insight of sublime importance, attributable to Saussure, it would seem in spite of himself. Poetic language can be understood as a site of the extermination of the relentless positivity of value, and its structural predicate, the law. The poetic is a site where symbolic exchange and reversion are evident within the field of language, and as such, Baudrillard argues, it reveals the ideological reduction at the heart of semiology, or linguistics.[1] This 'fundamental discovery' is apparently to be found, according to Baudrillard, in Saussure's *Anagrams*. He acknowledges that Saussure certainly does not claim any revolutionary portent in the principle he articulates through this work; he does not draw out what Baudrillard perceives to be the radical and critical consequences of the hypothesis that emerges. But Baudrillard does find the 'incredible scope' of the proposals Saussure makes is matched by the 'passion' he devotes to establishing the principle and arguing its case. However, when Saussure does not find the 'proof' he is looking for in what he proffers as the structure of Vedic, Germanic, and Saturnine texts, he gives up on that line of inquiry, and, in Baudrillard's words, '[goes] on to the edification of linguistic science' (SE&D: 195). Baudrillard observes that it has been necessary for it to take this time, half a century of the development of linguistic science, before it has been possible really to draw out the consequences of this early work of Saussure – his abandoned hypothesis – to be able to review how it holds the potential, or 'lays the foundations', for a 'decentring of all linguistics' (SE&D: 195).

Baudrillard refers to Jean Starobinsky, *Les Mots Sous Les Mots*, published in 1971, for this discussion of Saussure. The 'law of coupling' is the first rule of the poetic identified by Saussure. It has three components, which are cited by Baudrillard as follows:

1. A vowel has no right to figure within the Saturnine unless it has its counter-vowel in some other place in the verse (to ascertain the identical vowel, without attention to quantity). The result of this is that if the verse has an even number of syllables, the vowels couple up exactly, and must always have a remainder of zero, with an even total of each type of vowel.
2. The law of consonants is identical, and no less strict: there is always an even number of any consonant whatsoever.
3. . . . if there is an irreducible remainder either of vowels (unpaired verse) or consonants, then, contrary to what we might think, this does not escape condemnation even if it is a matter of a simple 'e': we will see it reappear in the following verse, as a new remainder corresponding to the overspill from the preceding one.

(SE&D: 195–6)

The second poetic rule is that of the 'theme-word', which apparently Saussure claimed he heard on listening to one or two Latin Saturnine verses. The theme-word referred to in this context is a proper name (generally), and the poet works the phonetic components of the theme-word into the verse, so that they appear dispersed through the text in the form of an anagram. According to Starobinsky's account, as Saussure listened, the phonemes of the theme-word, the proper name, became clearer and clearer (the examples given are Scipio and Agamemnon). In Saussure's terms, these two rules can coexist.

Baudrillard is quick to observe that it is not that these two simple 'laws' point to what is at the heart of the enjoyment (jouissance) proper to the poetic, or to its aesthetics. Indeed, he claims that Saussure has only considered the poet's 'inspiration' and not the 'reader's ecstasy' (SE&D: 197). But then again, although Saussure's preoccupation is with the logic of the signifier and not, according to Baudrillard, with poetic enjoyment, Saussure does make the following statement: 'the enjoyment derived from the poetic is enjoyment in that it shatters "the fundamental laws of the human word"' (SE&D: 197). Baudrillard refers to linguists who have acknowledged that the poetic anagram is entirely at odds with Saussure's two 'fundamental laws of the human word': the codified bond between the signifier and its signified, and the linearity of signifiers (citing Roman Jakobson). The response to this potentially radical subversion of the basis of linguistics is, according to Baudrillard, to 'recuperate the poetic as a particular field of discourse' so that it remains within the domain of linguistic study. Even though the poetic might defy the laws of signification, this defiance can be neutralised by incorporating its departure into a distinct field of linguistics. Or can it? Baudrillard thinks not, and asks 'what is a signified or signifier if it is no longer governed by a code of equivalence?' and 'what is a signifier if it is no longer governed by the law of linearity?', and adds 'what is linguistics without all this?' His answer: 'Nothing' (SE&D: 197).

Against what he describes as the attempt of linguists to 'annex the poetic to itself' with a complex series of manoeuvres that even serve to entrench further the field of poetics as an economy of term (signifier) and value (signified), Baudrillard mounts a contrary argument that poetics is 'a process of the *extermination of value*' (SE&D: 198). As such it belies the ideological move to construct it within the economic rubric of the linguistic law. A rigorous procedure of the poetry described and analysed by Saussure ensures that *'nothing remains of it'* (SE&D: 198). Linguistics, on the other hand, assumes that language functions in accordance with the economic law of production, accumulation, and distribution of language as value. The poetic, however, 'is irreducible to the mode of signification, which is nothing other than the mode of production of the values of language' (SE&D: 198). In other words, linguistics, as the science of this mode of production, cannot reduce the poetic to its own terms (although it assumes to do so). The repetitious duplication of vowels according to Saussure's law of coupling cannot be understood as an accumulation in the additive sense, but rather, according to Baudrillard, it has to be understood as *'the cyclical cancellation of terms, two by two, the extermination of doubling by the cycle'*. He cites Saussure (as cited in Starobinsky) making this very point: '[v]owels always couple up exactly, and must always give a remainder of zero' (SE&D: 199).

The anagrammatic dispersion of the name through the poetic text too can be analysed in terms of a process of reversion and annulment, rather than a solely productive accumulation of meaning or identity as value through signification. Baudrillard describes the theme-word as being 'diffracted' through the text. He uses an analogy from physics, suggesting that the word is 'analysed' by the verse: 'reduced to its single elements, decomposed like the light spectrum, whose diffracted rays then sweep across the text' (SE&D: 199). Baudrillard argues that the dispersion of the theme-word, like the coupling of vowels, accomplishes a reversion and extermination of value rather than an accumulative rendition of the Same. The theme-word is not reiterated, but is dis-integrated and scattered – annihilated, put to death rather than reinforced in its signification. The extermination of the name of God will lead to the 'end of the world'.[2] Baudrillard is in disagreement with the commentary on the significance of the *Anagrams* by Starobinsky, who reads into the process a reassembling of the component phonemes; a reuniting of the dismembered body. Moving to comment on Lacan's theory of symbolism in this context, Baudrillard also considers him 'wrong' in conveying the symbolic act as one of 'return', or a reconstitution of wholeness and identity after alienation. The symbolic act, Baudrillard insists against both Starobinsky and Lacan, inheres in 'the volatilisation of the name, the signifier, in the extermination of the term, disappearance with no return' (SE&D: 200).

Baudrillard points, of course, to the impossibility of the limits Saussure imposes on his own analysis; the form Saussure identifies, this poetic principle common to both 'laws', is not confined only to Vedic, Germanic, or Latin verse. It is Baudrillard's contention that seeking 'proof' to provide the basis for a 'hypothetical generalisation' is to miss the point. Today, he is quick to state, poets do not use the theme-word, for example, and he wonders if the ancients ever did. In other words, it is not a matter of finding 'proof' of specific usages of this form, but rather identifying what the 'form' itself is all about, and then recognising that the form of reversion Saussure distinguished traverses all languages. Baudrillard's consideration of that aspect of the poetic he claims Saussure overlooked, the 'reader's ecstasy' or the 'enjoyment' of reading, or hearing, the poetic, leads Baudrillard to argue that this enjoyment can only be understood in terms of this process of reversion and annulment, the extermination of terms.[3] As such, enjoyment bears witness to the sovereignty of this form of reversion within language. 'A good poem is one where nothing is left over, where all the phonemic material in use is consumed' (SE&D: 200), and correspondingly, bad poetry (or not poetry) is recognised as such when there is indeed a remainder, a surplus of signifying value that has not been consumed, re-versed, exchanged within the verse.

'The Festival of Reversible Speech'

> Only subjects dispossessed of their identity, like words, are devoted to social reciprocity in laughter and enjoyment.
>
> (SE&D: 233)

The enjoyment of the exchange within the poetic, where every phoneme, diphoneme, syllable, or term has been 'seized by its double', is contrasted by Baudrillard with the economic logic of a process of signification where value is precisely that which is assigned to the residue, the surplus. It is possible to see here how the logic of the economic is duplicated within the logic of the sign. The 'festival of reversible speech' evident in the poetic can be understood as a parallel to the exhaustion of economic value in the circulation of gifts. Where the surplus is accumulated, 'the birth of the economic begins' along with the split of signifier and signified, the instantiation of the code of equivalence, and an inexorable logic of the growth and expansion (productivity) of discourse.

Baudrillard adds a third dimension to the two 'fundamental laws of language' identified by Saussure to be 'shattered' by the poetic form: in addition to the equivalence of signifier and signified, and the linearity of the signifier, Baudrillard adds 'that of the *boundlessness, the limitless production of signifying material*' (SE&D: 201). He is referring here to the absolute nature of the assumption of a limitless expansion of signifying value that parallels the logic of growth, or increase, of economic value. The ideology of the latter is made possible through the notion of equivalence. The resulting 'freedom of discourse' is analysed by Baudrillard as a kind of stockpiling of residual significatory value that has not been reversed, exchanged, annulled; a form of pollution that he likens to that produced through the accumulation of capital (in fact, as mentioned in Chapter 1, he claims that industrial leftovers are nothing by comparison with the remains of language). Within this economic framing, language is viewed as an inexhaustible resource of signifying material freely available to all individuals, subjects, to 'express' whatever they want: 'to each according to his or her needs'. This exponential growth in the production of discourse is even more evident now than it must have appeared to Baudrillard writing *Symbolic Exchange and Death* in the first half of the 1970s, prior to the Internet, etc.; released from the constraints of print and face-to-face contact, will we drown in residual signification before the depleted ozone layer, global warming, and other environmental disasters resulting from industrialisation commit us to the illusory 'end'? Baudrillard's argument is that the productive logic of growth and accumulation is the point of commonality, whether it is evident in relation to discourse, demographics, or material goods. Equally, the infinite horizon of this proliferation is contrasted to the finite sphere circumscribed within the symbolic exchange, which, like that of the Rule, 'recovers a reversible space' (SEDN: 134).

The possibilities of this symbolic model of exchange are literally 'revolutionary' in Baudrillard's assessment, as subject and object eliminate one another through their exchange, their challenge and seduction. This contrasts with an order where such exchange is replaced by its impossibility, where individuals 'pass in transit as values through the models that engender or reproduce them in total "estrangement" to each other' (SE&D: 205), holding tight to their identities, mediated by a code of equivalence.

For the secret of a social parole, of a revolution, is also the anagrammatic dispersal of the instance of power, the rigorous volatilisation of every transcendent social instance. The fragmented body of power is then exchanged as social parole in the poetry of rebellion. Nothing remains of this parole, nor is any of it accumulated anywhere. Power is reborn from what is not consumed in it, for power is the residue of parole. In social rebellion the same anagrammatical dispersal is at work as that of the body in eroticism, as that of knowledge and its object in the analytic operation: the revolution is symbolic or it is not a revolution at all.

(SE&D: 205)

Against this revolutionary perspective, Baudrillard refers to the claim of linguists such as Jakobson regarding the radical importance of the ambiguity of the signified. Such a claim, while appearing to undermine the structuralist assumption of equivalence of signifier and signified, in Baudrillard's view does nothing, or very little, to the code of equivalence. The code stays firmly in place, the principle of identity is retained along with that of meaning and value. As Baudrillard points out, it only introduces 'floating values', renders identities 'diffuse', and makes the process of reference more complex, but changes very little, and certainly abolishes nothing (SE&D: 216). Baudrillard's critique of the import of the ambiguity Jakobson claims is distinctive to poetry could also be extended to the poststructuralist rhetoric of deferred meanings; although 'subjects become unsettled *in their subject-positions*', the positivity of discourse remains, as does the sign as value. Whether reference is made to 'polysemia', 'polyvalence', 'polyphony' of meaning, it does not change this fundamental observation of Baudrillard's: 'it is always a matter of the radiation of the signified', of a plurality of possible positively cast values.

Julia Kristeva's 'Poésie et négativité', in her 1969 book *Séméiotikè*, is the text that, when Baudrillard wrote *Symbolic Exchange and Death*, he found came closest to engaging a notion of the poetic which acknowledged the radicality he was himself proposing, building on the early Saussure. He cites her at length. To reiterate:

In this other space, where logical laws of speech have been weakened, the subject dissolves and, in place of the sign, the clash of signifiers eliminating each other is instituted. An operation of generalised negativity, which has nothing to do with the constitutive negativity of the judgement (Aufhebung), nor with the negativity internal to the judgement (binary logic: 0–1), an annihilating negativity (Sunyavada Buddhism). A zerological subject, a non-subject who comes to assume the thought that cancels itself.

(Kristeva, 'Poésie et négativité', p. 212 in *Séméiotikè*, 1969, cited in SE&D: 236)

In Baudrillard's terms Kristeva 'comes close', but in what appears to be a departure from the analysis cited above, her theorisation moves to 'fill' this 'other space' with positive substitutes (metaphor, metonymy), and to understand the 'relation' of Non-Being and Being in terms of a dialectic. Metaphor comes to have a positive value, a value that moves from one field to another to the point of the 'absorption of a multiplicity of texts (meanings) in the message' (Kristeva, p. 194, cited in SE&D: 220). Instead of the annulment and extermination of value (the non-valence of ambivalence), Kristeva transforms the movement of negativity into a harmonious combinatory of a plurality of values. This theory of intertextuality and Kristeva's semiotic project is, Baudrillard laments, another, even more subtle way of 'neutralising' the radical import of the poetic form. Kristeva too 'saves' the hegemony of linguistics 'under the cover of the ideology of "plurality"' (SE&D: 221). With the work of Kristeva as with Saussure, Marx, and Freud, the bar of linguistics (the bar of equivalence) and the bar of psychoanalysis (the bar of repression) remain. Baudrillard discusses this observation through a comparison of his notion of enjoyment in the reversion of the poetic with Freud's analysis of 'pleasure' in the joke.

The intensity of the poetic is precisely about the destruction of identity and not its repetition. In fact, Baudrillard speculates that 'enjoyment is a direct function of the resolution of every positive reference' (SE&D: 208), and develops a discussion on the enjoyment of the joke, *Witz*, or *mot d'esprit*, in Freud, building on the same line of argument (discussed briefly below).

Psychoanalysis and the 'Economy' of 'Pleasure'

In his exploration of the affinity or otherwise between the poetic and psychoanalysis, Baudrillard concludes that they are in fact widely divergent. Where the poetic marks a commonality with the reversibility of symbolic exchange and seduction, psychoanalytic discourse is complicit with the economic and the productive, even though its appearance is to contest the assumptions of presence and equivalence. In this discussion Baudrillard focuses particularly on the so-called 'primary processes' in psychoanalytic theory, those of displacement and condensation as these are evident in Freud's work on the joke, or *mot d'esprit*. He claims that Freud's theory of enjoyment, pleasure, or jouissance gives it a 'functional' quality, employing economic concepts to explain pleasure from the signifier in terms of the fulfilment of a desire. The joke has the effect of 'liberating' significations through taking a kind of 'short cut' to convey meaning. Baudrillard claims that in Freud's terms, it is always this 'ellipsis of psychical distance' that brings the enjoyment, as it 'liberates' energies, or affects that would not otherwise be 'unbound'. So there is a disinvestment of repressed energies, released unexpectedly through this short-circuit of the joke; 'enjoyment emerges from a residue, an excess or a differential quantum of energy made available by the operation of the *Witz*' (SE&D: 223).

This concept of a production or release of energies is portrayed and developed by Freud through metaphors that Baudrillard renders as fundamentally economic. The joke functions to produce enjoyment through its 'energy saving', calculated in terms of investments and the achievement of an 'energetic surplus value' (SE&D: 224). The unconscious contents of affects and representations of a libidinal economy are *produced* through repression. The resulting tensions incline towards equilibrium through the binding and releasing of energies. In the case of the joke, it is not the play of signifiers that pleases, but the movement of repressed energies, the satisfaction of a capital gain. Desire, in psychoanalytic theory, is predicated on the existence of a physiological need; without such a need, desire cannot invest libidinally in the body. The function of the organic, physiological level of need is diverted towards the fulfilment of desire, but as Baudrillard points out, the 'articulation' of the need and the desire remains unexplained, and any concept that is brought in to accomplish this task will simply provide a bridge between them, but not achieve anything more than this. The very division of the primary and secondary process and its attendant assumptions creates the problem, not the necessity to explain their 'relation'.

Baudrillard's point in relation to psychoanalysis in this context is to signal the illusory nature of its apparent subversion of the assumptions of linguistic equivalence, because psychoanalysis merely presents the flip-side of the coin, remaining firmly lodged within the economic paradigm. The psychoanalytic signifier manifests the absence of the signified, instead of its presence; Baudrillard places the emphasis on the manifestation, inevitably productive. Signifying the lost object in all its negativity, forever absent and repressed, is still signifying something. The bar establishing the signifier/signified remains, it is just that it is a bar of repression rather than a bar of equivalence; the signifier signifies in relation to the unconscious, even though the mobile and unidentifiable contents of the unconscious (signified) remain unrepresentable. Baudrillard argues, therefore, that although according to psychoanalysis the Sr/Sd relation is certainly entirely different from that of equivalence, it is not outside the paradigm of value. Referring to the psychoanalytic signifier: '[f]or all its "hesitation"[4] [*trébuchement*], it always designates what it represents as *value* in absentia, under the sign of repression. Value is no longer logically conveyed by the signifier, it haunts it phantasmatically' (SE&D: 227). The continued instantiation of the bar literally bars ambivalence. In other words there can be no dissolution of value where the bar splits the signifier and signified, and hence psychoanalysis is radically different from the poetic, where value is precisely volatilised.

A psychoanalytic 'reading' will lend itself, therefore, to the articulation or manifestation of the hidden meaning, silenced through each utterance. The assertion of meaning also has the function of silencing, within this framework, of repressing an unsaid, establishing a disjuncture between what is said and what is meant. It is always death, nothing, absence that is repressed and silenced. Baudrillard insists, by contrast, that nothing is silenced within the poetic form. In fact, death is symbolised and actively engaged within the poetic, rather than barred and manifested as a phantasmatic haunting of that which excludes it. The reversion and sacrifice of all residue cancel the economic, which is predicated on 'the remainder'; no bar of equivalence, and thus no signified behind the signifier, no bar of repression, and thus no repressed 'beneath' a repressing, latent beneath a manifest, primary behind a secondary process.

> Market value, signified value and unconscious/repressed value are all pro-
> duced from what remains, from the residual precipitate of the symbolic
> operation. It is always this remainder that is accumulated and fuels the
> diverse economies that govern our lives.
>
> (SE&D: 229)

Baudrillard concludes *Symbolic Exchange and Death* with a brief review of the implications his discussion on poetics has for materialist as opposed to idealist theories of language. Materialist critiques of idealism have postulated that the material existence of the world is not contingent on our ideas about it, whereas idealism postulates that the world is the effect of our ideas about it. Employing materialist assumptions, while also developing a critique of the notion that language takes its meaning from the structure of language and not from an extradiscursive reality, has led some to conclude that language, words, discourse have a materiality themselves – that words are things. The psychoanalytic interpretation of the *Witz*, of neuroses, of the dream posits just this, Baudrillard argues, and the signifier is the 'material' put to work by the primary processes. He comments critically on the assumed radicality associated with the questionable insight that 'words are things', materialised as well as materialising, arguing that, on the contrary, it simply represents an inverse or 'overturning' of idealism. Idealism's repressed and phantasmatic 'matter' is recast into a positivity of the material real. But Baudrillard's argument is that it is actually idealism that has posited the irreducible substance of the real, forged in the negative, for materialism to 'liberate'. Either way, signification marks the site of the Real as a positive reference, demarcated through a productive logic, where things/word-things are made to appear. Neither idealism nor materialism tolerates a void. The poetic, by contrast, vaporises language as a thing and as discourse; a kind of anti-matter.[5] 'The symbolic is already beyond the psychoanalytic unconscious, beyond libidinal economy, just as it is beyond value and political economy' (SE&D: 237).

Cool Seduction in a Digital World of Subjects without Objects

Where seduction, reversion, and the symbolic are best understood in terms of the order of the Rule, and psychoanalysis, signification, desire, production, and value of the order of the Law, Baudrillard argues that today we have moved into an era of norms and models, which cannot be understood in terms of the Law. The age of the Law has passed (SEDN: 155). If an era of symbolic exchange, regulated through rules and ritual exchange, was succeeded by an era of the Law, regulated through laws, contracts, and economic exchange, we are now in an era of the 'digital relation', regulated through signals and networked connectivity. A dual relation (duel, obligatory, agonistic) shifted to a polar relation (social, contradictory, antagonistic, dialectic) shifted to a digital relation, which is the relational residue left over when, through a radical dispersal of all relationality, the order of the law implodes into its own simulation. In other words, there is no relationality at all, just 'an endless play of models with their ever-changing combinations' (SEDN: 157).

> Everyone is moving in their own orbit, trapped in their own bubble, like satellites. Strictly speaking, no one has a destiny any more, since there is destiny only where one intersects with others. Now the trajectories do not intersect . . . They merely have the same destination.
>
> (PC: 143)

To draw out the distinctions between these eras, Baudrillard characterises the order of the Rule as one of 'tragic immanence': the duel encounter of challenge and counter-challenge where the delineation of stakes is immanent to the obligatory system of the Rule. The Law, on the other hand, is predicated on the transcendence of the system, its antagonistic stakes, and the transgression of the law. The order of the digital is one of 'cool immanence' of norms and models where all stakes have disappeared, poles are neutralised; no transcendence or transgression. This typology leads Baudrillard to suggest we are living through a kind of 'cool' or 'soft' seduction – 'the seduction of an "ambience," or the playful eroticization of a universe without stakes' (SEDN: 156).

Baudrillard describes this 'cool' or 'cold' seduction as 'ludic',[6] with its connotation of play; playing with networks and the combinatory possibilities of models within models. The actor is caught and suspended in this cybernetic play with a kind of fascinated absorption rather than cathected through a libidinal investment (temperature rising). This is a form of 'play' that is less about 'fun', and certainly not about the game in accordance with the Rule, but rather is about a pleasure derived from discovering the optimal functioning of a set of possibilities; the 'play' is in the choosing, deciding, moving, observing. It is the jouissance of the instrument panel. In this sense, Baudrillard claims that the 'ludic' is increasingly to be found everywhere, whether it is a matter of choosing a brand of laundry detergent, 'playing' computer games, or manipulating gene codes. The entire universe becomes 'combinatory, aleatory, ludic', with the genetic code serving as a '"biological" prototype' (SEDN: 159).

The cool seduction of the ubiquitous 'tele': everything can happen at a distance through digital compression and signal transmission. As Baudrillard suggests, communication systems circulating networked speech ensure that what we have to say no longer means anything: '[o]ne says that one is speaking, but by speaking one is only verifying the network and the fact that one is linked up with it' (SEDN: 164–5). Baudrillard attributes the characteristic of networked speech that reduces the possibility of 'meaning' to its binary scansion of 1/0. Unlike the meaning understood to emanate from a polarity of terms within discourse (Baudrillard refers in this context to Jakobson), digital constructs no longer present distinctive oppositions or differences. The 'bit' as 'the smallest unit of electronic impulse' cannot be understood in terms of a unit of meaning, but is rather 'an identificatory impulse' (SEDN: 165), registering either presence or absence, each a positive signal in itself.

Cool seduction is on a course of auto-, self-seduction where everyone becomes eroticised through his of her own self-monitoring and management; be your own terminal, sublime independence forever networkable and reproducible, '[a] digital Narcissus instead of a triangular Oedipus' (SEDN: 173), transparency of self to self as all information is fed back electronically. The metastatic expansion of these individual units that never intersect, Baudrillard claims, is most clearly modelled in the clone. Cloning is not even a self-engendering, but a kind of 'bud' from a segment, like taking cuttings. Baudrillard's argument that this process is metastatic rests on his observation of the similarities of the logic of cancer and the cloning of individuals, in that the code residing in the single cell provides the information for its proliferation; a proliferation that contains no endogenous mechanism to reverse the process. Self-seduction in the sense of becoming one's other, materialised through the clone: 'love your neighbour as yourself' – you are your neighbour, as Baudrillard writes, total love, total self-seduction (SEDN: 173). This 'cool seduction' is not reversible, but rather a strategy of producing subjects of desire who can then be entirely caught up in the project of fulfilling these desires: the simulation of seduction. Baudrillard reflects on this as a corrupted form of seduction, 'the seduction that remains when all the stakes have been withdrawn' (SEDN: 175), being nothing more than the 'social and technical lubrication required' for the smooth functioning of simulated 'relations' (SEDN: 174).

> No more other: communication.
> No more enemy: negotiation.
> No more predators: conviviality.
> No more negativity: absolute positivity.
> No more death: the immortality of the clone.
> No more otherness: identity and difference.
> No more seduction: sexual in-difference.
> No more illusion: hyperreality, Virtual Reality.
> No more secret: transparency.

No more destiny.
The Perfect Crime.

(PC: 109–10)

The entire deontology of western culture has involved the impulse to remove the negative, the evil, the destructive, and by extension expose the hidden, reveal the truth. This of course is predicated on the spurious assumption of the dichotomous separation of good and evil. Much of Baudrillard's work emphasises how this very ethos has produced the dominant and ubiquitous logics that are increasingly encircling the globe. In *The Perfect Crime*, he writes:

> [t]he best strategy for bringing about someone's ruin is to eliminate everything which threatens him [*sic*], thus causing him to lose all his defences, and it is this strategy we are applying to ourselves. By eliminating the other in all its forms (illness, death, negativity, violence, strangeness), not to mention racial and linguistic differences, by eliminating all singularities in order to radiate total positivity, we are eliminating ourselves.

(PC: 113)

Baudrillard refers in a number of his books to this resulting proliferation of the subject without object, self without other, a paradigm possibly best encapsulated in his description of the 'bubble child', kept sealed from any contaminants, who would die if encountering anything other than its 'self'.

In fact, this insistence on subjectivity, this obsessive preoccupation with self, Baudrillard argues, has meant the growth of a simultaneous indifference to everything else. Self becomes the object of our care, our desire, our suffering. We are 'doomed to our own image, our own identity' (PC: 131). What matter these 'other' selves who can all look after themselves, cast permanently in some parallel universe. Baudrillard suggests that this indifference actually generates a form of despair, which in turn animates an envious form of hatred when confronted with anything that exposes one's own indifference.

Faced with this hatred, the simulation of otherness becomes a necessity. Baudrillard claims that we are seeing a 'new victim order', as the other in the form of those/he/she suffering calamity of some sort is the 'easiest' to resurrect. It is difficult to argue with Baudrillard's assertion that the new identity is the 'victim's identity'. Not *as* victim, of course, but as he or she who has something to struggle for, some right to assert, some victory to achieve, some 'other' (male, coloniser, heterosexual, able-bodied, etc.) against which the identity is meaningful. Who on earth are you if you are not 'different' in some way? Baudrillard refers to Foucault and his argument that the confession of sex was definitional of a whole culture for a period. He claims that this has flipped into a 'confession of wretchedness' (PC: 138). All of the negativities that have defaced entire groups of people can now be 'laundered' and recast in the respectful positive as subjects, citizens of hyperreality. And once we are all included . . . ? It is the impossibility of this prospect that haunts this seemingly singular source of hope for politics of the so-called left as much as the so-called right.

Shadowing the Object

Baudrillard notes that 'yesterday' it was considered (by those of leftist, critical persuasion) that to divert subjects from their 'truth' was to divert them from the revolutionary truth of history, whereas today it is to divert them from the truth of their desires (SEDN: 175). In a philosophy of desire, the subject (who desires), no matter how 'de-centred', fluid, multiple, is privileged absolutely. The fate of the object is at best secondary. Baudrillard's contention is that this privilege has just about run its course. Viewed from the reversion of seduction, the object seduces and holds a power of dissolution of the fragile desiring subject. The object does not believe in its own desire; this is its secret. It does not live the weighty seriousness of the illusion of its desire as does the subject, which is infinitely vulnerable to its own needs being met, desires being fulfilled, autonomous identity being recognised and given due consideration. The object knows nothing of this. It is inalienable. Undivided, it has no 'meaning' or substance of its own. Baudrillard asserts, in *Fatal Strategies*, that the 'arrogant glory' of the subject is finished. It is unquestionably in for a hard time. Its secret is its knowledge and fear of its own fragility.

> We arrive then at this paradox, at this conjuncture where the position of the subject has become untenable, and where the only possible position is that of the object. The only strategy possible is that of the object. We should understand, by this, not the 'alienated' object in the process of de-alienation, the enslaved object claiming its autonomy as a subject, but the object such as it challenges the subject, and pushes it back upon its own impossible position.
>
> (FS: 113)

Baudrillard comments that the object 'knows nothing of the mirror phase'; it *is* the mirror, and 'the crystal takes revenge' (FS: 114) by catching the subject in its own trap, returning it to its inevitable transparency. Maybe then the subject is simply nothing but a reflecting mirror (EC: 93)?

> The object is what has disappeared on the horizon of the subject, and it is from the depths of this disappearance that it envelopes the subject in its fatal strategy. It is the subject that then disappears from the horizon of the object.
>
> (FS: 114)

Here Baudrillard confronts the objectification and reification intrinsic to the whole fabric of western life. There has been a considerable amount of work since Marx, both empirical and theoretical, developing critiques of reification as abstraction of the construction of 'the object' relative to the positioning of the 'subject'. These critiques, however, have tended to remain caught uncritically within the perspective of the economic. Baudrillard is possibly unique in analysing the implications of an extreme reification in the contemporary west whereby a 'cool seduction' effects the vanishing of the subject, where simulated desire precludes the encounter with an other; the subject as self-same has no alternative but to desire objects and to become 'its' own object of desire.

Baudrillard talked to Guy Bellavance about the difference between his use of the terms 'fatality' and 'banality' in relation to strategy, in an interview on his book *Fatal Strategies*, in 1983 (Gane 1993: 50). The fatality of the strategy refers to the inevitability of its course, and this inevitability can only be sought in the specifics of the context; obviously it has no universal application. Baudrillard comments that the strategy as a fatal strategy is always ironical: there is no subject 'behind it', so it cannot be tragic, sentimental, Romanesque. The banality of a strategy resides in its complicity with its own simulated form. For example, the response of the 'mass' (with all the provisos attached to this term, rehearsed in Chapter 3) to mediatised information about their 'opinions', surveyed and fed back to them, is to 'enjoy' seeing the fluctuations of polls, neutralising any attempt to produce 'meaning' or any attempt to render them a serious and responsible 'public' (see SSM: 17–18). Baudrillard notes elsewhere (*The Ecstasy of Communication*) that his use of the term 'fatal' is not intended as 'fatalistic' in the sense of 'apocalyptic', but rather he uses it to imply a 'metamorphosis of effects' through reversion (EC: 87). Quite simply, 'everything is metamorphosis' (EC: 91).

The subtitle of *Fatal Strategies* is *The Crystal Takes Revenge*. In the interview with Bellavance, Baudrillard is clear that the 'crystal' is the object: 'the pure object, the pure event, something which no longer really has an origin or end' (Gane 1993: 51). The 'object' that the subject has resolved to resurrect with an origin and a purpose is taking another tack. Baudrillard calls it 'revenge' to evoke something of the reversion in train; the fatality of the reversion and seduction of the subject and all the finalities on which it depends. He writes of how '[t]he Object and the world let themselves be surprised for a moment (a brief moment in the general cosmology) by the subject and science, but today they are violently reasserting themselves and taking revenge (like the crystal!)' (EC: 87). A passion of the object? Insofar as there is a passion in irony, indifference, ruse, yes indeed. A destiny of the object? Baudrillard proposes the order of destiny where there is no desire. Desire is of the order of the subject, of the interplay between determinacy, probability and chance. Destiny is of the order of seduction where events are played out in an infinitely open space where, not determined/caused, probable, or random, they are contingent on the symbolic encounters that precede and prefigure them; symbolic encounters that are seductive, understood in terms of the immanence of the Rule and not the reductive transcendence of the Law.

> For months I followed strangers on the street. For the pleasure of following them, not because they particularly interested me. I photographed them without their knowledge, took note of their movements, then finally lost sight of them and forgot them. At the end of January 1980, on the streets of Paris, I followed a man whom I lost sight of a few minutes later in the crowd. That very evening, quite by chance, he was introduced to me at an opening. During the course of our conversation he told me he was planning an imminent trip to Venice.
>
> Sophie Calle (SV: 2)

> To follow the other is to take charge of his itinerary; it is to watch over his life without him knowing it. It is to play the mythical role of the shadow, which, traditionally, follows you and protects you from the sun – the man without a shadow is exposed to the violence of life without mediation – it is to relieve him of that existential burden, the responsibility for his own life. Simultaneously, she who follows is herself relieved of responsibility for her own life as she follows blindly in the footsteps of the other. Again, a wonderful reciprocity exists in the cancellation of each existence, in the cancellation of each subject's tenuous position as a subject. Following the other, one replaces him, exchanges lives, passions, wills, transforms oneself in the other's stead.
>
> Jean Baudrillard (SV: 82)

Shadowing is a fatal, seductive strategy of the object (that is, both of the object shadowing and of the object shadowed).

> I walk the streets randomly. In the course of our conversation about Venice, Henri B. had alluded to a pensione: the San Bernadino. On the list of hotels that I obtained en route, I don't find a San Bernadino. That doesn't surprise me. There is a San Giorgio, a San Stefano. I arrive at Piazza San Marco and sit against a column. I watch. I see myself at the labyrinth's gate, ready to get lost in the city and in this story. Submissive.
>
> (SV: 6)

> I continue my search for Henri B. on the streets. I wonder if he's rich. I go into the luxury hotels. 'Do you have a guest named Henri B.?' At the Savoïa, the Cavaletto, the Londra, the Danieli, the San Marco, the answer is no. I know so little about him, except that he had rain and

fog the first days, that he now has sun, that he is never where I search. He is consuming me.

(SV: 10)

The 'cancellation' Baudrillard refers to is an intrinsic feature of the following Sophie Calle enacts: she has no desire, no will, no 'outcome' at stake in her quest and yet she fulfils it with a passionate intensity. It matters, but for no purpose. After dedicated inquiries and searching, she now knows his hotel.

> If Henri B. leaves the pensione when the street is empty, he won't escape me. But if he goes out at a crowded moment, I run the risk of missing him. One of two things may happen: Either he turns left to continue on foot or he goes right to board the boat. Given these alternatives, the only solution is to survey the street ceaselessly, without relaxing my attention. If he should see me . . .

(SV: 18)

The secret is imperative. And yet, once Henri B. is 'found' and followed, the possibility of the following being reversed is always present, in fact is integral to the seductive nature of the scene. It is the Rule of the game: the vertigo of anticipation of that moment.

> He's there, motionless, staring fixedly at the water. He's slung his camera back over his shoulder. He leans with his elbows upon the bridge wall, daydreaming. I'm afraid he'll turn abruptly and see me crouching in the garbage. I decide to pass silently behind him and wait a little farther along. Quickly with head lowered, I cross the bridge. Henri B. doesn't move. I could touch him.

(SV: 44)

> As soon as I'm outside, I see him, sitting at the landing of the Ponte Cavello, some ten meters to my right. He's looking at me. Concealing my emotions, I determinedly cross the piazza, circle around the monument, and pretend to study it. I feel his eyes on me. I walk along the hospital's right wing. There's an alcove. Finally I'll be out of his sight. I've got to get a hold of myself. I lean against a column and close my eyes.

(SV: 48)

The illusory subjectivity, will, desire of Henri B. is annulled in the act of being followed. The unknown shadowing is continually reversing the assumption of subjectivity. Following a subject who takes responsibility for fulfilling the demands of personal history and continuity of individual experience, who carries the 'burden' of existence, the very act of tracing her/his steps simultaneously reveals the absence of any essence deemed necessary for such continuity and erases its pretence. It is a truly fatal strategy, seduction in the act of creating absences through a secret presence. '11.30 A.M. I give him one last chance: I count to one hundred, he doesn't appear, I leave' (SV: 60). The act of photographing (appearance and disappearance), the structure of Venice with its narrow canals and alleyways, work to make the vanishing point more vivid. She, through following, and observing, photographing unseen, takes his path, his past, and as they enter her consciousness, they vanish elsewhere. Their vanishing is made perfect. No trace is to be seen in their reappearance.

Dissolution of Power and Meaning in the Illusion of the Real

Feminist theory, discourse, action is infinitely diverse, traversed as it is by a multiplicity of positions and trajectories within constructs and experiences of identifications with numerous sources of 'difference', generally figured in terms of 'politics' in some form. The examples of contemporary western feminist theories of gender, or sexual difference, I have considered in relation to the challenges raised by Baudrillard have shown a tendency for these theories to pivot on combinations of concerns including the importance of the 'female subject', 'women's identity', 'women's desire/feminine desire', the 'nomadic subject', the multiplicities of 'desiring subjects', the notion of gender as 'performative', the intersection (and inextricability) of 'gender' with 'other' sources of 'difference' (race, culture, class, sexuality, and so on). Where there is a concern to subvert identity, all the tropes of the productive, of positivity in Baudrillard's terms, remain firmly in place: 'power' understood as 'productive'; the 'real' is produced and these productions are contested and resignified, re-produced; identity as self-same reappears in the guise of plurality, becoming, multiple subjects with no objects, nomadic and fluid.

These concerns and foci of analysis and deconstruction are undeniably driven by an assumption of the inevitability of the economic (needs, production, value), the inevitability of the law (the bar that structures identity/ difference, subject/object), even taking into account the attempts at deconstruction and rewriting from a position of a different 'difference', and of the inevitability of power. There is no seduction here. These theories unilaterally fail to engage the historically and culturally specific interweaving of the construct of the economic and the structure of representation which, in Baudrillard's analysis, figures our ontological assumptions.

Donna Haraway is a feminist theorist who departs from the constraints of some of the epistemological and ontological presuppositions critiqued by Baudrillard. Her 'Manifesto for cyborgs' (in Haraway 1991) shows a determination, like Baudrillard's, to develop an analysis that is grounded culturally and historically. There are evident in Haraway's work none of the universal questions or constructs that tend to creep into the works of those other feminist theorists discussed, in spite of their claims to support what Haraway has called 'situated knowledges'. Nevertheless, Vicki Kirby (1997) takes Haraway to task for instituting the 'specific' as the binary opposite of the 'universal', a move Kirby questions as one potentially reinstalling 'the *cogito* as the subject who only speaks for him or herself' (1997: 161). Kirby's interest in an ontology and epistemology that deconstruct this binary and rethink the question of 'position' in relation to the speaking subject is important.

Haraway (1991) proposes the figure of the irreverent cyborg, a 'creature in a post-gender world', with whom she tracks a critical understanding of key facets structuring a world that is also postmodern. The breaching of the boundaries constructing the human is central to her inquiry. But these are boundaries that are still 'transgressed' (in accordance with the law). Haraway is concerned at what she views as the need to 'resist world-wide intensification of domination that has never been so acute' (1991: 154). This domination functions according to dynamics that are different from those confronted by a socialist feminism of an earlier era; the question of 'political struggle' remains, however, itself unquestioned by Haraway. A reading of Baudrillard throws the whole notion of the 'political', contemporarily, into question.

Haraway's cyborg manifesto recognises both the dangers (the grid of control) and the possibilities (ways out of the 'maze of dualisms') of the 'New World Order'. Haraway develops a critical theorising on the situated decline in influence and potency of myths of origin (post-gender, a world without gender, without genesis, without end), of totalising epistemologies, of politics defined through immobile identities, of discourses both of unity and of contradiction. She proposes a schema of categories to distinguish the transition from what she describes as 'the comfortable old hierarchical dominations' to the 'scary new networks' which she calls 'the informatics of domination' (1991: 161). This chart of dual categories reflects, in idealised form, a listing characterising what we have moved from (on the left side) and what we have moved to (on the right). Haraway has no reference to Baudrillard in this work apart from the sole point of a definition of 'simulacra', yet her portrayal of contemporary social dynamics, and more specifically her chart, have significant resonances with Baudrillard's analyses of hyperreality and simulation. Indeed, at the top of Haraway's list is 'representation' replaced by 'simulation', although the shift remains untheorised. The informatics of domination marks a world where:

> communications sciences and modern biologies are constructed by a common move – the translation of the world into a problem of coding, a search for a common language in which all resistance to instrumental control disappears and all heterogeneity can be submitted to disassembly, reassembly, investment, and exchange.
>
> (Haraway 1991: 164)

Baudrillard's work develops a critical theorising of precisely this phenomenon; a theorising that leads to a more cautious reflection on the possibilities for 'political struggle', and possibly a more nuanced questioning of the implications of a post-gender world. It is noteworthy that Haraway's chart does not include the 'political' on the left side, against which we might suggest 'cool, ludic seduction' on the right, as a simulated politics endlessly recast as yet another market niche. On the contrary, the 'political' appears in Haraway's essay to assume a meta-position straddling both 'eras' (power as a universally applicable and non-situated concept?). How does the question of political 'representation' transpire if representation itself has imploded into simulation?

Haraway's 'Manifesto for cyborgs' is followed by her more recent work, *Modest_Witness@Second_Millennium. FemaleMan©_Meets_Oncomouse™* (1997). To take one tiny example of a point of connection with Baudrillard's work, the 'time-space regime' inhabited by her cyborg figures is marked, amongst other things, by a 'temporal modality' of 'implosion' (1997: 12). Given the extent to which the movement of implosion is so central to Baudrillard's theorising of contemporary shifts in signification and value, the fact that Baudrillard, writing prior to Haraway, is not referred to once in this lengthy and important work is, again, noteworthy. A part of the project of the present book is to suggest that Baudrillard's work has important points of inter-connection with feminist critique, and indeed serves to extend debates on the nature of our contemporary world and how we might, as feminists, formu-late and engage with the problems we find here. Haraway's identification of the site of technologies as crucial to exploring possibilities of undermining the 'grid of control' is commensurate with aspects of Baudrillard's thinking. On the basis of his theorising, he is less optimistic, however, and certainly does not write in terms of a manifesto, thus manifesting his concern to critique some of the anchoring points of the kind Haraway employs to ground a 'politics'.

Kirby (1997) criticises Haraway for embracing a vision of the cyborg as one revealing Haraway to be unaware of its 'Cartesian recuperations' and uncritical of its additive logic of grafting the one identity onto the other. My reading of Haraway is that she is indeed aware of these permutations of the 'disassemble, reassemble' model, but her wish is to strategise with a clear eye focused on precisely these realities. Referring back to the 'Manifesto for cyborgs', the cyborg is important not in a utopian sense, but because it is our predicament right now. And the increasing digitisation and simulation of the 'human' and its various interfaces not only bear out Haraway's earlier (and more recent) contributions, but reinforce her contention that this is a point, a position, from which our action as feminists inevitably emerges. Kirby is con-cerned that the Cartesian dualism of mind and body is already inscribed in the technological developments of a cyborgian world. Where the cyborg is fully digitised, it is hard to see how this could be the case, except in the form of a continued reliance on ostensibly inactive metaphors. The dualism of mind and body is a formulation predicated on an oppositional logic of consciousness and pre-existing objects of perception. In a world predicated on simulation, where the logic undergirding the whole of the social space tends to reduce everything and everyone to digitised information and models, this dualism is dissolved. From a feminist perspective it becomes important to analyse critically the relationship between the mind/body dualism and the contemporary dynamics of simulation, remembering too Foucault's insistence that modernity is decidedly anti-Cartesian (1966, trans. 1970).

In a hyperreal world of the precession of the model, where the ascendancy of sign value accompanies a fractal logic of the irradiation of value and representation in pure positivity in all directions, where all the 'relations', understood in dialectical terms, giving meaning to 'politics' have imploded – for someone concerned about the gendering of oppression, violence, totalitarianisms of increasingly sinister kinds (those residual mutations that remain when totalitarianism takes the radical action of self-dissolution), what 'position' makes any sense? Baudrillard has been asked this kind of question in a number of interviews (without the emphasis on gender), and it no doubt has motivated at least some of his work. If the west has indeed 'signed its own death warrant' by systematically seeking to eradicate all aspects of the symbolic and reversion, and in doing so has terminated (its) history, recuperating it as a hyperreal artefact, feminism is now confronted with its own project. In other words, what is feminism now opposing, and what are the stakes? The various trends of analysis woven throughout the chapters of this book present Baudrillard's challenge, which I perceive to be the requirement for a paradigm shift away from feminism's preoccupations (fascination?) with the structure of the subject/object dichotomy and with feminine subjectivity, towards an immediate engagement with contemporary dynamics of simulation and the myriad of singularities that remain irreducible to codification, models, and simulation.[7]

As Baudrillard has said, 'critical radicality' is (now) useless (FS: 186). If there is any strategic terrain, it is that of indifference (Baudrillard in Gane 1993: 175). It is indifference, not in the banal sense of shrugging one's shoulders and being literally 'indifferent' to the fate of the planet (where, ambiguously, Baudrillard writes that 'the human species seems to be staging its disappearance' in Gane 1993: 185); rather, it is an indifference that emerges from the radical (ex)termination of any shred of humanism: the shift from that of subject to that of object. But not where the 'object' is simply the inverse of the subject; rather where the representable ontology of the object is always only illusory, 'it' has no substance, or 'thingness'. Baudrillard writes of this 'enigma' of indifference through analogy. Once it was understood that it was the Sphinx that posed to human beings the question of human beings, of 'man'. In other words, the human was posed the question of the enigma of itself; the question, Baudrillard suggests, Oedipus thought he had answered. Baudrillard's thought is that today the focus of this enigma has been inverted: it is the human, or 'man', who poses to the Sphinx, the non-human, the question of the non-human (FS: 190). That world which is not of the order of the subject, which has a fatal indifference towards us subjects, which has a fickleness towards our objective laws, such a world is the object of our challenge; but to seduce we have to be seduced. Baudrillard asks, 'what remains but to side with this enigma?' (FS: 191).

The object challenges and seduces in an exchange where death, dissolution, and evil are in constant exchange and interplay with life, production, good. 'The transparency of evil' does not refer to evil having the quality of our being able to see through it, but rather its tendency to appear everywhere, to 'show through', no matter how resolute the determination to eradicate it (IE: 40). Furthermore, it is not a question of *reconciling* these incomparable domains in some kind of mystical cycle, reuniting them into the great one. Baudrillard is intensely critical of any monistic assumption, insisting that this is precisely, perversely, the ascendant trend contemporarily: the denial of otherness, of strangeness, the repudiation of negativity, of 'evil', to ensure reconciliation around the self-same and its figures of incest, autism, cloning (PC: 129). The agonistic encounter of seduction is not one of reconciliation of 'opposites'; on the contrary, it 'safeguards' non-reconciliation and what Baudrillard refers to as the fatality of strange attractors.

My interpretation of Baudrillard's project is to view it as one of enjoyment in the challenge he both responds to and presents. His analysis has no impetus to 'find' or portray 'what is', but rather to respond to the challenge 'it' presents him. The challenge he is presented with appears to me to reside in the relentless materialisation of the world, the real, and the social dynamics he 'lives' precisely through inhabiting the social world so constructed. He responds to this challenge by exposing its foundations through a process of critical inquiry, but also, probably more importantly, by returning its illusion through the reversion of seduction, by 'making things appear and disappear' (in Gane 1993: 182). Is seduction destiny, or is this the wrong question? Possibly the challenge is to wager that seduction is destiny, as Baudrillard suggests (SEDN: 180). It certainly is not about 'politics'. According to Baudrillard, the political 'died with the great empires' which, resurrected to a second life, are 'retroviral', 'genetically infecting all their wastes, all their by-products, all their basic cells' (IE: 50). This is no longer political, but 'transpolitical', in the sense that the boundaries are con-fused, with 'evil' (negativity) becoming increasingly immanent, confined to the interstices. The illusion of the political is refracted as from a smooth surface.

In Baudrillard's terms, power, meaning, and reality are illusory. This does not mean that the real is a figment of our imaginations! In fact, possibly the 'reality' of the real is so unbearably not a figment of our imaginations that we attempt to render it bearable (apparently controllable) through ideologically reducing the metamorphosis of the real (the play of illusory appearances) to a transcendent instance. It is then truly of the order of illusion. To dissolve power and meaning through the reversion of their illusion is to dissolve ontology of any essence; to return it to the symbolic order of appearances.

Notes

Introduction

1 All emphases appearing in quoted material throughout are as in original, unless otherwise stated.

1 Ideologies of Meaning and Value

1 I take issue on this point, with Kellner (1989) who criticises Baudrillard for not defining the use of the term 'code', suggesting that this absence is a major flaw (p. 29). Poster (1994) raises the same concern (p. 83). In my view, although Baudrillard does not spell it out in strictly 'definitional' terms, the meaning of the code is abundantly clear and used consistently throughout these texts.

2 I want to acknowledge that it is insufficient to attempt to characterise 'feminist poststructuralism' in any singular manner. Numerous authors actively respond to the challenge posed by the logics of identity that rest on the construction of meaning through exclusions, and thus problematise the assumed positivity of identity. I have not read one, however, that develops the kind of critique discussed here in relation to the work of Baudrillard.

3 Baudrillard contrasts the 'science' of Saussurian linguistics with the early work of Saussure on anagrams and the poetic, which Saussure later abandoned. Baudrillard's interpretation of Saussure's work on anagrams and poetry is discussed in Chapter 6.

4 On numerous occasions, Kellner (1989) states that Baudrillard *uses* neo-Saussurian linguistics 'to analyze and critique consumer society' (p. 19). In my view this interpretation not only misses the point but actively sidelines what is probably one of the most important arguments Baudrillard is making in these early works, that is, that the structural facets of the construction of the value of objects and the linguistic construction of subjects and objects have parallel characteristics that can be understood in theoretical terms, and this parallel is neither accidental nor innocent.

5 The absolute quality of the dichotomous logic of identity/difference originates with Aristotle in the west. Frequently the positive term is called the 'unmarked' term, signalling its status as the universal norm, a standard from which the 'other', the 'not the same', is marked. I prefer to refer, as Baudrillard does, to the positive term as 'marked', to accent the positivity of the logic of identity.

6 Foucault (1966, trans. 1970) examines precisely this emergence of 'man' as a 'transcendental doublet'; a figure who is simultaneously the subject and object of knowledge.

7 For example, and in simple terms, the UV of a loaf of packaged bread as a commodity is an effect of the structuring of social life, whereby a majority of people situated as workers/consumers are compelled to exchange part of their wage/income for such a commodity (EV) and are in no position to grow wheat, mill flour, and bake bread for themselves, as a myth of a prior UV to satisfy needs would assume.

8 The assumption that language, and the relation between words and things, could be theorised within a transhistorical, transcultural, universalised frame has been overturned by the work of Foucault (1966, trans. 1970), who has analysed the European history of just this relation, arguing that a number of eras of distinct modes of representation can be delineated.

9 Foucault's argument (1966, trans. 1970) regarding the emergence of 'man' as both subject and object of knowledge complements Baudrillard's analysis here.

10 In doing so, Baudrillard is not concerned with anthropological and/or historical scholarly analyses of the symbolic, or whether his notion of the symbolic is the same as that defined by previous scholars, or even whether it can be said to characterise accurately specific 'other' societies. Through this notion of the symbolic he critically points at something that is excluded, that threatens, relentlessly haunts, and challenges (to death) the modern and 'postmodern' order.

11 In what is now called the postmodern order, this notion of the economic has been subsumed into a code of signification, as discussed in the following section.

12 Consider, for example, the symbolic relation of members of a given tribe to its totemic ancestor animal. When they say they are 'red kangaroos', it does not mean that they 'identify' with such an animal. They point at a complex process of exchange, challenge, and seduction with the place they inhabit, and with the other entities present there that ritually establish them as a specific tribe, that is at heart profoundly non-economic, even if, from a western point of view, it appears to encompass some economic features.

13 See Chapter 2 for a discussion of Baudrillard's analysis of power.

14 See Grace (1989, 1991). Bauman (1993), considering Baudrillard's postmodernity, discusses a similar phenomenon regarding the dissipation of resistance and dissent in a 'postmodern world', arguing that 'losers have no less reasons than the winners to wish that the game goes on, and that the rules stay in force; and no more reason to want the game to be proscribed or its rules overhauled. Postmodernity enlists its own discontents as its most dedicated storm-troopers. At no other time has dissent resided so dangerously close to collaboration' (p. 44).

15 I cite this version in *Revenge of the Crystal* (1990) because I think it is a preferable translation.

16 Gane (1991a) provides an insightful discussion of Baudrillard's analysis of work in the hyperreal context; work that becomes 'a simulation of its former self, and is, in the process, dramatically emptied of all real content. It is a form which now has to reproduce itself for its own sake' (p. 80).

17 Baudrillard is critical of the structural and political implications of the displacement of the real from a position of reference (objectivist) to a simulated form (idealist). He develops this critique from the standpoint of the symbolic that cannot be understood within an objectivist nor idealist ontology. MacCannell and MacCannell's view (1993) unfortunately neglects to account for this critical standpoint and they claim, erroneously, that Baudrillard's critique of the hyperreal reveals his nostalgia for a 'naive positivism', and 'objective reality' (p. 131).

18 Where 'seduction' is the counter to production, as that which removes from the realm of the visible, of identity, and is marked by ambivalence. Baudrillard's concept of seduction is discussed in more detail in Chapter 5.

19 An example of the failure to grasp the significance (ontological and political) of this shift to sign value is provided by Kellner (1989), who, although Baudrillard warns readers of the pitfall of this possible, superficial reading ('The *form* sign must not be confused with the *function* of social differentiation by signs', MOP: 122), continues to discuss and critique Baudrillard's depiction of sign value as a message, as a commodification that signifies particular positions within a hierarchy of social status, positions that are then conferred on the consumer. While such a depiction is an aspect of

contemporary life that has been touched upon by Baudrillard and discussed and analysed at length by many others, this interpretation negates the import of the far more fundamental critique developed by Baudrillard.

20 Pataphysics means the science of imaginary solutions.

21 Thomas Tierney (1997) is clear on this point in his discussion of Baudrillard's analysis of death in *Symbolic Exchange and Death*, reminding his readers that Baudrillard, in making claims about the significance of symbolic exchange, 'is not offering them as historical truths' (1997: 64). Tierney's view is that Baudrillard precisely offers symbolic exchange as 'a utopian alternative to modernity's more rigidly demarcated stance toward death, as a sort of counter-myth to the story that moderns have been telling themselves about death for the last few centuries' (p. 64). His conclusion is that we have to evaluate these claims, not in terms of their historical veracity, but rather for the way they 'reveal and challenge' what may otherwise go unnoticed. The epistemological 'standard' he identifies in Baudrillard's work is the effect that the historical claims made have in disrupting uncritically accepted convictions. He writes 'I endorse this implicit standard, and think Baudrillard should be applauded for avoiding the epistemological moat that neo-Kantians have dug around every interesting question' (p. 75, footnote 16). By contrast Chow (1995), with reference to another author (one among many to make this kind of comment), characterises Baudrillard's evocation of non-western cultures as 'self-serving romanticism' full of 'factual errors' (p. 235, endnote 48).

22 See Mauss (1966), Sahlins (1974), Bataille (1967, trans. 1988) and Hyde (1979).

23 'Communication' in this sense is structured in accordance with emitter–message–receiver; hence the message is codified and the process is one of encoding and decoding.

24 See PES: 30.

25 Since 1982 the Anti-Utilitarianism in Social Sciences Movement (M.A.U.S.S., Mouvement Anti-Utilitariste dans les Sciences Sociales), headquartered in Paris, has developed a systematic, varied, and rich critique of the universality of the economic paradigm, furthering the pioneering work of Mauss, Bataille, and others.

26 Baudrillard, along with a number of other French authors, often uses the word 'logic' in a mathematical sense that is difficult to render in English. It refers to that which underpins the dominant or emerging patterns of trends, which Baudrillard singles out, analyses, and criticises within the prevailing hyperreal social order. I gratefully acknowledge discussions with Louis Arnoux on this point.

27 Rojek continues this line of objection to Baudrillard's 'theorising' in his chapter 'Baudrillard and politics' (1993), where he asserts that Baudrillard 'commits himself unequivocally to reporting and interpreting' (p. 121), and that his statements are not 'supported with evidence'. In other words, what constitutes analysis and evidence within the sociology that Rojek supports and is familar with does not accord with what he reads in Baudrillard's work. However, even formal logic would tell us that this does not mean that Baudrillard's work is devoid of analysis and evidence; it has to be understood in different terms. These terms are neither esoteric nor 'unscientific' but supported by a reputable and long-standing critical epistemological tradition. Turner (1993) is also critical of Baudrillard's work for the same kind of reason, claiming that his 'sociological fictions' are not 'ultimately convincing' even though his style is rich in various rhetorical devices that make it 'poetic and striking' (p. 82). Gane (1991a), on the other hand, finds, for example, Baudrillard's 'analyses' in *The Consumer Society* 'lucid and brilliant', noting that 'very few have grasped [their] true theoretical force and originality' (p. 53).

28 Rojek and Turner are certainly not alone in this interpretation of Baudrillard's comment on the Gulf War. Many commentators have made this erroneous judgement. The most recent example I have read is that of Zillah Eisenstein (1998: 16).

29 Kellner (1989) also discusses his claims that Baudrillard's stance is 'idealist' (p. 188). Cf. Gane (1991a), who argues that it would be 'wrong to conclude that Baudrillard wishes to present an idealist theory' (p. 3). Gane takes issue with numerous points of Kellner's interpretation of Baudrillard's work.

30 For Baudrillard's reflections on theory, see also 'Why theory?' in EC: 97–101.

2 The Fictions of Identity, Power, and Desire

1 I am referring here to Laqueur's theory (1990) of the shift in eighteenth-century Europe from a long history of a one-sex model, where sexual 'difference' was conceptualised as two versions of the same (with the female version as inferior), to the predominance of the two-sex model, where sexual difference was conceptualised as incommensurable and absolute, and anchored in the biological reality of the body.

2 A number of other authors have, in complementary ways in the late 1970s, analysed this biological and/or naturalistic ideological anchoring, in particular in connection with the contemporary imposition of the economic order (see Fradin 1976, 1978; Goux 1978; Maertens 1978).

3 Centrally to his critical epistemology of the social sciences, Latouche (1984) similarly refers to the non-essentialist character of ontology by using the word 'gesture' rather than 'thing'.

4 Maertens's five-volume analysis of the logic of rituals provides ample support to Baudrillard's analysis (Maertens 1978).

5 Baudrillard is not alone in making this critical observation. Foucault (1963, trans. 1973) analyses the contribution of Bichat to the development of pathological anatomy in nineteenth-century France in these terms, pointing to the way death was the only possibility of giving life a positive truth (see p. 145). Latouche (1989, trans. 1996) refers to the meaninglessness of life and death which accompanies their dichotomous separation in the increasing exaltation of 'biological life' so characteristic of the west (see p. 55–6).

6 The word 'usually' is inserted here to acknowledge the parallel structure whereby a dualism (for example, creating a distinction within the human group as male and female) is usually (but not of intrinsic necessity) overlaid by a representational logic of A/Not-A, whereby the A term, the dominant term, is identified by its oppositional split from that which it is not.

7 Weir (1996) comments on this same 'paradox' in Irigaray's work, whereby she simultaneously affirms and rejects a feminine identity, noting that this paradox 'is a constant source of frustration for feminist scholars' (p. 106).

8 Weir (1996) claims there are a number of 'paradoxes' or 'double gestures' in Irigaray's work. Consistently with this claim, she interprets Irigaray making a point which seems to be similar to Baudrillard's here (but in a context different from that of the discussion of Merleau-Ponty): that is, for Irigaray, 'the idea of a primal unity and the idea of the separate autonomous self are one and the same' (p. 99).

9 This view is consistent with that of Irigaray, who finds the notion of 'androgyny' particularly objectionable, claiming its advocates are 'decadents plunged in their own world of fantasy and speculation . . . producing an even weirder culture for bodies that produce it' (1987, trans. 1993: 123). In this context she refers to her concern that 'sex morphology' will be 'again suppressed'.

10 There is a curious statement in this connection in her chapter on Deleuze that possibly points to an uneasiness I have with her work, and indeed that of others who appear to adopt a similar stance in relation to theorising. She writes: '[i]n order to announce the death of the subject one must first have gained the right to speak as one' (Braidotti 1991: 122). Surely announcing the death of the subject results from an analytic process and does not (or certainly not necessarily) mean that the author of the announcement is deemed actually to have done the deed.

11 Indeed, Irigaray has stated that the 'horizon of sexual difference' has a kind of fundamental necessity: '[n]o world is produced or reproduced without sexed difference. Plants, animals, gods, the elements of the universe, all are sexed' (1987, trans. 1993: 178).

12 Weir (1996) is also critical of what she terms Butler's 'totalizing theory of identity' (p. 113). Weir's criticism is, however, grounded on a different assumption from mine. Weir is concerned with any theory of identity that understands identity only within a logic of identity/difference, which she refers to as a logic of sacrifice. That said, she is critical of the implicit omnipotence and intransigence of a theory of identity which has no 'outside'. I discuss her critique very briefly in the next section.

13 In her more recent work, however, Kristeva (1998) invokes a process of 're-volt' as that which is not of the order of the Law. By renewing the challenge of psychoanalysis, Kristeva posits a notion of 're-volt' that encompasses both the most intimate aspects of the critique of the self, and an engagement with the hyperreal contemporary social world.

14 Over ten years ago Elizabeth Spelman (1988) analysed the problem of adding 'different' components of 'identity' to the fundamental identity category of 'woman' as the 'ampersand problem' in feminism.

15 The mathematical concept of 'identity' stresses the integral notion of criteria. A scale or calculable reference point is necessary to establish a relation of identity. For example, to develop a method for stacking apples at the supermarket, plastic models of apples could be developed. The plastic 'apples' would be identical to the apples to be stacked according to the criteria of size, shape, weight, and so on. They would have the 'identity' 'apple' for this purpose. But for the purpose of modelling taste and texture, the plastic 'apples' would not have the 'identity' apple.

16 The present 'one-world' global economy as analysed by Greider (1997) illustrates this analysis vividly: a global economy irreversibly engaged in an ever-increasing growth of economic agents jostling to remain competitive, that is with the sole net aim of producing some positive sign value, in its crudest form some positive accumulation of dollar signs in a forever floating global financial sphere.

17 It needs to be acknowledged that Lacanian psychoanalytic theory does indeed open onto the symbolic (in Baudrillard's terms) through its understanding of castration as the impossibility of 'saying it all'; hence its critique of pure ontology, of positivity. Baudrillard's critique in this context appears to be directed towards the predominant form of psychoanalytic theory and practice which negates the challenge of this critical edge, a challenge implicit at the origins of psychoanalysis. Kristeva's most recent work (1998), centred on her notion of re-volt, exemplifies and actively engages this psychoanalytic challenge.

3 Simulated 'Difference', Simulated 'Politics'

1 See Braidotti (1989) for an explicit defence of essentialism.

2 In mathematics 'modulo' refers to a criterion, or set of criteria, used to define a congruence or relation of equivalence between members of a set or class of elements.

3 Such a distinction is also at the heart of Jewish and Muslim (Sufi) philosophy/epistemology, and that of Zen.

4 This same trend is observed and analysed by others such as Verschueren and Blommaert (1998) and Chow (1995).

5 Maori are the original inhabitants of Aotearoa, or New Zealand.

6 'Pakeha' are non-Maori New Zealanders, mainly of European, or specifically British, descent.

7 More than fifteen years later, relatively few authors have critiqued economic development as decisively as Latouche, and revealed its illusory character.

8 *Campus Review*, Australia, 7, 20, 28 May–3 June 1997.
9 Latouche (1989) characterises 'the west' by its trends towards uniformity, standardisation, and universalisation. 'Deculturation' is a process whereby the imposition of a single scale of cultural identity is the model from which 'cultural difference' proliferates. 'Cultural difference' is then embraced and promoted.
10 The residual cultural elements are those that cannot be integrated into the logic of sign value, and that therefore comprise a 'remainder', or residue. They include those the Europeans now call the excluded (previously the Fourth World), solid and liquid waste, wastelands, the 'environment' (Arnoux and Grace 1997).
11 For example, in his discussion on 'Baudrillard for sociologists', Turner (1993) makes this very point. Citing de Certeau, he claims that 'sociological research on mass audiences shows that there is no ground for believing that media messages are received, consumed or used in any standardised manner, and the majority of social scientists working on culture have attempted to argue that cultural objects in the age of mass media are appropriated, transformed and consumed in diverse forms and according to various practices' (p. 83). Emily Martin (1994) similarly reads Baudrillard to be rendering mass absorption of media images as simplistic against ethnographic explorations which reveal a more complex reality (p. 62).
12 This discussion refers to 'The orders of simulacra' as it appears in the Semiotext(e) translation of *Simulations*. This same text appeared originally as a chapter in *Symbolic Exchange and Death*.
13 The Treaty of Waitangi was signed between the British Crown and a number of chiefs of Maori tribes in 1840.
14 Baudrillard also discusses this phenomenon of 'the masses' in *Fatal Strategies* (pp. 94, 98). In *Seduction*, he writes that, '[i]n the last analysis, the masses are simply the sum of all the systems' terminals – a network travelled by digital impulses (this is what forms a mass)' (p. 173).
15 Baudrillard's early works, *The Consumer Society* (CS) and *The System of Objects* (SO), were cited in the food engineering literature in the 1960s in France, with respect to their relevance to the marketing of consumer products.
16 Bauman (1992) and Kellner (1989) cited above, appeared, however, to be referring to Baudrillard's work in *The Silent Majorities*.
17 Bauman (1989) has made a similar distinction.
18 This information was reported in the *Public Health Association News* (NZ), 10, 5, October 1998: 6, from speeches made by James Love during a visit to New Zealand in July 1998.

4 Hyperreal Genders

1 For example, Stephen Whittle (1998), in his introduction to a journal issue on 'transgendering', recognises the importance of Butler's 'huge contribution to Queer theory by compressing all gender into performativity' (p. 270).
2 A full discussion of this shift and its implications appears in Chapter 1.
3 This question of 'otherness' in connection with sex and gender will be discussed in more detail in Chapter 5. 'Loss' here suggests a kind of nostalgia for something valued which is gone. This would be a problematic interpretation. In Chapter 5 I will address the question of how Baudrillard depicts 'otherness' and how this differs from the assumptions found in the works of those feminist authors discussed in Chapter 2.

5 The Inevitable Seduction

1 In support of this thesis, Power and Aiello (1997) hypothesise the correlation of abundant red pigment associated with female ritual performances and the onset of a

symbolically structured division of labour on the basis of sex. They cite numerous examples of fossil and archaeological evidence that support this correlation, in addition to ethnographic sources.

2 It is important to draw attention to the fact that the authors refer to 'symbols' and not 'signs'. The symbolic remains enigmatic, an active part of the process of creating human relationships that are not 'representational' as such, cannot be 'decoded', in contrast to a 'sign' that is precisely to be decoded without ambiguity, as in the prevalent hyperreal economic order. The fact that Derrida and others point out that meaning is constantly deferred in a reading of signifiers does not detract from this point, since the hyperreal sign precisely functions without meaning 'attached' to it. Possibly what haunts Derrida's 'différance' is an unavowed symbolic.

3 This Maori proverb is cited by Mauss (1966: 69), and is translated by his source as follows: 'Give as much as you receive and all is for the best.' Mauss notes that a literal translation might rather read 'As much as Maru gives, so Maru receives, and all is well', where Maru is god of war and justice.

4 This is an alternative translation from Irigaray's 1977 work.

5 Goshorn (1994) suggests there is a contradiction in Baudrillard's '"advice" to women to not . . . abandon [their] historical advantage', and asks which is worse, a traditional hierarchy with overt power associated with one gender, and covert power with the other, or a society 'with the overt *signs* of "liberation," that are too often only those of commercial "hype" functioning as the basis and pretext for developing the formerly subjugated group as an expanded market of consumption' (p. 282). My interpretation of Baudrillard suggests that he would probably agree with the implications of the question as framed, but that it does not re-present the issue at hand. The order of the symbolic, or reversion and seduction, precisely annuls power; the so-called 'overt' power of the masculine is continually reversed. It is only with the order of the productivist logic of the economic, which bars the symbolic, that seduction is also barred.

6 Baudrillard discusses pornography in a number of his works, particularly *Symbolic Exchange and Death*.

7 There is an irony in this depiction of women when considered in relation to Power and Aiello's (1997) thesis of the emergence of symbolic ritual and taboo in 'sham menstruation'. In accordance with this theory, as outlined above, 'sham menstruation' was a seductive ritual creating women precisely as not 'continuously available', in conjunction with the evolutionary loss of oestrus.

8 Conversely, the explosion of pornography as media (the medium is the message) is an epiphenomenon of consumerism, where there is an obscenity in the consumption of any good or service.

9 In terms of Baudrillard's epistemology, the question of 'what is' can never be rendered in absolute terms; such attempts will always fail. Any comment on, or analysis of, social processes can only emerge from a critique resolutely situated in action. Frequently, feminist theorists appear to adopt a similar critical epistemology, and yet still insist on contributing a rendering of 'what is'. For example, Judith Butler critiques sex as 'natural' and yet still posits it as 'performative'; a logic along the lines of 'it's not that, it's this', as if 'performativity' has some transcendent quality to anchor an understanding of 'sex'. 'Sex' posited as objectively verifiable as natural, and sex as socially constructed, can really be viewed as the flip sides of a coin. Both are reliant on an assumption to claim a knowledge of 'what is'.

10 Desire in many non-western cultures is arguably closer to Baudrillard's notion of seduction.

11 Baudrillard explicitly critiques the claim that women's position has 'since time immemorial' been one of defeat, passivity, repression, awaiting 'liberation' through opening 'the doors of desire under the auspices of revolution and psychoanalysis'

(SEDN: 19). This form of commiseration, he claims, is in fact at the heart of sexism, and racism.

12 For Baudrillard's reference to this 'position', see interview with Nicholas Zurbrugg in Gane (1993: 168).

13 Spivak (1988) develops a critique of 'use value' with reference to a number of key authors who have employed the term (including Marx) but astoundingly does not mention Baudrillard's work.

6 Feminism and the Power of Dissolution

1 I do not claim expertise in analysing poetry, or wish to situate this discussion in relation to debates and scholarly work on what poetry may or may not 'be'. My intention is to present Baudrillard's reflections on the significance of Saussure's early work on poetics, to demonstrate how language might be traversed by seduction, by the symbolic.

2 Baudrillard (SE&D: 210) refers to a science-fiction story by Arthur C. Clarke about a brotherhood of lamas who, in the foothills of Tibet, are dedicated to the task of reciting the nine million names of God. When this is accomplished and the names have all been stated, the lamas prophesy, the world will come to an end; the cycle of existence will be reversed and annulled. The religious 'delirium' of the lamas is to be found in this process of exhausting the totality of the signifiers of God, undoing their presence one by one. When IBM computers are introduced to the scene by American technicians to speed things up by recording and decoding the names, the time to complete the task shrinks from many centuries to three months. Once the task is done, the IBM technicians flee the monastery in fear that the lamas will turn on them because the prophecy is not fulfilled. As the technicians flee, and as the last of the nine million words has been recited, the Americans see the stars going out one by one.

3 He precisely does not use the word 'pleasure', which he designates as that associated with the productive logic of 'desire' (SE&D: 241, n. 16).

4 Note alternative translation: to miss a step, stagger (Louis Arnoux, personal communication).

5 Goshorn (1994) is of the view that Meaghan Morris (1984) presents the most sustained discussion of the work of Baudrillard written by a feminist. Morris's conclusion, however, that Baudrillard's work (to the date of her writing in 1984) returned us to 'the prison house of language', is a perplexing one to say the least. Given Baudrillard's portrayal of the significance of reversion for the poetic dematerialisation of language, and the fact that this observation is consistent with the direction of his entire work, focusing as it does on the interweaving of the structures of signification and the economic and the barring of the symbolic, to conclude that his work leads us to the confinement of signs is unintelligible.

6 It is noteworthy that Baudrillard uses the same word as Ebert in her title *Ludic Feminism* (1996). She is critical of 'ludic feminism' for its departure from 'materialist' concerns and politics, and condemns those male theorists whom she perceives to be the originators of such 'postmodern' philosophies, including Baudrillard. It is clear, on the contrary, that Baudrillard is also ardently critical of 'ludic' tendencies, although from a very different point of departure.

7 In a recent series of interviews (Petit 1997), Baudrillard stresses how the negativity systematically eradicated in the simulated hyperreal world keeps oozing through countless singular points; 'singular' because they cannot be reduced to, or captured by, the simulation process.

Bibliography

Works of Baudrillard cited

AM   *America* (1986) translated by Chris Turner (1988), London: Verso.

CM   *Cool Memories 1980–85* (1987) translated by Chris Turner (1990), London: Verso.

CS   *The Consumer Society. Myths and Structures* (1970) translated by 'C.T.' (1998), London: Sage.

EC   *The Ecstasy of Communication* (1987) translated by Bernard and Caroline Schutze (1988), New York: Semiotext(e).

EOP The end of production. Chapter in *Revenge of the Crystal. Selected Writings on the Modern Object and its Destiny, 1968–83* (1990) from *Symbolic Exchange and Death*, translated by Paul Foss and Julian Pefanis, London: Pluto Press.

FF   *Forget Foucault* (1977) translation 1987 (translator not cited), New York: Semiotext(e).

FS   *Fatal Strategies* (1983) translated by Philip Beitchman and W.G.J. Niesluchowski (1990), New York: Semiotext(e)/Pluto Press.

IE   *The Illusion of the End* (1992) translated by Chris Turner (1994), Cambridge: Polity Press.

MOP *The Mirror of Production* (1973) translated and introduced by Mark Poster (1975), St. Louis, Mo.: Telos Press.

PC   *The Perfect Crime* (1995) translated by Chris Turner (1996), London: Verso.

PES *For a Critique of the Political Economy of the Sign* (1972) translated and introduced by Charles Levin (1981), St Louis, Mo.: Telos Press.

SE&D *Symbolic Exchange and Death* (1976) translated by Iain Hamilton Grant and introduced by Mike Gane (1993), London: Sage.

SEDN *Seduction* (1979) translated by Brian Singer (1990), London: Macmillan.

SIM *Simulations* (1981) translation 1983 (translator not cited), New York: Semiotext(e).

SO   *The System of Objects* (1968) translated by James Benedict (1996), London: Verso.

SSM *In the Shadow of the Silent Majorities, or the End of the Social* (1978) translated by Paul Foss, Paul Patton, and John Johnston (1983), New York: Semiotext(e).

SV   *Suite Venitienne* (by Sophie Calle) and *Please Follow Me* (by Baudrillard) (1983) translated by Dany Barash and Danny Hatfield (1988), Seattle: Bay Press.

TE   *The Transparency of Evil. Essays on Extreme Phenomena* (1990) translated by James Benedict (1993), London: Verso.

Interviews

Gane, Mike (1993) *Baudrillard Live. Selected Interviews*, London: Routledge.

Moore, Suzanne and Johnstone, Stephen (1989) Politics of seduction. An interview with Jean Baudrillard. *Marxism Today*, Jan., 54–5.

Petit, Philippe (1997) *Paroxysm. Interviews with Jean Baudrillard* translated (1998) by Chris Turner, London: Verso.

Williamson, Judith (1989) An interview with Jean Baudrillard. Translated by Brand Thumim, *Block*, 15: 16–19.

References

Arnoux, Louis (1998a) *The Network Revolution on the NASDAQ Stock Exchange*, Indra-Net float information, IndraNet Technologies Limited. *http://www.indranet.co.nz*

—— (1998b) *The Global Network Revolution*, IndraNet Technologies Limited. *http://www.indranet.co.nz* (and *http://www.indranet-technologies.com*).

—— (1998c) *Crisis? What Crisis? The Global Investment Context and IndraNet*, Indra-Net Technologies Limited. *http://www.indranet.co.nz*

Arnoux, Louis and Grace, Victoria (1997) Critical futures. Paper presented at the Environmental Justice, Global Ethics for the 21st Century Conference, University of Melbourne, Australia, Oct. 1–3.

Bataille, Georges (1967) *The Accursed Share*, translation 1988, New York: Zone Books.

Bauman, Zygmunt (1989) Sociological responses to postmodernity. *Thesis Eleven*, 23: 35–63.

—— (1992) *Intimations of Postmodernity*, London: Routledge.

—— (1993) The sweet scent of decomposition, in Rojek, Chris and Turner, Bryan (eds) *Forget Baudrillard?*, London: Routledge.

Bordo, Susan (1990) Feminism, postmodernism, and gender-skepticism, in Nicholson, Linda (ed.) *Feminism/Postmodernism*, New York: Routledge.

Bornstein, Kate (1994) *Gender Outlaw. On Men, Women, and the Rest of Us*, New York: Routledge.

Braidotti, Rosi (1989) The politics of ontological difference, in Brennan, Teresa (ed.) *Between Feminism and Psychoanalysis*, London: Routledge.

—— (1991) *Patterns of Dissonance. A Study of Women in Contemporary Philosophy*, Cambridge: Polity Press.

—— (1994a) *Nomadic Subjects. Embodiment and Sexual Difference in Contemporary Feminist Theory*, New York: Columbia University Press.

—— (1994b) Feminism by any other name. Interview with Judith Butler. *Differences. A Journal of Feminist Cultural Studies*, 6, 2–3: 27–61.

Burchill, Louise (1984) Either/or: peripeteia of an alternative in Jean Baudrillard's *De La Séduction*, in Frankovitz, A. (ed.) *Seduced and Abandoned: The Baudrillard Scene*, NSW: Stonemoss Press.

Butler, Judith (1990) *Gender Trouble. Feminism and the Subversion of Identity*, New York: Routledge.

—— (1993) *Bodies that Matter. On the Discursive Limits of 'Sex'*, New York: Routledge.

—— (1994) Gender as performance. Interview with Judith Butler. *Radical Philosophy*, 67: 32–9.

—— (1997) *Excitable Speech. A Politics of the Performative*, Routledge: New York.

Butler, Judith and Scott, Joan (eds) (1992) *Feminists Theorize the Political*, New York: Routledge.

Butler, Rex (1999) *Jean Baudrillard. The Defence of the Real*, London: Sage.

Caillé, Alain (1989) *Critique de la Raison Utilitaire. Manifeste du MAUSS (A Critique of Utilitarian Rationality. The Manifesto of MAUSS)*, Paris: Éditions la Découverte.

Caufield, Catherine (1998) Selling a piece of your mother. *Whole Earth*, 94: 58–73.

Charles, Nickie (1996) Introduction, in Charles, Nickie and Hughes-Freeland, Felicia (eds) *Practising Feminism. Identity Difference Power*, London: Routledge.

Chen, K-H. (1987) The masses and the media: Baudrillard's implosive postmodernism. *Theory, Culture & Society*, 4, 1: 71–88.

Chow, Rey (1995) *Primitive Passions. Visuality, Sexuality, Ethnography, and Contemporary Chinese Cinema*, New York: Columbia University Press.

Cook, Deborah (1994) Symbolic exchange in hyperreality, in Kellner, Douglas (ed.) *Baudrillard. A Critical Reader*, Oxford: Blackwell.

Crosby, Christina (1992) Dealing with differences, in Butler, Judith and Scott, Joan (eds) *Feminists Theorize the Political*, New York: Routledge.

De Beauvoir, Simone (1949) *The Second Sex* translated by H.M. Parshley (1953), London: Jonathan Cape.

Debord, Guy (1967) *The Society of the Spectacle* translated by D. Nicholson-Smith (1994), New York: Zone Books.

—— (1988) *Comments on the Society of the Spectacle* translated by M. Imrie (1990), London: Verso.

De Lauretis, Teresa (1987) *Technologies of Gender. Essays on Theory, Film, and Fiction*, Bloomington: Indiana University Press.

—— (1990) Eccentric subjects: feminist theory and historical consciousness. *Feminist Studies*, 16, 1: 115–50.

Di Stephano, Christine (1990) Dilemmas of difference: feminism, modernity, and postmodernism, in Nicholson, Linda (ed.) *Feminism/Postmodernism*, New York: Routledge.

Drucker, Peter (1989) *The New Realities*, Oxford: Heinemann.

Ebert, Teresa (1996) *Ludic Feminism and After. Postmodernism, Desire, and Labor in Later Capitalism*, Ann Arbor: University of Michigan Press.

Eisenstein, Hester and Jardine, Alice (eds) (1990) *The Future of Difference*, New Brunswick: Rutgers University Press.

Eisenstein, Zillah (1998) *Global Obscenities. Patriarchy, Capitalism, and the Lure of Cyberfantasy*, New York: New York University Press.

Epstein, Julia and Straub, Kristina (eds) (1991) *Body Guards. The Cultural Politics of Gender Ambiguity*, New York: Routledge.

Favret-Saada, Jane (1977) *Les Mots, La Mort, Les Sorts (Words, Death, Spells)*, Paris: Gallimard.

Ferguson, Kathy (1993) *The Man Question. Visions of Subjectivity in Feminist Theory*, Berkeley: University of California Press.

Foucault, Michel (1963) *The Birth of the Clinic. An Archaeology of Medical Perception* translation 1973, New York: Tavistock Publications.

—— (1966) *The Order of Things. An Archaeology of the Human Sciences* translation 1970, New York: Random House.

Fradin, J. (1976) *Les Fondements Logiques de la Théorie Néoclassique de L'Echange (The Logical Foundation of the Neoclassical Theory of Economic Exchange)*, Paris: Pug-Maspero.

—— (1978) Introduction sommaire à une nouvelle économie politique. (Brief introduction to a new political economy). *Cahiers du CEREL*, 9: 1–19.

Fraser, Nancy (1992) Introduction, in Fraser, Nancy and Bartky, Sandra Lee (eds) *Revaluing French Feminism. Critical Essays on Difference, Agency and Culture*, Bloomington: Indiana University Press.

Fraser, Nancy and Nicholson, Linda (1990) Social criticism without philosophy: an encounter between feminism and postmodernism, in Nicholson, Linda (ed.) *Feminism/Postmodernism*, New York: Routledge.

Friedman, Lenore (1987) *Meetings with Remarkable Women. Buddhist Teachers in America,* Boston: Shambala.

Fuss, Diane (1989) *Essentially Speaking. Feminism, Nature and Difference*, New York: Routledge.

Gabb, Jacqui (1998) Marginal differences? An analysis of the imag(in)ed bodies of Del LaGrace. *Journal of Gender Studies*, 7, 3: 297–305.

Gallop, Jane (1987) French theory and the seduction of feminism, in Jardine, Alice and Smith, Paul (eds) *Men in Feminism*, New York: Methuen.

Gane, Mike (1991a) *Baudrillard's Bestiary. Baudrillard and Culture*, London: Routledge.

—— (1991b) *Baudrillard. Critical and Fatal Theory*, London: Routledge.

—— (1993) *Baudrillard Live. Selected Interviews*, London: Routledge.

Genosko, Gary (1999) *McLuhan and Baudrillard. Masters of Implosion*, London: Routledge.

Godbout, Jacques T. and Caillé, Alain (1992) *The World of the Gift*, translated by D. Winkler (1998), Montreal: McGill-Queen's University Press.

Goshorn, A. Keith (1994) Valorizing 'the feminine' while rejecting feminism? Baudrillard's feminist provocations, in Kellner, Douglas (ed.) *Baudrillard. A Critical Reader*, Oxford: Blackwell.

Goux, Jean-Joseph (1978) *Les Iconoclastes* (*The Iconoclasts*), Paris: Seuil.

Grace, Victoria (1989) The marketing of empowerment and the construction of the health consumer: a critique of health promotion in New Zealand. PhD thesis, Christchurch, NZ: University of Canterbury.

—— (1991) The marketing of empowerment and the construction of the health consumer: a critique of health promotion. *International Journal of Health Services*, 21, 2: 329–43.

Greider, William (1997) *One World, Ready or Not*, New York: Simon and Schuster.

Grosz, Elizabeth (1989) *Sexual Subversions. Three French Feminists*, Sydney: Allen and Unwin.

Gunew, Sneja (1990) Postmodern tensions. Reading for (multi)cultural difference. *Meanjin*, 49, 1: 21–33.

Gunew, Sneja and Yeatman, Anna (eds) (1993) *Feminism and the Politics of Difference*, St Leonards: Allen and Unwin.

Halberstam, Judith (1994) F2M: the making of female masculinity, in Doan, Laura (ed.) *The Lesbian Postmodern*, New York: Columbia University Press.

Haraway, Donna (1991) *Simians, Cyborgs, and Women*, New York: Routledge.

—— (1997) *Modest_Witness@Second_Millennium. FemaleMan©_Meets_Oncomouse™*, New York: Routledge.

Hyde, Lewis (1979) *The Gift. Imagination and the Erotic Life of Property*, New York: Vintage Books.

Irigaray, Luce (1974) *Speculum of the Other Woman* translated by Gillian C. Gill (1985), New York: Cornell University Press.

—— (1977) *This Sex Which is Not One* translated by Catherine Porter (1985), New York: Cornell University Press.

—— (1980a) When our lips speak together, translated by Carolyn Burke. *Signs: Journal of Women in Culture and Society*, 6, 1: 69–79.

—— (1980b) Book review of *Seduction*. *Histoires d'Elles*, 21, Mar.

—— (1984) *An Ethics of Sexual Difference* translated by Carolyn Burke and Gillian C. Gill (1993), New York: Cornell University Press.

—— (1987) *Sexes and Genealogies* translated by Gillian C. Gill (1993), New York: Columbia University Press.

Jeffreys, Sheila (1997) Transgender activism: a lesbian feminist perspective. *Journal of Lesbian Studies*, 1, 3/4: 55–74.

Kellner, Douglas (1989) *Jean Baudrillard. From Marxism to Postmodernism and Beyond*, Cambridge: Polity Press.

—— (ed.) (1994) *Baudrillard: A Critical Reader*, Oxford: Blackwell.

Kirby, Vicki (1997) *Telling Flesh. The Substance of the Corporeal*, New York: Routledge.

Kristeva, Julia (1998) *L'Avenir d'une Révolte*, Paris: Calmann-Lévy.

Laqueur, Thomas (1990) *Making Sex. Body and Gender from the Greeks to Freud*, Cambridge, Mass.: Harvard University Press.

Lash, Scott (1990) *Sociology of Postmodernism*, London: Routledge.

Latouche, Serge (1973) *Épistemologie et Économie (Epistemology and Economics)*, Paris: Editions Anthropos.

—— (1979) *Critique de L'Impérialisme (A Critique of Imperialism)*, Paris: Editions Anthropos.

—— (1982) Le sous-développement est une forme d'acculturation. (Underdevelopment is a form of acculturation). *M.A.U.S.S. Bulletin*, 2: 35–50.

—— (1984) *Le Procès de la Science Sociale. Introduction à une Théorie Critique de la Connaissance (Social Science on Trial. An Introduction to a Critical Theory of Knowledge)*, Paris: Editions Anthropos.

—— (1986) *Faut-Il Refuser le Développement? Essai sur L'Anti-Économique du Tiers-Monde (Should We Refuse Development? An Essay on the Anti-Economics of Third Worldism)*, Paris: Presses Universitaires de France.

—— (1989) *The Westernisation of the World. The Significance, Scope and Limits of the Drive Towards Global Conformity* translated by Rosemary Morris (1996), Cambridge: Polity Press.

—— (1991) *In the Wake of the Affluent Society. An Exploration of Post-Development* translated by M. O'Connor and R. Arnoux (1993), London: Zed Books.

Lennon, Kathleen and Whitford, Margaret (eds) (1994) *Knowing the Difference. Feminist Perspectives in Epistemology*, London: Routledge.

Levin, Charles (1996) *Jean Baudrillard. A Study in Cultural Metaphysics*, London: Prentice Hall.

MacCannell, D. and MacCannell, J.F (1993) Social class in postmodernity, in Rojek, Chris and Turner, Bryan (eds) *Forget Baudrillard?*, London: Routledge.

Maertens, Jean-Thierry (1978) *Ritologiques (Ritologics)*, Paris: Aubier.

Maezumi, Hakuyu Taizan (1978) *The Way of Everyday Life*, Los Angeles: Zen Centre of Los Angeles.

Maltz, Robin (1998) Real butch: the performance/performativity of male impersona-
  tion, drag kings, passing as male, and stone butch realness. *Journal of Gender Studies*,
  7, 3: 273–86.
Martin, Emily (1994) *Flexible Bodies. The Role of Immunity in American Culture from the
  Days of Polio to the Age of AIDS*, Boston: Beacon Press.
Mauss, Marcel (1966) *The Gift*, London: Cohen and West.
Moi, Toril (1985) *Sexual/Textual Politics. Feminist Literary Theory*, London: Routledge.
Moore, Suzanne (1988) Getting a bit of the other – the pimps of postmodernism, in
  Chapman, Rowena and Rutherford, Jonathon (eds) *Male Order: Unwrapping Mascu-
  linity*, London: Lawrence and Wishart.
Morris, Meaghan (1984) Room 101 or a few worst things in the world, in Franko-
  vitz, A. (ed.) *Seduced and Abandoned: The Baudrillard Scene*, NSW: Stonemoss Press.
Namaste, Ki (1994) 'Tragic misreadings': queer theory's erasure of transgender sub-
  jectivity, in Beemyn, Brett and Eliason, Mickey (eds) *Queer Studies. A Lesbian, Gay,
  Bisexual and Transgender Anthology*, New York: New York University Press.
Nataf, Zachary (1996) *Lesbians Talk Transgender*, London: Scarlet Press.
Plant, Sadie (1992) *The Most Radical Gesture. The Situationist International in a Post-
  modern Age*, London: Routledge.
—— (1993) Baudrillard's woman: the eve of seduction, in Rojek, Chris and Turner,
  Bryan (eds) *Forget Baudrillard?*, London: Routledge.
Porter, Roy (1993) Baudrillard: history, hysteria and consumption, in Rojek, Chris
  and Turner, Bryan (eds) *Forget Baudrillard?*, London: Routledge.
Poster, Mark (1994) Critical theory and technoculture: Habermas and Baudrillard, in
  Kellner, Douglas (ed.) *Baudrillard. A Critical Reader*, Oxford: Blackwell.
Power, Camilla and Aiello, Leslie (1997) Female proto-symbolic strategies, in Hager,
  Lori (ed.) *Women in Human Evolution*, London: Routledge.
Raymond, Janice (1979) *The Transsexual Empire: The Making of the She-Male*, Boston:
  Beacon.
Rojek, Chris (1993) Baudrillard and politics, in Rojek, Chris and Turner, Bryan (eds)
  Forget Baudrillard?, London: Routledge.
Rojek, Chris and Turner, Bryan (eds) (1993) *Forget Baudrillard?*, London: Routledge.
Rubin, Gayle (1978) The traffic in women, in Jaggar, A. and Struhl, P.R. (eds)
  Feminist Frameworks, New York: McGraw-Hill.
Sahlins, Marshall (1974) *Stone Age Economics*, London: Tavistock Publications.
Said, Edward (1989) Representing the colonized: anthropology's interlocutors. *Critical
  Inquiry*, 15: 205–25.
Spelman, Elizabeth (1988) *Inessential Woman: The Problem of Exclusion in Feminist
  Thought*, Boston: Beacon Press.
Spivak, Gayatri (1988) Scattered speculations on the question of value, in *In Other
  Worlds: Essays in Cultural Politics*, New York: Routledge.
—— (1989) In a word. Interview, Ellen Rooney with Gayatri Spivak. *Differences*, 1,
  2: 124–56.
Stone, Sandy (1991) The *Empire* strikes back: a posttranssexual manifesto, in Epstein,
  Julia and Straub, Kristina (eds) *Body Guards. The Cultural Politics of Gender
  Ambiguity*, New York: Routledge.
Strathern, Marilyn (1988) *The Gender of the Gift. Problems with Women and Problems
  with Society in Melanesia*, Berkeley: University of California Press.

Strickland, Susan (1994) Feminism, postmodernism and difference, in Lennon, Kathleen and Whitford, Margaret (eds) *Knowing the Difference. Feminist Perspectives in Epistemology*, London: Routledge.

Stryker, Susan (1998) The transgender issue: an introduction. *GLQ: A Journal of Lesbian and Gay Studies*, 4, 2: 145–58.

Sussman, Gerald (1997) *Communication, Technology, and Politics in the Information Age*, Thousand Oaks, Calif.: Sage.

Tierney, Thomas (1997) Death, medicine and the right to die: an engagement with Heidegger, Bauman and Baudrillard. *Body and Society*, 3, 4: 51–77.

Turner, Bryan (1993) Baudrillard for sociologists, in Rojek, Chris and Turner, Bryan (eds) *Forget Baudrillard?*, London: Routledge.

University of Otago (1998) *Report of the Panel Appointed to Review the Women's Studies Section*, September.

Varela, Francisco, Thompson, Evan and Rosch, Eleanor (1991) *The Embodied Mind. Cognitive Science and Human Experience*, Cambridge, Mass.: MIT Press.

Verschueren, Jef and Blommaert, Jan (1998) *Debating Diversity. Analysing the Rhetoric of Tolerance*, London: Routledge.

Von Foerster, Heinz (1995) Metaphysics of an experimental epistemologist @ *http://www.vordenker.de/metaphysics/metaphysics.htm*

Walters, Suzanna Danuta (1996) From here to queer: radical feminism, postmodernism, and the lesbian menace (or, why can't a woman be more like a fag?). *Signs*, 21, 4: 830–69.

Weedon, Chris (1987) *Feminist Practice and Poststructuralist Theory*, Cambridge, Mass.: Blackwell.

Weir, Allison (1996) *Sacrificial Logics. Feminist Theory and the Critique of Identity*, New York: Routledge.

Whittle, Stephen (1998) Guest editorial. *Journal of Gender Studies*, 7, 3: 269–72.

Wiegman, Robyn (1995) *American Anatomies. Theorising Race and Gender*, Durham: Duke University Press.

Zinn, Maxine and Dill, Bonnie (1996) Theorising difference from multiracial feminism. *Feminist Studies*, 22, 2: 321–31.

Index